T0272520

NO
DEMOCRACY
LASTS
FOREVER

NO
DEMOCRACY
LASTS
FOREVER

How the Constitution Threatens
the *United* States

ERWIN CHEMERINSKY

Liveright Publishing Corporation

A Division of W. W. Norton & Company
Independent Publishers Since 1923

Frontispiece: Volunteers help roll up a giant banner printed with the Preamble to the United States Constitution during a demonstration against the Supreme Court's *Citizens United* ruling at the Lincoln Memorial on the National Mall, October 20, 2010, in Washington, D.C. The rally at the memorial was organized by brothers Laird and Robin Monahan, who spent the last five months walking from San Francisco, California, to Washington to protest the court decision, which overturned the provision of the McCain-Feingold law barring corporations and unions from paying for political ads made independently of candidate campaigns.
(Photograph by Chip Somodevilla / Getty Images)

For information about permission to reproduce selections from this book, write to Permissions, Liveright Publishing Corporation, a division of W. W. Norton & Company, Inc., 500 Fifth Avenue, New York, NY 10110

For information about special discounts for bulk purchases, please contact W. W. Norton Special Sales at specialsales@wwnorton.com or 800-233-4830

Manufacturing by Lake Book Manufacturing
Production manager: Anna Oler

ISBN 978-1-324-09158-5

Liveright Publishing Corporation
500 Fifth Avenue, New York, N.Y. 10110
www.wwnorton.com

W. W. Norton & Company Ltd.
15 Carlisle Street, London W1D 3BS

1 2 3 4 5 6 7 8 9 0

For Catherine

CONTENTS

PART III

Can the *United* States Be Saved?

PROLOGUE

The U.S. Constitution, which created a government that succeeded so well for so long, now itself threatens American democracy. In the 2020s, Americans' confidence in all branches of the federal government is justifiably at an all-time low. The government, by every measure, seems increasingly dysfunctional. Few believe that it has the ability to deal with the urgent issues, such as climate change, that threaten our society and the world. The United States is more politically polarized than it has been at any time since Reconstruction. Many have begun asking whether what unites us as a country is greater than all that divides us.

Although our democracy faces a widespread sense of a crisis, most Americans do not realize how much the Constitution itself is responsible. In fact, the Constitution had serious flaws from the outset as a result of compromises that were made to get it enacted. Some of those defects, such as its treatment of race, have haunted the nation throughout its history.

No Democracy Lasts Forever focuses on how, over the last half-century, the American political landscape has changed in ways that have made the Constitution a threat to democracy as never before. Some of its flaws—such as the framers' distrust of democracy in using the Electoral College to choose the president and its creation of a Senate that accords every state equal representation regardless of size—have become dramatically and dangerously problematic because of changes in demographics and national politics. Poor choices made along the way, such as allowing partisan gerrymandering and permitting almost unlimited Senate filibusters, have contributed to the increasing failure of American government. The Supreme Court's allowing corporations and rich people to spend unlimited sums to get their candidates elected has spawned seemingly ineradicable cynicism about our electoral process. Social media, which has many virtues in facilitating speech, has also fomented polarization and easily spreads dangerous falsehoods that undermine democracy in ways that the Founding Fathers never could have fathomed. The First Amendment, so crucial to democracy, has itself become a threat to it.

The Constitution created a structure of government that was suited for a small, not wealthy country in which a tiny segment of white, male landowners governed everyone else. Thankfully, we no longer believe that form of government is legitimate. But sophisticated political actors, using powerful computers and social media that could not have been imagined in science fiction, have figured out how to use the Constitution's undemocratic structure to create permanent minority rule.

Moreover, our reverence for the Constitution has kept us from seeing how much it has become the root of the problem. We praise it effusively, and some evangelicals even claim it was divinely inspired. Elementary school students memorize its Preamble, and students across the country, as well as immigrants seeking citizenship, are tested on its content. A hit Broadway musical was made about one of its primary drafters. The Supreme Court, in making decisions today, looks increasingly to the framers' intentions at the time when it was adopted, as if they had some omniscient if not messianic wisdom. As a society, we turn to the Constitution, and its interpretation, to resolve many important disputes. It has been described as our civic religion.

This reverence, however, comes at a great cost. For too long we have ignored or at least accepted the Constitution's serious flaws. In many ways, the government that it has given us is not functioning and has lost the confidence of a huge swath of the American people. The Constitution has played a role in creating a society that is flagrantly unequal, especially along the lines of race and class. Its very existence as a largely unchanged guiding document has become a sledgehammer wielded by a minority to prop up a system that engenders polarization and festering national discord. Small wonder that its proponents protect it so vociferously, given their fear of what they could lose.

Despite these troubles, the situation is not hopeless. It is both possible and essential to cure the defects and save American democracy. Many meaningful changes can be made without constitutional amendment. The Senate can change its rules to eliminate the filibuster. Congress, by legislation, can end partisan gerrymandering for seats in the House of Representatives, and the Supreme Court can end partisan gerrymandering altogether. The size of the House of Representatives can be increased to make it more democratic. Congress can create term limits for federal judges. It can pass new legislation to protect voting rights.

The Constitution also can be amended where that is necessary. Amending the Constitution is enormously difficult, but it is not impossible. Virtually every flaw in the document can be fixed by constitutional amendment if we have the will to do so. Except for the allocation of two senators per state, which cannot be modified by amendment, every other problem in the Constitution—and the Supreme Court's interpretation of it—can be solved through amendments. Although amendments have been rare in recent decades, at other times in American history they have been more common. From 1913 to 1920, the country passed four amendments: authorizing an income tax, creating the popular election of senators, providing women the right to vote, and imposing Prohibition. Our sense of a crisis and a real need for changing the Constitution may again open the door to amendments.

Beyond a spate of separate amendments, it is imperative, after two hundred years, that Americans begin to think of drafting a new constitution to create a more effective, more democratic government. It's absurd to use a document written for a small, poor, and relatively inconsequential nation in the late eighteenth century to govern a large country of immense wealth in the technological world of the twenty-first century. We must begin to think about crafting a new governing document that keeps the strengths of the existing Constitution but fixes its manifest flaws.

I do not minimize the difficulty of significant change. Amending the Constitution, let alone replacing it entirely, appears to have little chance of happening right now, and many would regard me as a dreamer to even suggest it. Making such changes would require a consensus that is the antithesis of the current moment of division. But then we must contemplate the consequences of failing to institute dramatic constitutional reform. Some predict that the United States could drift to an authoritarian government, as other former democracies have done. Disturbing notes of authoritarianism recurringly sound in today's political rhetoric. The events of January 6 have made political violence a reality in this country as never before.

Without substantial and meaningful change, I think calls for some form of secession will increase. Opinion polls show that it already is on the minds of *both* Democratic and Republican voters. Latent secession movements exist in California and Texas, albeit from different political directions. I certainly am not advocating secession, but I believe that if the problems with the Constitution are not fixed—and if the country stays on its current path—we are heading to serious efforts at secession. Paradoxically, the Constitution has put the *United* States in grave danger. It is time to begin thinking about what secession might mean and contemplating what shape it could take that would preserve what is best about the United States.

My hope is that facing this reality will motivate meaningful change. The breakup of the United States would not be in anyone's interest. It would have unfathomable international consequences as Russia and China surely would exploit whatever emerged from the former United States. If there is to be a radical change, it should come from careful planning, not from angry attempts to break the country apart.

A decade ago the premise of this book—that American democracy is imperiled—likely would have been dismissed as hyperbole. But few today, on the left or the right, are sanguine about the direction of the country or about its future if it hews to its current path. Saving the *United* States is possible; the defects in government can be fixed, and American democracy can be strengthened. But to go forward, we must acknowledge that the root of many problems is the Constitution itself, and we need to confront the enormously difficult task of repairing or replacing it. That is what I seek to do in this book.

NO
DEMOCRACY
LASTS
FOREVER

A noose is seen on makeshift gallows as supporters of President Donald Trump gather on the west side of the U.S. Capitol in Washington, D.C, on January 6, 2021. Trump's supporters stormed a session of Congress held that day to certify Joe Biden's election win, triggering unprecedented chaos and violence at the heart of American democracy and accusations the president was attempting a coup. *(Photograph by Andrew Caballero-Reynolds /AFP via Getty Images)*

PART I

THE CRISIS FACING
AMERICAN DEMOCRACY

1

There Is a Crisis

American Democracy in Grave Danger

Democracies are there until they are not. No form of government lasts forever. Only arrogance would cause us to believe that the United States is somehow immune to pressures for authoritarianism and that its current form of government somehow can endure indefinitely.

The events of late 2020 and early 2021 caused many Americans to realize how fragile our democracy is and how easily we could have lost it. What if Republican election officials or legislators in Georgia and Michigan and Pennsylvania had given those states' electoral votes to Donald Trump despite Joe Biden winning the popular vote there? Or what if Mike Pence, as vice president, had ruled to make Trump the winner, as John Eastman proposed and as Trump urged? The core feature of democracy—that elections decide who holds power—would have ended in the United States after 233 years.

But the threat to democracy was not just about the attempted coup. If just 42,921 votes had changed in Arizona, Georgia, and Wisconsin, Donald Trump would have been reelected president, even though he lost the popular election by almost seven million votes. The Republicans then would have controlled the evenly divided Senate as well. If the losing political party controlled the government yet again, it would have been impossible to regard the United States as still a democracy in any meaningful sense.

On January 6, 2021, the first armed insurrection in American history took place at the U.S. Capitol. It is tempting to write it off as an aberration caused by a demagogic president, but that people stormed the Capitol armed with weapons must be seen as a symptom of a deeper disquiet and threat to democracy. Likewise, that 70 percent of Republican voters continue to believe that the election was stolen, without a shred of evidence to support that belief, is a sign that something is really wrong.

After January 6, the majority of Americans heaved a collective sigh of relief, and the media was filled with self-congratulations about how the guardrails of democracy had held. But I fear that this emotion has caused us to overlook the real threats to democracy that have developed over the last half-century. The existential danger to democracy remains, even after Trump left the White House.

Signs abound that democracy is in grave danger. For one, Americans' confidence in the institutions of government is at an all-time low. The Pew Research Institute, which has been tracking public trust in government since 1958, found that it has gone from a high-water mark of 77 percent in 1964 to our contemporary 20 percent.[1] In a poll in September 2023, only 4 percent of those surveyed said that the American political system "works well."[2] This dramatic decline should be of great concern.

The president's approval ratings consistently hover in the low thirties.[3] Congress's approval rating is 18, and that may be eighteen people, not 18 percent.[4] The Supreme Court has its lowest approval ratings in history. A Gallup poll revealed that only 25 percent of the American people expressed confidence in the Supreme Court.[5] And a Marquette University poll in July 2022 had 38 percent approving the Court and 61 percent disapproving.[6]

The loss of public confidence in the institutions of government is not sudden—it has been steadily eroding for decades. Overcoming the Great Depression, fighting World War II, and battling the Cold War once unified Americans and provided a widespread sense of need for a strong national government. But by the 1960s, this unity was dissipating. The civil rights movement, which led to the end of the legal apartheid that existed in every Southern state, divided the North and the South and caused a realignment of our political parties that continues to this day. The senseless tragedy of the Vietnam War and the lies surrounding it, followed by the corruption of Watergate, did lasting damage to public trust in government. Ronald Reagan ran for president, in large part, by campaigning against the federal government and especially its social programs. The government's failure to deal with the huge problems that people see—climate change, a deteriorating infrastructure, a growing wealth gap, the unhoused on our streets—engender great doubt in its capacity to address them at all. The persistent claims, however baseless, of election fraud undermine the faith of many in the legitimacy of those who hold public office.

For many reasons, the country has become much more polarized, and politics have become much more toxic, which heightens concern over the future of American democracy. Donald Trump's election and prominence in national politics are simultaneously a reflection of this polarization and a cause for it worsening.

Indeed, by many measures, Americans are more politically polarized than at any time since Reconstruction. Over the course of Trump's presidency, an average of 87 percent of Republicans approved of his handling of the job, compared with an average of just 6 percent of Democrats.[7] That, by far, is the largest gap in history. In August 2022, about eighteen months into Biden's presidency, his approval rating among Democrats was 78 percent and among Republicans just 12 percent, a gap of 66 percent, which is less than during the Trump years, but still stunning and reflects a deeply cleaved country.

The division of views is pronounced on every issue. The COVID pandemic, instead of unifying the country, furthered the split. When the Supreme Court was considering whether the federal government could require workplaces with over one hundred employees to require employees to be vaccinated, a national poll by the University of South Florida found that 50 percent of Democrats, but only 15 percent of Republicans, regarded COVID as the most serious problem facing the country.[8] The poll found that 88 percent of Democrats, but only 22 percent of Republicans, favored the vaccination requirement. In the summer of 2022, over 90 percent of Democrats, but only 60 percent of Republicans, were vaccinated. A public health crisis involving a communicable disease that killed over one million Americans should have been an occasion of coming together, but that was impossible in our divided times, and instead became a further basis for fervent ideological disagreements.

All this has taken a toll on American democracy. According to international rankings, democracy is eroding faster in the United States than in other major Western democracies. Today the United States is more on par with Brazil, Bangladesh, Turkey, and India, according to the global think tank V-Dem Institute's 2020 democracy report.[9] The Economist Intelligence Unit also downgraded the United States to a flawed democracy in 2016.[10] Public confidence in democracy is at its lowest point on record in the United States; in fact, Americans who are dissatisfied with democracy now outnumber those who are satisfied with it.

To be sure, many commentators today are warning of the serious threats to American democracy. But insofar as they fail to recognize how much those threats stem from compromises and choices made in creating the Constitution in 1787, they are missing an essential element in understanding and ultimately solving the crisis. Quite crucially, most have insufficiently recognized that changes in the last half-century have magnified the problems inherent to the Constitution's design. Americans have revered the Constitution from its inception. Thomas Grey observed that the Constitution "has been, virtually from the moment of its ratification, a sacred symbol, the potent emblem . . . of the nation itself."[11] But this reverence has caused us to overlook how much the document's defects are responsible for the current crisis in government. Unless we address the constitutional flaws, American democracy is in serious danger.

Flaws at the Foundation

The framers made some Faustian bargains in creating the Constitution. They made these decisions in order to produce a document that the Constitutional Convention and the states would approve. But those decisions came at the cost of a document with serious flaws. Although the Constitution is revered and many brilliant choices were made in its drafting, it is also profoundly anti-democratic and, in many ways, was from the outset a bad blueprint. The framers made three especially poor choices in drafting the Constitution.

First, they distrusted democracy. Of the four institutions of government created by the Constitution—the president, the Supreme Court, the Senate, and the House of Representatives—only one, the House, was democratically elected or accountable. The president was and still is chosen by the Electoral College. The Constitution does not even require that states allow people to vote for president or that they accord their electors to the winner of a popular vote. It is hard for us to fathom, but in the early decades of American history, in some states it was their legislature, not the voters, that decided who would be that state's electors in the Electoral College.

The Constitution provided that state legislatures, not the people, choose U.S. senators, and this did not change until the Seventeenth Amendment was adopted in 1913. One of the Constitution's most anti-democratic features is that each state, regardless of its size, has two senators.

Justices of the Supreme Court and lower federal courts are chosen by the president and confirmed by the Senate. And they hold their positions for life. This arrangement certainly has the virtue of enhancing judicial independence, but it is yet another anti-democratic choice that the framers made in 1787.

The Constitution's anti-democratic nature is reflected in and highlighted by the enormous difficulty of changing it. Amending the Constitution requires the approval of two-thirds of both houses of Congress and three-quarters of the states. There have been only twenty-seven amendments since 1787, and only seventeen since the Bill of Rights was added in 1791. And two of those were to create and then repeal Prohibition. The difficulty of amending the Constitution has been lauded as one of its virtues, but just as it makes undesirable reforms more difficult, it makes needed and even essential changes almost impossible.

Second, the Constitution explicitly protected the institution of slavery, and it contained no provision to ensure that all citizens had equal protection of the law. In 1787 the Southern states would not have accepted a constitution that eliminated slavery. They insisted on provisions that prevented Congress from banning the importation of enslaved persons for twenty years (one of the only constitutional provisions that was exempt from the possibility of amendment), treated enslaved people as three-fifths of a person for purposes of apportioning seats in the House of Representatives (greatly benefiting slave states in the Electoral College as well), and required the return of escaped enslaved persons. Nothing in the Constitution even hinted at equal protection or any limit on discrimination. These compromises are a tragic flaw that has haunted the country throughout its history, and they continue to plague us with a racially divided and unequal society.

Nor did the Constitution make any effort to protect the rights of Native Americans, who were here long before the first European settlers arrived. The Constitution makes few references to them, which in itself is telling. Article I of the Constitution gives Congress the power to regulate commerce with Native tribes. It also provides that in apportioning seats in the House of Representatives, "Indians not taxed" would not count at all. Nothing in the document even hints at an obligation for the United States to respect the rights of Native Americans and their long heritage. This absence had tragic consequences. Abuses of Native Americans increased after the adoption of the Constitution. The election of Andrew Jackson finally gave the expansionists a president who was willing to use force. Just over a year after taking office, President Jackson signed the Indian Removal Act of 1830.[12]

The discovery of gold on tribal land accelerated expansionist enthusiasm. In Georgia, gold was discovered on the land of the Cherokee Nation, whereupon the state legislature enacted laws to "protect the gold" and evict the Cherokee from the land. Forced off their land, the Cherokee Nation embarked westward on the "Trail of Tears," during which one in three perished.[13] By 1850, most of the tribes that occupied eastern states had been removed. The Constitution's failure to protect Native Americans, like its failure to protect Americans of African descent, reverberates to this day.

Third, the Constitution vigorously protected states' rights. The framers regarded a national government with the power to act as a necessary evil; they desired to leave most governance to the states and to empower them. In a crucial compromise, they gave each state two senators, to be chosen by the state legislatures, regardless of population. In so doing, they would limit Congress to powers "herein granted" and protect the states with the Tenth Amendment. All this had the effect of limiting the authority of the national government and granting states significant power.

Over the course of American history, vital federal laws have been invalidated in the name of federalism. For example, the Civil Rights Act of 1875 prohibited places of public accommodation from discriminating based on race; in 1883 the Supreme Court struck it down as exceeding Congress's powers.[14] How very different our society might have been if racial discrimination by hotels and restaurants and other businesses had remained illegal after 1875. The first federal law prohibiting the use of child labor was struck down by the Supreme Court in 1918 as infringing states' rights.[15] Many children died or were maimed or suffered greatly because of this misguided decision. More recently, in 1997, the Supreme Court used states' rights to declare unconstitutional a provision of federal law, the Brady Handgun Violence Prevention Act, which required state and local law enforcement to do background checks before issuing permits for guns.[16] Indeed, states' rights were the basis for opposing the abolition of slavery and desegregation, and the argument had sufficient force to delay both for decades.

To be clear, the framers had to make these choices, or at least many of them, to ensure that the convention would adopt the Constitution and that the states would ratify it. Whether these compromises were worth it is a fascinating question, one I raise with my students. Was it better to have one nation with a constitution that institutionalized slavery, or would it have been better for the country in 1787 to split into two smaller countries, one that banned slavery and one that allowed it? But that question is not my focus here. I prefer to think of the three defects I've described as Faustian bargains that the framers struck in order to create a constitution for a single country, the United States of America.

Most of all, it is crucial for Americans today to recognize these choices made in 1787 are directly responsible for our crisis of democracy. And recognizing these problems with the original document should make us suspicious of the current Court's approach of saying that the Constitution's meaning is limited to the framers' original intentions. We must never forget that the Constitution was written and drafted exclusively by white men who owned property. Today's Court, in interpreting the Constitution, increasingly focuses on the framers' intent and original meaning and excludes the voices and interests of those who were not part of the process at all.

Why It Has Gotten Worse

All these defects were in the Constitution from the beginning, but changes in the last half-century have combined with them to create the crisis of democracy that we face today. Historical accidents, good fortune, and good will allowed the Constitution to undergird effective government for an extended period. But about fifty years ago, certain changes in society and our political system began to occur that caused the Electoral College and the Senate to emerge as more significant threats to democracy. Because these changes have occurred gradually over time, separate from one another, it has been easy to overlook how much their cumulative effect has undermined democracy. It's helpful to look at these changes as they unfolded chronologically.

First, by the 1960s, the American population was shifting, so that certain states gained disproportionately more residents than others. At the time when the Constitution was written, the most populous state (Virginia) had twelve times more people than the least populous state (Delaware). According to the 2020 census, the most populous state (California) has sixty-eight times more people than the least populous state (Wyoming).[17] This discrepancy makes the Senate and the Electoral College egregiously undemocratic.

At the same time, a political realignment was under way. Beginning with the 1964 presidential election and coming to fruition in 1968, the Southern states left the Democratic coalition. Thereafter the political parties came to be defined far more by ideology than they had been in the past.

The population shift and the political realignment, taken together, have make it far more likely today—and for the foreseeable future—that a presidential candidate who loses the popular vote can win in the Electoral College and become president. It never happened in the twentieth century, but it has already occurred twice in the twenty-first, and it almost happened twice more.

In fact, today, in theory, states that are home to only 22 percent of the country's population can choose the president.[18] That cannot be reconciled with the most elementary notion of democracy, that the winner of an election governs. Even the framers, who distrusted democracy, would likely find the current reality greatly disturbing.

To put these changes in stark terms: A president who had lost the popular vote, Donald Trump, picked as Supreme Court justices Brett Kavanaugh and Amy Coney Barrett, who were both confirmed by senators representing 44 percent of the population. Kavanaugh was fifty-three years old at his confirmation, and Barrett was forty-eight; they likely will serve on the Supreme Court for over thirty years. No plausible definition of democracy makes this situation reasonable, let alone desirable.

Since the 1970s, the Senate has become much more anti-democratic. It was always anti-democratic in that the Constitution allocates each state two senators regardless of size. But its anti-democratic nature has gotten much worse. The same political realignment and population shift described above have made the Senate much less representative. In the first two years of the Biden presidency, when the Senate was evenly split between the parties, the fifty Democratic senators represented 42 million more people than did the fifty Republican senators.[19]

In the 1970s, the Senate revised the rules concerning the filibuster, which further increased the body's anti-democratic nature. Now a minority of senators representing a minority of the population can block any piece of legislation. In the beginning, from 1788 to 1806, the Senate functioned without a filibuster. Debate over legislation could be ended at any time by a majority vote. From 1806 to 1917, although the Senate had no formal way to end debate, the body continued to function normally because maintaining a "speaking" filibuster required a senator to hold the floor continuously (like Jimmy Stewart in *Mr. Smith Goes to Washington*), or to act in carefully choreographed relays to prevent a vote on the merits. Senators maintained a few successful filibusters, most notoriously to block anti-lynching and other civil rights legislation, but only when their opposition to the legislation was so passionate that they were willing to endure the physical and logistical rigors of seizing the Senate floor and refusing to let go.

Beginning in 1975, the original "speaking filibuster" was transformed into the modern virtual version. A filibustering senator no longer had to hold the floor physically for a long period of time, as the filibuster was confined to a short window in the morning session. And most important, supporters of the filibuster no longer had to worry about maintaining a one-third floor presence since it was now the job of opponents to marshal a fixed sixty votes to end debate. Supporters of the filibuster could stay home in bed. As a result, the Senate suffered no institutional cost for maintaining a filibuster, since it could conduct business as usual for the rest of the day.

The net result was an explosion in the number of filibusters. The filibuster, once a relatively rare device intended to protect the conscience of the minority in a few deeply felt settings, morphed into a de facto supermajority voting rule. Proponents of virtually all legislation were now required to secure sixty affirmative Senate votes for passage. Conversely, senators representing less than 25 percent of the population can block any legislation. This heightens the undemocratic nature of an already profoundly undemocratic institution. By making legislation far more difficult to enact, it contributes to the widespread sense that government is broken.

The Constitution created the House of Representatives as the only democratic body, but partisan gerrymandering undermines it. Partisan gerrymandering is the practice by which the political party that controls the legislature draws election districts to maximize safe seats for that party. It is nothing new. In fact, the practice is named for Massachusetts governor Elbridge Gerry, who in 1812 signed a bill that redrew the state senate election districts to benefit his Democratic-Republican Party. But since the 1980s and 1990s, its use has grown to the point that it increasingly thwarts democracy. What has changed are the sophisticated computer programs and detailed population statistics that make partisan gerrymandering far more effective than ever before.

Consider the case of North Carolina.[20] It is essentially a purple state, leaning red. Barack Obama carried it in 2008, but Mitt Romney won it in 2012 and Donald Trump in 2016 and 2020. All these elections were decided by a narrow margin. When Republicans got a slight majority of the votes cast for the state legislature, they drew election districts to give themselves a supermajority in both of the state's legislative houses.

Republicans then drew districts for districts for the congressional delegation from North Carolina, using what they called "partisan advantage" criteria. Their expressly stated goal was to draw the districts so they would guarantee ten Republicans and three Democrats. They had a computer draw three thousand possible ways of creating election districts, and they then chose the one most likely to result in Republicans winning ten of thirteen congressional seats. It worked. In 2016 the statewide vote for members of Congress was nearly tied, but Republicans won ten of thirteen races. The same result occurred in 2018.

Both Democrats and Republicans, when they control state legislatures, engage in partisan gerrymandering. It is objectionable no matter who is doing it. It allows a political party to entrench itself in power. Voters are supposed choose their elected officials; in partisan gerrymandering, elected officials choose their voters. The whole point of partisan gerrymandering is to have elections that don't reflect the will of the "great body of society," which James Madison described as the core of democratic self-government.[21] Rather, it greatly weights elections toward the will of the partisan incumbents who draw the maps. Even Justice Antonin Scalia, who wrote an opinion that partisan gerrymandering cannot be challenged in the federal courts, spoke of "the incompatibility of severe partisan gerrymanders with democratic principles."[22]

In June 2019, the Supreme Court ruled, 5–4, that challenges to partisan gerrymandering cannot be heard in federal courts.[23] Thus state legislatures know that when they redraw districts—for congressional seats and state legislative districts—they can gerrymander with impunity. Except for a handful of states that use independent redistricting commissions, partisan gerrymandering is endemic and allows the political party that is in power to remain there.

In the twenty-first century, the Supreme Court has increasingly undermined democracy and heightened the constitutional crisis. First, the Court returned to enforcing states' rights and limiting fed-

eral power. From 1937 to 1995, it did not strike down a single federal law for exceeding the scope of congressional power or infringing
states' rights. That changed in 1995 and led, among other decisions,
to the Court declaring essential provisions of the Voting Rights Act
of 1965 unconstitutional.[24] The Court gutted the Voting Rights Act,
which in itself poses a real threat to democracy. In 2021 eighteen states
controlled by Republican legislatures adopted laws to restrict voting,
with the clear effect of disadvantaging Democratic voters and, particularly, voters of color. These laws will be much harder to challenge
successfully since the Supreme Court invalidated crucial provisions of
the Voting Rights Act.

Second, the Supreme Court has become involved in the political process to an unprecedented extent and in a manner inimical to
democracy. It has struck down campaign finance laws and allowed
corporations and the rich to dominate the political process. Its ruling
in *Citizens United v. Federal Election Commission*, in 2010, permitted
corporations to spend unlimited money in elections to get candidates
elected or defeated.[25] Ever since then, huge amounts of money have
been spent in elections, often "dark money" whose source is never
known. And often these expenditures are decisive in determining
who is elected. The Court thereby gave the wealthy and the powerful,
who always have an advantage in the political process, vastly more
influence and control.

Third, the entire judiciary has become even more anti-democratic
over time. In part, this is because of much longer life spans. In 1787
the average life span was thirty-eight years. Justices, who have life tenure, were unlikely to remain for decades. But now justices commonly
remain on the Court for decades. Clarence Thomas became a justice
in 1991 at forty-three. If he remains on the Court until he is ninety,
the age at which Justice John Paul Stevens retired, he will have been a
justice for forty-seven years. Amy Coney Barrett was forty-eight when
she was confirmed. If she remains until she is eighty-seven, the age at
which Justice Ruth Bader Ginsburg died, she will be a justice until the
year 2059.

In part, too, accidents of history have caused the Supreme Court to
be more unrepresentative. Between 1960 and 2020, the United States
has had thirty-two years with Republican presidents and twenty-eight

years with Democratic presidents. But during that period, Republican presidents placed fifteen justices on the Court, while Democratic presidents placed only eight. Put another way: President Donald Trump chose three justices in his four years as president. But the prior three Democratic presidents—Jimmy Carter, Bill Clinton, and Barack Obama—served a combined twenty years in the White House and placed only four.

Some of this inequity results from when the vacancies occurred. Richard Nixon placed four justices on the Court in his first two years as president; Jimmy Carter placed none. But vacancies are not the only factor. Republicans blocked Merrick Garland's confirmation and rushed through Amy Coney Barrett. Also, to please the Republican base on the issue of abortion, Republican presidents over the last quarter-century have picked almost entirely very conservative Catholics. Of course, no justice should be picked or rejected on account of religion, but we have a Court with six Catholic justices because Republican presidents wanted to send a message that their justices would vote to overrule *Roe v. Wade.* And they did.

Between the timing of vacancies and the pressures of politics, we now have a Court that is much more conservative than most of the American people, and it is likely to be that way for a long time to come. Not only is the Court a much more undemocratic institution, it is actively working to undermine democracy.

Over the last decade, a new threat to democracy has developed that the Constitution's framers could not possibly have imagined: the rise of social media. The nature of communications has changed dramatically. Social media and the internet have significantly benefited speech, and they have democratized users' ability to reach a mass audience. In the past, in order to reach a large number of people, a person had to be wealthy enough to own a newspaper or get a broadcast license. Now anyone with a smartphone or a modem can do so. In addition, citizens now have immediate access to unlimited information.

But social media have a downside: when speech is easy and cheap, false speech can readily be transmitted. The development of deepfakes, digitally altered images that are false but seem real, makes the problem of false speech even worse. Current First Amendment law protects false political speech and poses "more speech" as the remedy. But that approach often fails to counter false speech in elections. The challenge is to preserve social media as an unprecedented tool for free speech, while addressing the real danger of false speech for elections and democracy. Also, the proliferation of social media, allowing people to choose their message, has furthered political polarization, which further threatens democracy. Finally, the internet and social media allow foreign interference in elections in an unprecedented manner. These threats only will increase in the years ahead.

Racial inequalities continue largely unabated. To be sure, civil rights laws were finally adopted in the 1960s, but the last major civil rights law was enacted in 1991. But enormous racial inequalities persist. Twenty-four percent of African Americans and 21 percent of Latinos live below the poverty level, compared to 9 percent of whites.[26] Forty percent of African American children live in poverty—a Black child born today has a 4 in 10 chance of being born into an impoverished family—compared to 14 percent of white children. The incarceration rate among African American men is more than 3,000 per 100,000 citizens, roughly four times the national average and roughly six times the rate among white men. An African American male born in 2001 has a 32 percent chance of serving time in prison at some point in his life, while a white male born at the same time would have a 6 percent chance. The median income level of African American families has increased over the last two decades, but it is still less than two-thirds that of white families. Moreover "middle-class blacks earn seventy cents for every dollar earned by middle-class whites, but they possess only fifteen cents for every dollar of wealth held by middle-class whites."[27]

These racial disparities stem from the tragic choices that the framers made in 1787 in drafting a constitution that protected the institution of slavery.

All the changes I described above—the shifts in population and party realignment, the increased role of the Electoral College in choosing the president, the Senate rule changes that make the filibuster easier, the composition of the Supreme Court, and even social media—come together to make meaningful progress toward racial equality ever more difficult.

More generally, the growing gap between haves and have-nots in our society itself poses a threat to democracy. Income inequality in the United States increased by about 20 percent from 1980 to 2016.[28] As the Council on Foreign Relations noted, "Income and wealth inequality in the United States is substantially higher than in almost any other developed nation, and it is on the rise."[29] Those who see themselves as permanently left behind are more receptive to the appeals of authoritarian leaders who prey on the disaffected. World history shows that vast wealth gaps in a society are a threat to a democracy's survival.[30]

Can American Democracy Be Saved?

The constitutional reforms that are essential to save American democracy are not difficult to identify. They must include popular election of the president, the allocation of Senate seats based on population, the abolition or at least reform of the filibuster, term limits for Supreme Court justices, the elimination of partisan gerrymandering, the clearer empowerment of Congress especially with regard to civil rights, limits on campaign spending, greater advancement of racial equality, and more protection of voting rights.

What are the paths forward? One would be to not address the problems and to assume that American democracy will be what it has been for over two hundred years, flawed but functional. The reality is that this path is the most likely. And perhaps politicians or events will emerge that unify the country and allow it to be effectively governed. But I fear that this scenario is unlikely, and the more probable one is that dissatisfaction with our government will grow, and the political divide will increase. It is difficult to point to any signs that our government is becoming more effective or that political polarization is diminishing. We all then must face the question of whether American democracy can survive if it continues on its current path.

We have no way of knowing what will happen if major structural changes in government are not implemented. I have been frightened by the political right's embrace of authoritarian regimes. Donald Trump praises Vladimir Putin. The Conservative Political Action Committee held its 2022 convention in Hungary and celebrated Viktor Orbán, its authoritarian leader.[31] In the summer of 2022, CPAC invited Orbán to Texas, where attendees gave him the longest ovation.

The appeal of authoritarianism to a significant fraction of the American people is cause for great worry. "A scale measuring propensity toward right-wing authoritarian tendencies found right-leaning Americans scored higher than their counterparts in Australia, Canada, and the United Kingdom," a *Morning Consult* poll found. "Twenty-six percent of the U.S. population qualified as highly right-wing authoritarian, . . . twice the share of the No. 2 countries, Canada and Australia."[32]

It thus is imperative to explore the paths to meaningfully improve, and perhaps even to save, American democracy. One path is to fix many things by statute and by constitutional interpretation, without changing the document itself. Congress, for example, could pass a law mandating that independent commissions draw election districts for congressional seats. It could arguably create term limits for Supreme Court justices. The Senate could change its rules to abolish the filibuster. And the Supreme Court could declare the Electoral College unconstitutional as violating the Fifth Amendment's assurance of equal protection. At the very least, the Court could find "winner take all," which increases the likelihood of the losing candidate becoming president, is unconstitutional.

But these changes have a very low probability of occurring. In Congress, the very forces that are the problem—partisan gerrymandering of seats in the House of Representatives, the filibuster in the Senate— make it unlikely that it will enact positive reforms. And the current majority of the Supreme Court appears not even to perceive a problem, let alone to interpret the Constitution to provide a solution. After all, its decisions—protecting the right of corporations to spend unlimited sums in elections, gutting the Voting Rights Act of 1965, preventing federal courts from hearing challenges to partisan gerrymandering— all contribute significantly to the threat to democracy.

That said, reforms that can be done in Congress and in the courts must be pursued, but realism is necessary; essential changes seem highly unlikely.

Another path to explore is to amend the Constitution. Almost all the flaws in the document can be solved by amending it. A notable exception is Article V, which provides that every state has equal representation in the Senate; it explicitly states that this provision cannot be amended. But are any constitutional amendments realistically possible? A crucial flaw in the Constitution—reflecting its profoundly anti-democratic character—is the enormous difficulty of amendment. It requires two-thirds of both houses of Congress and then three-quarters of the state legislatures to pass an amendment. That is why it is has been amended only seventeen times since 1791, and two of those were to impose and then repeal Prohibition.

If change is essential but cannot happen by legislation, interpretation, or amendment, we must contemplate a more radical path: we must face the question of whether it is time for a new constitution. We need to stop venerating a document written in 1787 for an agrarian slave society and imagine what a constitution for the twenty-first century should look like.

Creating a new constitution will be a daunting task, but I want to argue that it is possible. The first step is to recognize that our Constitution is failing. Opinion polls show a dramatic loss of faith in American democracy and government on both the left and the right. It is important for Americans to see that these failures stem from the Constitution itself.

Article V creates a mechanism for drafting a new constitution. Two-thirds of the states can call for a constitutional convention, and then Congress must convene one. Or Congress could do so on its own.

Trying to draft a new constitution would be risky and may not even be possible at a time when there is no social consensus on any major issue and when the country is so deeply divided. Many fear that a new constitution would be worse than the existing one. Those concerns are not trivial, and I share them.

We must hope that the men and women chosen to draft a new constitution will rise to the occasion, as the framers in Philadelphia did in 1787, and draft a document that keeps the best features of the current Constitution and addresses its flaws. Those gathered at a new constitutional convention will know that the document they draft must have a chance of being enacted.

The largest challenge—and there will be many—will be to avoid replicating the worst defects in the Constitution, such as the Electoral College and two senators per state. We will have to give careful thought to choosing the delegates to the constitutional convention and to ratifying the document they propose. If seats at the convention are allocated by state, and if ratification requires approval of three-quarters of the states, then the new constitution will be doomed from the outset. Governments of states that benefit from the Electoral College and that have disproportionate representation in the Senate are not going to approve a document that harms them politically. We need a mechanism to appoint delegates from throughout the country who do not see themselves as representing particular states. And most of all, the proposed constitution would have to be submitted to the people for a national vote. It is a radical suggestion but an essential one if we are ever to have a new constitution that cures the defects in the existing one. Otherwise state governments that benefit from the current structure have sufficient numbers to block amendments for reform.

Is it possible to revise or replace the Constitution in a manner that does not follow the procedures for change that it specifies? There actually is precedent for it. The Articles of Confederation, which preceded the Constitution, required unanimous consent of the states for change. But the draft Constitution, in Article VII, said that it could be adopted if approved by three-quarters of the states. Our new constitution should provide that it will be adopted if approved by a majority of the voters in the United States.

The reader's instinctive reaction may be that adopting a new constitution is impossible to contemplate at a time when the country is so deeply polarized. But that was true in 1787 as well. New York ratified the Constitution by three votes, 30–27, and Virginia by just ten votes, 89–79. Rhode Island, the last state to ratify, passed it by two votes. Waiting for a time when the country is not ideologically divided would mean never engaging in the essential reforms.

I recognize that the new constitution, like the existing one, will require compromises on most major issues. Perhaps it will be impossible to get rid of the Electoral College and the allocation of two senators per state. But we must begin to think and talk about it. At some point, the United States will have a new constitution. We should start that conversation now.

We must also contemplate what could happen if all these paths prove futile and dissatisfaction with government mounts. We need to acknowledge the substantial sentiment that now favors some form of secession. The country could come apart into two or more separate nations. The Constitution contains no mechanism for secession, but rumblings about it are being heard from the left in California and from the right in Texas. I expect that if we ever get a conservative Republican president and a Republican Congress, calls for secession in California and some other states would go from fringe to mainstream. Likewise, if a liberal Democrat is elected president with a Democratic Congress, conservative states will begin serious talk of secession. The reality is that what divides the most liberal and the most conservative states is much greater than what unifies them. The differences always were there—dramatically so with regard to slavery and civil rights, but the gulf between red and blue states is ever growing.

The image of secession in the United States is based on history, in which Southern states seceded in 1861 and precipitated the Civil War. But secession need not be violent and could be a mostly amicable divorce. Quite importantly, secession need not take the form of the dissolution of the United States. Power could radically devolve to the states for most things, while retaining a national government for the military and foreign affairs. We could return to a form of government more like the Articles of Confederation or the European Union.

To be clear, I am not advocating secession. Nor do I think it is likely in the foreseeable future. It certainly is not imminent, but rumblings are there and may grow, so we need to begin thinking about the unthinkable. If nothing else, looking into this abyss may give rise to pressure for fundamental, essential reforms.

Looking at all the possible paths to reform should reassure us that while major change is difficult, it is not impossible. And we must recognize that at some point, if things continue to get worse, major change inevitably will happen. It is better to carefully consider the ways to make it succeed in the best possible way than to ignore them.

Too Apocalyptic?

Perhaps you think I am being too apocalyptic. After all, the United States has thrived under the Constitution for over two hundred years, despite all its flaws, and it remains the wealthiest, most powerful nation in the world.

But no country stays in that position forever. And we must recognize that even as the American government has become increasingly dysfunctional, it faces problems of existential significance: climate change, with the planet warmer than at any time "in the history of modern civilization";[33] a pandemic that is unlikely to be the last; and the rise of China as a dominant world power. The need for effective government has never been more urgent, but few are confident that our government institutions have the capacity to act effectively.

It is strange to write a book based on a premise—that American democracy is in grave danger—that I hope is wrong. But the problems with our current government are too overwhelming to ignore. I thus think it imperative that we try to understand the causes of our flawed system of government and how to fix it. And that means we must focus on the deep-seated problems in the Constitution and what can be done about them.

Scene at the Signing of the Constitution of the United States, with George
Washington, Benjamin Franklin, and Thomas Jefferson at the Constitutional
Convention of 1787; oil painting on canvas by Howard Chandler Christy,
1940. The painting is 20 by 30 feet and hangs in the United States
Capitol building. *(Photograph by GraphicaArtis / Getty Images)*

PART II

HOW THE CONSTITUTION BECAME A THREAT TO DEMOCRACY

2

The 1960s

Population Shifts and Political Realignments
Undermine Democracy

To draft a constitution that would be approved at the Constitutional Convention in Philadelphia and then ratified by the states, the framers had to make compromises. States with slavery would never have approved a constitution that abolished it, yet they wanted their enslaved population to count as part of their political strength in the composition of Congress and in choosing the president. Small states insisted on a senate that accorded each state equal representation. Those who opposed these choices, and they were many, realized that they had to accept them in order to have a new constitution; otherwise the country would have to continue under the Articles of Confederation, which were leading it to bankruptcy and open revolt.

These choices—the Electoral College choosing the president, and the Senate comprising two senators per state—were problematic from the beginning because of their profoundly anti-democratic nature. Limiting rule by the majority certainly has its virtues, but it is hard to see how either of these institutions help protect against tyranny or enhance checks and balances.

But the undemocratic nature of these governmental institutions has become much worse in the last half-century because of population shifts and political realignments. To understand their significance, it is necessary to go back to the beginning and grasp the choices that the framers made in drafting the Constitution. These choices were the diseased roots that grew into the current crisis of democracy.

The Constitutional Convention: An Illegal Enterprise?

Fifty-five white men gathered in a crowded room in 1787 and ignored their assigned task. They were supposed to revise and propose modest changes to the Articles of Confederation, but they took it upon themselves to write a new constitution. They did not want anyone to know what they were doing and pledged secrecy. This questionable process gave birth to the Constitution by which the United States has governed itself for well over two centuries.

Winning the Revolutionary War and creating a government are vastly different enterprises. Those who fought the Revolutionary War were deeply suspicious of national power and feared the tyranny of centralized government, as they lamented in the Declaration of Independence. A consensus emerged that the new government had to avoid the worst aspects of English rule and lack significant central authority. The document they created for that new government was the Articles of Confederation.

The Articles of Confederation regarded a federal government as a necessary evil that had to be minimized as much as possible. "Each state," the document declared, "retains its sovereignty, freedom, and independence, and every power, jurisdiction, and right, which is not by this confederation expressly delegated to the United States, in Congress assembled." The Articles of Confederation provided for no federal judiciary and chief executive who was very weak and served a one-year term. The powers of the Congress of the Confederation (sometimes called the Confederation Congress or the Second Continental Congress) were greatly circumscribed. It had the authority to wage war, coin money, establish post offices, and deal with Indian tribes, but it had no power to tax or to regulate commerce among the states. The only authority that the Articles of Confederation granted to Congress were the noncontroversial powers that Parliament and the Crown had exercised under the colonial system.[1] The national government created by the Articles of Confederation was intentionally designed to have no power over individuals, businesses, or even state governments.

Not surprisingly, serious problems developed under the Articles of Confederation. Most notably, states adopted laws that discriminated against goods and services from other states. For instance, New York, as a state with a port, imposed duties on goods that were destined for other states. To retaliate, those states then enacted taxes on commerce with New York. Many states tried to erect trade barriers to help their own economic interests. Congress was powerless to it all. Also, problems developed because of the lack of national executive or judicial authority. For instance, there was no way to ensure that states would comply with the laws Congress adopted.

By 1786 the new nation was essentially bankrupt, and rebellions began to break out in the states. That year representatives of five states met in Annapolis, Maryland, in a gathering titled "Meeting of Commissioners to Remedy Defects of the Federal Government." They especially focused on curing the trade barriers that had developed between the states. But they realized that not enough of the states were represented there to make a difference, so they called for a meeting of representatives of all the states.

In February 1787 the Confederation Congress passed a resolution calling for a convention for the "sole and express purpose of revising the Articles of Confederation." The Confederation Congress passed it grudgingly and wanted the convention to have a limited scope, focusing on the trade barriers. After all, those who served believed in the institution and did not want to see it eliminated. They wanted to fix the existing government, not abolish it.

The meeting was to be held in Philadelphia, which was the largest American city at the time, although still quite small by modern standards. It had only forty thousand residents; New York would soon surpass it in population and stature.[2] Travel to Philadelphia was difficult, and it was a hot summer.

The meeting was held in the Assembly Room of the Pennsylvania State House, a place that could barely hold all the delegates. Fifty-five men, from twelve of the thirteen states, met there from May 25 to September 17, 1787. Rhode Island chose to send no delegates. Not all of the men attended every meeting, and some of them avoided meetings so as to not have to go on record about slavery. Ultimately only thirty-nine of them signed the document.

Although the delegates' explicit and limited task was to fix the Articles of Confederation, they quickly decided on a very different undertaking. Their first vote, on May 30, was to adopt of a resolution "that a national government ought to be established consisting of a supreme legislative, judiciary and executive."[3] In other words, early in the convention, the delegates abandoned their assigned task of repairing the Articles of Confederation and instead embarked on drafting a new document.

The arrogance of this act is obvious, and furthermore, it was illegal. The Articles of Confederation required unanimity to make any change. The Constitution they drafted said in Article VII that it would be effective only when nine of the thirteen states ratified it. In fact, North Carolina did not ratify it until November 1789, over six months after George Washington had been inaugurated as president on April 30, 1789. And Rhode Island did not ratify it until a year later, on May 29, 1790. Rhode Island was critical of the Constitution's compromises on the issue of slavery, and it resisted ratifying until the U.S. government threatened to sever commercial relations with the state.

The Constitutional Convention delegates were not typical of the residents of the country. The youngest delegate, Jonathan Dayton, was twenty-six; the oldest was Benjamin Franklin, age eighty-one, who had to be carried to sessions in a sedan chair. In 1775 there were only three thousand college graduates in a population of 2.5 million, but over half of the delegates—twenty-nine—had graduated from college.[4] Over half were lawyers or had some legal education. Many had played a role in forming the nation: eight had signed the Declaration of Independence, twenty-seven had been officers in the Revolutionary War, and thirty-nine had served in Congress under the Articles of Confederation.

Twenty-five of the delegates—or 45 percent—were slave owners. These included George Washington, who presided over the Constitutional Convention, and James Madison, who took its official notes. But support for slavery was far from unanimous. Some, such as Franklin and Alexander Hamilton, opposed slavery and became members of anti-slavery societies.

The Constitutional Convention was conducted entirely in secret, behind closed doors.[5] The delegates agreed not to discuss the proceedings with the press or public and not to publish their notes for at least fifty years.[6] After Jefferson, who was in France at the time, learned of this secrecy rule, he strongly objected in a letter to John Adams: "I am sorry [the convention delegates] began their deliberations by so abominable a precedent as that of tying the tongues of their members. Nothing can justify this example but the innocence of their intentions, and the ignorance of the value of public discussion."[7] But those at the convention knew they were abandoning their assigned task of fixing the Articles of Confederation and doing something much more controversial: writing a new constitution.

The Constitution as Compromises

The U.S. Constitution was a reaction to what preceded it, the tyranny of British rule and the failure of the Articles of Confederation. It was also a product of compromises on all the major issues. The delegates at the Constitutional Convention disagreed sharply on crucial questions. This reflected the differing interests of the states—large as opposed to small, slave as compared to nonslave—as well as political disagreements. The only way to craft a constitution that all could support was to effect a series of compromises. (If we are to contemplate a new constitution for the United States, we must recognize at the outset that every major issue will again require a compromise.)

The framers of the Constitution have long been venerated. Increasingly, the current Supreme Court says that the Constitution's meaning is limited to the framers' views and the public's understanding at the time. In a June 2022 decision, the Court, in interpreting the clauses of the First Amendment concerning religion, declared that "the line that courts and governments must draw between the permissible and the impermissible has to accor[d] with history and faithfully reflec[t] the understanding of the Founding Fathers."[8]

I have always been baffled as to why the country should be governed by the views of those who lived in an agrarian slave society in the late eighteenth century, almost half of whom owned slaves.[9] It also is deeply disquieting to be governed by their views in light of their strong distrust of democracy, let alone their views on matters of race and gender.

On the one hand, the Constitution starts with a seemingly ring-ing endorsement for popular governance. Its first words, found in its Preamble, proclaim that the Constitution is created by "we the peo-ple." The people are sovereign. This phrase makes clear that the United States is to be a democracy, not a monarchy, a theocracy, or a totali-tarian government—the dominant forms of government throughout the world in 1787.

But contrary to what schoolchildren have been taught for gener-ations, the government that the framers created in Philadelphia in 1787 is anything but a democracy. To begin with, they did not imag-ine women or enslaved people, or even freed Blacks, ever having the right to vote. In many places in the country, the franchise was limited to property owners. Nothing in the original Constitution protected a right to vote. Not until the ratification of the Fifteenth Amendment in 1870 did the Constitution say that the right to vote could not be denied on account of race or previous condition of servitude. And it was not until the adoption of the Nineteenth Amendment in 1920 (131 years after the Constitution was ratified) that women were accorded the right to vote.

The framers' distrust of democracy, though, did more than reflect the discriminatory and exclusionary views of the time. The govern-ment they designed was profoundly anti-democratic. It reflected a group of elites—and the drafters were elites—who distrusted the masses of the people. The Constitution creates four institutions of government: the president, the Supreme Court (and the lower federal courts if Congress should choose to create them), the Senate, and the House of Representatives. Only the last was elected by the people. The choices that the framers made in creating the other institutions reflect their antipathy toward democratic rule. And the anti-democratic design of the Constitution is highlighted by one of its most celebrated features: it is enormously difficult to change by amendment.

The Electoral College

The only number that matters in a presidential election is 270. That is the number of electoral votes it takes for someone to be elected presi-dent of the United States. There are 538 electors, and victory requires getting a majority in the Electoral College. If no candidate receives a majority, then the House of Representatives chooses the president, with each state getting one vote.

The number of electors a state has is equal to the sum of its senators and representatives. Additionally, the Twenty-third Amendment allocates three electors to the District of Columbia. The six states with the most electors are California (55), Texas (38), New York (29), Florida (29), Illinois (20), and Pennsylvania (20). The seven smallest states in population—Alaska, Delaware, Montana, North Dakota, South Dakota, Vermont, and Wyoming—each have three electors.

Each state determines its own method for choosing electors. Today all states select the electors based on who wins the popular vote. The Supreme Court recently ruled that a state may direct how an elector is to vote, eliminating the problem of the "faithless elector" who does not follow the popular vote in that state.[10] But in the early nineteenth century, about half of the states had their state legislatures choose their electors. An open issue today is whether under the Constitution a state legislature may disregard the popular vote and award the state's electors to the candidate who lost the popular vote in the state. That possibility arose in the 2020 presidential election and likely will arise again in the future.

Even though its title implies a collective body, the Electoral College does not actually meet. Rather, the electors gather in each state on the Monday after the second Tuesday in December and determine how the state will allocate its electoral votes. In other words, the "electoral college" is not a single entity but "an aggregation of fifty-one different bodies, each of which meets and votes separately."[11] It is actually mandated by the Constitution. Both Article II and the Twelfth Amendment require that the electors meet to cast their ballots "in their respective states." Although this likely reflected concerns about travel at a time when it was far more difficult than it is today, it also was intended to prevent the group from deliberating as a collegial body where votes could be changed by discussion and compromise.

The Electoral College emerged as the way of choosing the president late in the deliberations at the Constitutional Convention. Many different methods of selecting the president had been debated, such as direct popular election, selection by the state governors, and election by Congress, as in a parliamentary system.[12] The Electoral College, once proposed, attracted widespread support at the Constitutional Convention.

In large part, the Electoral College reflected the framers' distrust of majority rule. Although it is an embarrassment for a country committed to democracy, for them the appeal was doubtless that it left choosing the president to the elites, not to the people. Alexander Hamilton, in *Federalist* No. 68, explained that the "immediate election [of the president] should be made by men most capable of analyzing the qualities adapted to the station."[13] He said that a "small number of persons, selected by their fellow citizens from the general mass, will be most likely to possess the information and discernment requisite to such complicated investigations." This anti-democratic aspect of the Electoral College was enthusiastically embraced, as Hamilton said that "if the manner of [presidential election] be not perfect, it is at least excellent. It unites in an eminent degree all the advantages the union of which was to be desired."

Moreover, small states strongly favored the Electoral College because it gave them much greater influence than they would have in the direct election of the president. In fact, today, in theory, states with only 22 percent of the country's population can choose the president.

But the Electoral College was also very much a product of the compromises concerning slavery that were at the core of the Constitution's drafting and ratification. Prior to considering the method of choosing the president, the convention delegates agreed to the Three-Fifths Clause, the provision in Article I that counted enslaved individuals as three-fifths of a person for the purpose of determining population for allocating seats in the House of Representatives. But since enslaved persons obviously could not vote, Southern states would not get the benefit of this population in direct presidential elections. The Electoral College provided a huge benefit for states with slavery: electors would be allocated based on seats in Congress, and enslaved persons counted toward that. If the president were directly elected by the voters, voters in the North would outnumber Southern voters because the South's half-million enslaved people were not voters. With the Electoral College, each Southern state could count its slaves as three-fifths of a person in its share of votes.

This was explicitly understood and expressed at the Constitutional Convention. Oliver Ellsworth of Connecticut proposed that state legislatures appoint the "electors,"[14] based on population, so that small states would have no special advantage. In response, James Madison, a slaveholder from Virginia, said that "one difficulty . . . of a serious nature" made election by the people impossible. The "right of suffrage," he observed, was "much more diffusive in the Northern than the Southern States; and the latter could have no influence in the election on the score of the Negroes."[15] As Paul Finkelman notes, "In order to guarantee that the nonvoting slaves could nevertheless influence the presidential election, Madison favored the creation of the electoral college."[16]

Hugh Williamson, a delegate to the Constitutional Convention from North Carolina, was even more explicit. Direct election of the president, he noted, would put Virginia at a disadvantage because "her slaves will have no suffrage."[17] The same would be true for all the Southern states.

As Yale law professor Akhil Reed Amar has repeatedly pointed out, the Electoral College "was originally much more about slavery than about a big-state, small-state balance."[18] This, in itself, should make us deeply uncomfortable with it.

Most fundamentally, the Electoral College is inconsistent with the core constitutional value of democratic governance. Five times in American history, including twice in the early part of the twenty-first century—in 1824, 1876, 1888, 2000, and 2016—the candidate who lost the popular vote became president. On November 6, 2012, Donald Trump tweeted, "The electoral college is a disaster for a democracy." For once, I can say that Trump was right. The United States is the only country in the world that chooses its chief executive this way, and the only nation where a person who loses the popular vote can be chosen. The Electoral College is antithetical to democracy, and any president chosen after losing the popular vote inherently lacks legitimacy.

The Senate

The method of choosing the president did not lead to a major fight at the Constitutional Convention, but the method of allocating representatives in Congress led to an intense battle. Not surprisingly, the more populous states disagreed with those with the smallest number of people. The states with the most people—Virginia and Pennsylvania—wanted representation in Congress to be allocated based on population. In their proposal, known as the Virginia Plan, representation in two houses in Congress would have been allocated on the basis of population.

But the smaller states—New Jersey and Delaware—wanted equal representation for each state. Their New Jersey Plan would have had one house in Congress, with every state having an equal number of representatives.

The delegates argued over this issue for more than six weeks. It was a dominant subject of discussion, and the disagreement could have derailed the entire enterprise. But finally the delegates from Connecticut—Roger Sherman and Oliver Ellsworth—offered a compromise. There would be two houses of Congress: a House of Representatives with representation based on population, and a Senate with each state having two senators.

Although we take this structure for granted, the Constitutional Convention reached no consensus in favor of the proposal. Five states supported it, four states opposed it, and the delegates of Massachusetts were divided. But the Connecticut Compromise passed and created the structure of Congress that has existed ever since. The importance of this decision both for the success of the Constitutional Convention and for American government cannot be overstated. Gordon Wood, a preeminent historian of this period, wrote: "Most historians consider July 16, 1787, the decisive day in the Constitutional Convention. That was the day on which the Connecticut Compromise, also known as the Great Compromise, was adopted, which gave each state, however large or small, equal representation in the Senate."[19]

No doubt this compromise was essential to creating the Constitution. But undeniably, the compromise made the Constitution significantly undemocratic from the start. As the Supreme Court said in the 1960s, the core of democratic governance is the one-person, one-vote rule.[20] The Constitution requires that for any elected body, all districts must be of about the same size. Only in that way does every person have an equal chance to affect the outcome of an election. Chief Justice Earl Warren said that of all the cases decided during his tenure on the Supreme Court, the most important were the rulings that required all districts for a legislative body to be about the same in population. He wrote: "Simply stated, an individual's right to vote for state legislators is unconstitutionally impaired when its weight is in a substantial fashion diluted when compared with votes of citizens living in other parts of the State."[21]

The one-person, one-vote rule is followed for *every* city council with election districts, for every house of every state legislature, and for seats in the U.S. House of Representatives. Only one elected body in the United States does not have to comply with this requirement: the Senate. Allocating two senators for every state gives disproportionate influence to smaller states and their voters. This was already true in 1787, but it is vastly more important today because the population disparities between small and large states have grown enormously.

Equal representation in the Senate was essential to the convention delegates from smaller states and later to the ratifying conventions in these states. So vitally important is this provision that it is one of only two provisions in the entire Constitution that are exempt from being amended. Article V, which governs the amendment process, says that the provisions that prohibited Congress from banning the import of slaves could not be amended until 1808. The other provision that cannot be changed by amendment is "that no State, without its Consent, shall be deprived of its equal Suffrage in the Senate."

The Senate's anti-democratic character was a bargain struck so that the delegates and the states would approve the Constitution. It was unquestionably necessary to secure approval, but it created an inequality in representation that was troubling to many in 1787 and that is far more disturbing today, as the disparity in population among the states has grown enormously over time.

Moreover, the Senate's anti-democratic character was heightened by the choice to have senators selected by state legislatures and not by the people in the states. Unlike the rule allocating senators, the provision that state legislatures would choose senators was not controversial at all during the Convention. The framers were afraid that a democratic majority could become tyrannical. They distrusted the masses and wanted the elites to control elections. So they took the choice of senators away from the people and put it in the hands of state legislatures. As Robert Caro explained, "In creating a Senate for the new nation, its Founding Fathers had tried to create within the government an institution that would speak for the educated, the well-born, the well-to-do, that would protect the rights of property, that would not function as an embodiment of the people's will, but would stand—'firmly'—as a great bulwark against that will."[22]

Not until 1913—126 years after the Constitution was drafted—was this part of the Constitution changed. The Seventeenth Amendment requires the popular election of senators. This was an essential, democratic reform. But it only highlights that the framers did not believe in the principles of democracy that are widely held today.

Why Is It So Much Worse Now?

The defects in the Constitution have been there since 1787. Why, then, are they only now causing a serious crisis in American government? I would quarrel with the premise of that question, that the problems are just emerging now. After all, the choices made at the Constitutional Convention with regard to slavery ultimately led to a Civil War and to deeply embedded racial inequalities that have existed throughout American history. The lack of constitutional protection for Native Americans contributed to their genocide and persecution. The defects in the structure of government—the Electoral College, the Senate, the emphasis on states' rights—have caused great problems at many points in history. The failure to enact any major civil rights laws for almost a century after Reconstruction was a direct result of these choices made at the government's founding. And to our good fortune, the loser of a presidential election has won in the Electoral College only a relatively few times. Also, the growth of the country over time, initially geographically, then economically, then in international power, has caused a sense of great satisfaction with the government created by the Constitution.

But things have undoubtedly gotten worse, and the crisis for the future of American democracy is greater than ever before. Why? The story is complex and cannot be reduced to a simple explanation, but the demographic and political changes that began in the 1960s and that have continued over the last half-century have contributed greatly to the flaws in the Constitution manifesting themselves far more than before.

Twice in this century—in 2000 and 2016—a candidate who lost the popular vote became president, and it almost happened two more times. If John Kerry had won Ohio in 2004, he would have become president despite losing the popular election to George W. Bush. In 2020, if 42,921 votes had changed in Arizona, Georgia, and Wisconsin, Donald Trump would have been reelected president despite losing the popular election by almost seven million votes.

What has changed? What makes it ever more likely that the loser in a presidential election will nevertheless become president? It is hard to think of anything more inconsistent with the idea of democracy than the winner of an election not prevailing. And a president who takes office having lost the popular vote will inherently lack legitimacy.

Population shifts and political realignments that began in the 1960s are directly responsible for the real risk in every presidential election that the popular vote winner will not prevail in the Electoral College. The twenty-first century has so far brought two presidential elections that were not decided by the popular vote, but the concept of a non-popularly elected president was not new. It is a mistake to think that this flaw in the Constitution began to manifest itself only recently, even if it has become more of a risk now than it was before.

In the 1824 presidential election, there were four candidates: John Quincy Adams, Henry Clay, William Crawford, and Andrew Jackson. Jackson won the plurality of the popular vote and in the Electoral College, but with four candidates running, no one received a majority in either. The Constitution requires that a candidate receive a majority in the Electoral College in order to become president, and Jackson's failure to do this meant that the election would be decided by the House of Representatives. In 1824 a deal was struck in the House—often referred to as the "corrupt bargain." Clay threw his support to Adams in exchange for being named secretary of state.[23]

When no candidate gets a majority in the Electoral College, the procedure prescribed by Constitution is even less democratic: every state, regardless of size, gets one vote in the House in selecting the president. This procedure had been used once. The 1800 presidential election deadlocked because presidential candidate Thomas Jefferson received the same number of Electoral College votes as his vice-presidential candidate, Aaron Burr. On the thirty-sixth ballot, the House chose Jefferson as the new president.

In 1876, in the race between Democrat Samuel Tilden and Republican Rutherford B. Hayes, Tilden won 200,000 more votes than Hayes, but he won only 184 of the 185 Electoral College votes that he needed to become president. Hayes had only 165 electoral votes. Twenty Electoral College votes were in dispute in the South—in Florida, Louisiana, and South Carolina—as well as in Oregon. Congress set up a commission, chaired by Supreme Court justice Joseph Bradley, to determine who would receive the contested votes. The commission had fifteen members: five chosen by the Senate, five by the House, and five associate justices of the Supreme Court. Seven were Democrats and seven were Republicans, with the swing vote supposed to be Justice David Davis, an independent. But then Davis got elected to the Senate and Bradley, a Republican, was chosen as his replacement.

Bradley joined the seven Republicans on the commission in awarding, by an 8–7 vote, the electoral votes to the Republican, Hayes, as part of a bargain: the Democrats agreed that Hayes would be president in exchange for an end to Reconstruction.[24] As a result, the substantial racial progress that had been achieved was quickly undone. Vigilante violence against Black individuals became rampant, and soon laws were adopted throughout the South to mandate segregation of the races and deprive Blacks of all civil rights.

In 1888 the race between Democratic president Grover Cleveland and Benjamin Harrison was fraught with scandal: candidates bought votes, and Black votes were suppressed. Cleveland received over ninety thousand votes more than Harrison, yet Harrison won in the Electoral College, 233 to 168.[25]

In the twentieth century, however, no loser in the popular vote won in the Electoral College, so the country paid relatively little attention to the Electoral College. Then in 1968, the country came close to an electoral crisis in which the winner of the popular vote would not become president.

The 1968 election was a three-way race between Richard Nixon, Hubert Humphrey, and George Wallace. Wallace, the governor of

Alabama and an ardent defender of segregation, received almost ten million votes and came in first in the balloting in five states: Georgia, Alabama, Mississippi, Arkansas, and Louisiana, winning him a total of forty-six electoral votes. Nixon ultimately won both the popular vote and the Electoral College, but a switch of fewer than 78,000 votes in two states, Illinois and Missouri, would have dropped him below an electoral vote majority and forced the election into the House of Representatives to choose the president.[26]

Some think the country has just been lucky that so few popular vote losers have become president. As Robert M. Alexander has observed, "Nearly 40 percent of all elections would have resulted in either a different winner or an Electoral College deadlock with a change in less than just thirty thousand votes. And 20 percent of all presidential elections have come down to less than just ten thousand votes between the winning ticket and the losing ticket."[27]

But today this luck has run out. Already in the first fifth of the twenty-first century, the popular vote loser has twice become president because of the Electoral College. Al Gore, who had been vice president during the Clinton administration, received 200,000 more votes than George W. Bush. The outcome in the Electoral College depended on the results in Florida, where the vote was exceedingly close. The Florida Supreme Court, pursuant to federal and state law, ordered a counting of all of the uncounted votes in the state. But on December 12, 2000, the U.S. Supreme Court, in a 5–4 decision split along ideological lines, ordered an end to the counting. Bush received Florida's electoral votes, meaning that he won 271, while Gore won 266.[28] For the first time in American history, the Court effectively decided a presidential election. We do not know who would have prevailed if all the uncounted ballots had been tallied. But when the counting was stopped, Bush was ahead of Gore by only 537 votes out of almost six million cast (0.009 percent). The popular perception, justifiably, was that the five most conservative justices, all of whom had been appointed by Republican presidents, had handed the election to the Republican candidate George W. Bush.

In 2016 the disparity between the popular vote and the Electoral College outcome was even more dramatic in the race between Donald Trump and Hillary Clinton. Trump lost by more than 2.8 million votes, yet he won in the Electoral College, 304–227.[29] Clinton would have won the presidency with only a shift of 39,000 votes (0.006 percent of all votes cast) in Pennsylvania, Michigan, and Wisconsin.[30]

As I mentioned earlier, twice more in this century, the popular vote loser almost won in the Electoral College. In the 2004 presidential election, George W. Bush beat John Kerry by over three million votes and by a 286–251 margin in the Electoral College. But if Ohio alone had come out differently, Kerry would have won in the Electoral College despite decisively losing the popular vote. A "shift in less than 60,000 votes out of more than 5.6 million total votes cast in Ohio," observes Alexander, "would have earned Kerry the presidency with 271 electoral votes in spite of trailing Bush by 3 million votes cast from across the country."[31]

In 2020 Joe Biden beat Donald Trump by seven million votes in the popular election and by seventy-four votes in the Electoral College. From that perspective, the election does not seem close at all. But Biden won Arizona by less than 11,000 votes, Georgia by less than 12,000, and Wisconsin by slightly more than 20,000. A shift of 43,000 votes, less than needed to fill a football stadium, would have made Donald Trump president again.

The Electoral College was a mistake from the beginning, because it was based on distrust of the people and the desire to protect the political power of states with slavery. But the likelihood of the losing candidate becoming president is much greater today than it was earlier in American history.

The most frequently advanced justification for the Electoral College is that it encourages candidates to pay attention to smaller states.[32] But that is hardly as important as the core value of democratic governance. In reality, candidates inevitably pay more attention to some states than to others. Because swing states tend to matter most in the Electoral College, candidates often focus their campaigns on these states and ignore the vast majority of other states. In the 2000 election, notes the historian Allen Guelzo, "the campaigns rightly spent more time in Florida than any other state (47 visits). The campaigns also targeted Michigan (39 visits), Pennsylvania (36 visits), California (34 visits), Wisconsin (31 visits), Missouri (30 visits), Illinois (29 visits), Ohio (27 visits), and Iowa (27 visits)."[33] In 2016, he continues, "94 percent of all campaign speeches, rallies, or town hall meetings took place in just 12 states. Put another way, 94 percent of all campaigning occurred in less than a quarter of the country."[34] Resources are concentrated in battleground states, and these resources encourage or discourage turnout rates depending on party desires. Hence they affect outcomes.[35] I live in California, and I never saw any political ads for the presidential candidates in 2016 or 2020. But when I went to Pennsylvania during those election seasons, candidate ads were everywhere. Everyone, especially the candidates, knows that presidential elections now are likely to turn on a handful of potential swing states: Arizona, Georgia, Michigan, Nevada, Pennsylvania, and Wisconsin. That, understandably, is where candidates focus their attention.

When the result in the Electoral College matches that of the popular vote—as it did in every election in the twentieth century—it is easy for people to largely forget about it. No longer, though, can we ignore the Electoral College. The experiences of 2000 and 2016, and the close calls in 2004 and 2020, are not coincidences. Real changes are making it much more likely that the popular vote loser will become president again and again in the years ahead.

One aspect of the Electoral College that is not provided for in the Constitution contributes to the likelihood that the losing candidate will prevail: most states award their electoral votes on a winner-take-all basis. In every state except Nebraska and Maine, the candidate who wins the statewide popular vote—even by the narrowest margin—gets all the electoral votes from that state.

Effectively, winner-take-all means that in 2020, say, a vote for Donald Trump in California or a vote for Joe Biden in Texas had absolutely no effect on the outcome of the election. That in itself should be troubling. In terms of determining who will be president, it's as if the vote were not cast at all. Nebraska and Maine allocate electoral votes by congressional district—the elector for each congressional district votes for the candidate who got the majority of the votes there, and the remaining electors are chosen statewide. Nebraska and Maine thus have a much more proportional allocation of electoral votes than all other states, where the principle is winner-take-all.

The Electoral College count, therefore, magnifies the winning candidate's margin of victory relative to the total popular vote count.[36]

For instance, in 1980, Ronald Reagan won just over 50 percent of the popular vote but nearly 91 percent of the Electoral College vote. In 1912, Woodrow Wilson captured 42 percent of the popular vote but 82 percent of the Electoral College vote.[37]

But winner-take-all is pernicious because it increases the likelihood that the popular vote loser can win in the Electoral College. If every state allocated its electors proportionately to its popular vote, as Nebraska and Maine do, then the vote in the Electoral College would much more likely be the same as the vote of the people. But as it is, a candidate who wins enough states by a small margin can win in the Electoral College, even if he or she loses in other states by a very large margin and loses the popular vote. This is what occurred in 2016: Trump won the presidency by winning several large states (such as Florida, Pennsylvania, and Wisconsin) by very narrow margins, gaining all their electoral votes in the process, even as Clinton claimed other large states (such as California, Illinois, and New York) by much wider margins. Trump's share of the popular vote, in fact, was the seventh-smallest winning percentage since 1828.[38]

Population shifts over the last half-century are one reason the Electoral College has been increasingly likely to choose the candidate who lost the popular vote. It inherently underrepresents more populous states and overrepresents less populous ones, because each state has electors equal to the sum of its senators and representatives and each state gets two senators regardless of size. For example, Wyoming has about one electoral vote per 195,000 people, while California has one for about 710,000 people. This in itself is anti-democratic and inconsistent with the one-person, one-vote rule that the Supreme Court has mandated for other elections.

California has about 10 percent of the electors, but 12 percent of the nation's population. At first blush, a difference of 2 percent does not seem significant. But in close elections, the difference between the winning and losing candidates is less than 2 percent. Giving each state at least three electors was meant to lessen the gap between the overpopulous states and smaller states in choosing the president, but now smaller states are overrepresented. The larger a state's population, the more it is underrepresented.[39]

The mis-weighting of votes based on a state population is only worsening. According to the Census, "Americans are, increasingly and rapidly, moving into big cities."[40] Between 2000 and 2012, our urban populations increased by 12 percent. "Cities are growing especially in the biggest states, where each individual vote means the least: in California, New York, North Carolina, Illinois, and New Jersey."[41] But as a result, the residents of the "increasingly sparsely populated Southern and Midwestern states have electoral college votes that are growing in power."[42] The political implications cannot be ignored: the Southern and Midwestern states that have disproportionate power in the Electoral College are red, while the states with the largest underrepresented urban populations are blue. Not surprisingly, then, given the current political configuration, Republicans have won solely because of the Electoral College.

In addition to demographic shifts, political realignment also has increased the likelihood that the popular election loser will win the Electoral College. From the 1930s until 1964, the Democratic Party was a coalition of liberal Northern states and conservative Southern states. The South was solidly Democratic in both presidential and senatorial elections. This was a lingering effect of Republicans being the party of Lincoln and Reconstruction, whereas Democrats had supported states' rights and brought about the end of Reconstruction. Frederick Douglass said, "I knew that however bad the Republican Party was, the Democratic Party was much worse. The elements of which the Republican party was composed gave better ground for the ultimate hope of the success of the colored man's cause than those of the Democratic Party."[43]

Beginning in 1955, Democrats held unbroken control of the Senate for twenty-six years. Between 1933 and 1995, Democrats controlled the House for all but four years. Franklin Delano Roosevelt's original coalition of white Southerners, white ethnics, and the white working class allowed for a period of domination that has never been seen before, or since, in American politics.

In 1960 Democratic candidate John F. Kennedy won decisively in Southern states, such as Alabama (59 percent to Nixon's 41 percent), Georgia (63 to 37 percent), and Louisiana (50 to 29 percent). He prevailed more narrowly in Arkansas, Mississippi, South Carolina, and Texas. He also carried Connecticut, Illinois, Massachusetts, New

York, and Pennsylvania. That coalition is unfathomable from today's perspective, but it was the core of the Democratic Party for decades.

At the same time, the Republican Party also spanned the ideological spectrum. Some Republican senators were liberal, like Jacob Javits from New York, Clifford Case from New Jersey, and Edward Brooke from Massachusetts. Prominent Republicans such as Nelson Rockefeller—who was governor of New York and vice president under Gerald Ford—were much more liberal than any prominent Republicans today. It is a surprise now to read the Republican Party platform from 1960, which declared: "In such a nation—a nation dedicated to the proposition that all men are created equal—racial discrimination has no place. It can hardly be reconciled with a Constitution that guarantees equal protection under law to all persons. In a deeper sense, too, it is immoral and unjust."[44]

The political alignment began to change in the 1964 presidential election. Although Republican Barry Goldwater lost overwhelmingly to incumbent president Lyndon Johnson, he carried five Deep South states—Louisiana, Mississippi, Georgia, Alabama, and South Carolina—that had been alienated by Democratic civil rights policies. Lyndon Johnson is rumored to have said that in signing the Civil Rights Act of 1964, "We have lost the South for a generation."[45] Whether this statement is apocryphal or was actually made, it certainly was accurate.

The political realignment intensified in 1968. With a campaign focused on attacking civil rights and integration, George Wallace won Arkansas and all the states that Goldwater had carried in 1964, except South Carolina. Nixon won Virginia, Tennessee, North Carolina, South Carolina, and Florida. Texas was the only Southern state won by Humphrey.

Nixon consciously pursued a Southern strategy. Among his first picks for the Supreme Court were Clement Haynsworth and Harold Carswell—from South Carolina and Georgia, respectively. (Both were denied confirmation by the Senate.) In the 1972 presidential election, Nixon won every state except Massachusetts, winning more than 70 percent of the popular vote in most of the Deep South (Mississippi, Alabama, Georgia, Florida, and South Carolina) and more than 65 percent of the votes in the other states of the former Confederacy. The

realignment of the political parties that began in 1964 came to fruition in 1968, and it has remained in place ever since.

The realignment in presidential politics was followed by shifts in
the Senate. It was increasingly uncommon to see Democrats elected
from Southern states. Gradually, the Republican Party lost any sem-
blance of having a liberal wing, while the Democratic Party lost
its conservatives.

The result is that today in presidential elections, Republicans can
count on a bloc of solidly red Southern and Midwestern states, while
Democrats know they will prevail in very populous Northern states
like New York, New Jersey, Connecticut, Illinois, and California. But
states in the former category are more numerous than those in the
latter category, which means that the Electoral College's favoring of
smaller states makes it more likely that it will choose the popular vote
loser as president. The scholar Robert Alexander rightly points out
that changing demographics may make misfire elections much more
common.[46] In the twenty-first century, a handful of closely divided
states—Pennsylvania, Wisconsin, Michigan, Georgia, Nevada, and
Arizona—have determined Electoral College outcomes.

An important aspect of this shift is the enormous economic disparity between the Democratic and Republican states. A report by
the Brookings Institution found that 15 percent of American counties generate 64 percent of the U.S. gross domestic product. Most of
the country's economic activity takes place on the East Coast, West
Coast, and a few metropolitan areas in between. The prosperous parts
of America include about fifteen states having thirty senators, while
the less prosperous areas encapsulate thirty-five states having seventy senators.[47] Because of the Electoral College (and the Senate), the
thirty-five states with less economic activity have disproportionate
power to choose presidents and dictate public policy.

Another aspect of our population shifts and population growth is
often overlooked: the fixed, relatively small size of the House of Representatives contributes to the problems with the Electoral College. We
know the Senate is unrepresentative because each state gets two senators regardless of size. But the House is increasingly unrepresentative,
too, because it remains at 435 seats even as the population grows. It
is becoming ever more difficult to draw districts in a way that accu-

rately reflects the population. Keeping the House of Representatives the same size makes it increasingly unrepresentative, again to the detriment of large metropolitan areas. In a 2003 study, two mathematicians found that if in 2000 the House had had 830 members, Al Gore would have won the presidency.[48]

All this combines to mean that the candidate who loses the popular vote is ever more likely to become president of the United States. The only solution that has been advanced so far is the National Popular Vote Interstate Compact. It is a proposed compact—an agreement among the states—that they will assign their electoral votes to whatever candidate wins the popular vote. It is meant to ensure that the candidate who receives the most votes nationwide is elected president. It would apply only when it would have the effect of ensuring that the popular election victor wins in the Electoral College.

Fifteen states and the District of Columbia have approved the compact, but they are all blue states. It seems unlikely that any red states will agree to it. Republicans rightly perceive that the Electoral College greatly increases their chances of winning the presidency, as it did in 2000 and 2016. The compact will go into effect when states possessing a majority of the electoral votes—that is, enough to elect a president (270 of 538)—enact it, but that seems unlikely to happen. There are not enough blue states to ratify it, and even if they did, not enough are participating to achieve the goals of the compact.

Also, it is unclear whether the compact would be constitutional. Some states would be awarding their electoral votes to candidates who *lost* the popular vote in their states, which would violate laws in those states requiring that the popular vote winner receive that state's electoral votes. And it is at best uncertain whether such a major change in the law can be done via an interstate compact.

Even more important, the compact is unenforceable. Imagine a presidential election, like 2004, where the Republican candidate won in the popular vote but was going to lose in the Electoral College, except for the National Popular Vote Interstate Compact. Imagine that California voters overwhelmingly favored the Democratic candidate, but if California electors adhered to the compact, they would have to cast their votes for the Republican rather than the Democrat. Does anyone believe that California would do this? And there is nothing in the compact—and nor can there be—that could force the state to adhere to its promises.

The simple, sad reality is that there is no easy fix for the Electoral College. It was always a deeply troubling way to choose a president, but it has gotten much worse and will continue to plague the country by choosing popular vote losers to be the chief executive. Nor is a constitutional amendment to eliminate the Electoral College likely to be adopted. Small states that benefit from the Electoral College are surely not going to ratify an amendment to decrease their political influence. Since the 2016 election, unsurprisingly, abolishing the Electoral College has become a partisan issue. In 2012, according to a Gallup poll, "54 percent of Republicans and 69 percent of Democrats were in favor of amending the constitution to eliminate the Electoral College. By late November 2016, 19 percent of Republicans and 81 percent of Democrats were in favor of such a constitutional change."[49] This makes a constitutional amendment to eliminate the Electoral College, requiring approval by two-thirds of both houses of Congress and three-quarters of the states, an impossibility.

Population Shifts Create an Ever Less Democratic Senate

The Senate, with each state having two senators regardless of size, was always inconsistent with majoritarian democracy. But as the population difference between large and small states has grown, the problem has gotten far worse. In 2020 California had a total population of 39.35 million, while Wyoming, the smallest state in population, had 565,000 residents. The population of California is about seventy times larger than that of Wyoming. Put another way, each senator in California represents seventy times more constituents than does a senator from Wyoming.

In 1787 the population difference between the largest and the smallest states was far more modest. The most populous was Virginia with 747,610 people, while Rhode Island was the least populous with 69,112 people. That is a difference of about ten to one, far less than exists today.

Adam Jentleson has pointed out that "the twenty Senate seats representing the ten smallest states are evenly split between Democrats and Republicans, with each party holding ten."[50] That's true, but on the other hand, rural, less populated states do lean heavily Republican. Democrats, increasingly centralized in urban settings, are increasingly distributed in a way that keeps them from exerting their electoral might in the Senate. The result is that after the November 2020 election, Republicans and Democrats each had fifty votes in the Senate, but the fifty Democratic senators represented 60 percent of the population and the fifty Republican senators represented 40 percent of the population. The anti-democratic nature of the Senate has grown greatly as the population disparity between large and small states has increased enormously.

The bargains that were struck in 1787 to create a constitution—an Electoral College to choose the president and a Senate allocating two senators per state—were always undesirable. Neither can be reconciled with democracy or defended as a way to provide checks and balances. Although these institutions have been disturbing from the outset, the population and political shifts of the last half-century have made their anti-democratic nature much worse and contribute greatly to the crisis of American democracy.

3

The 1970s

The Senate Becomes Even
More Anti-Democratic

F ew movie images are more endearing than that of an exhausted Jimmy Stewart staging a one-person filibuster against corruption in Frank Capra's iconic 1939 film *Mr. Smith Goes to Washington*. Stewart's character nobly holds the Senate floor until he collapses and shames his opposition into submission. But movies don't necessarily provide accurate information about government, and that scene should not obscure the serious problems with the filibuster and the Senate rules that permit it. Since the 1970s, the filibuster has operated in a very different way than it did in 1939. The filibuster, as practiced in recent years, is driven by motives less heroic and produces effects more pernicious than those depicted in *Mr. Smith Goes to Washington*.

Simply stated, the filibuster enables a minority of U.S. senators to block action that a majority of the Senate, the House of Representatives, and the president all favor. The only way the Senate can overcome a filibuster is by a vote of sixty senators to end debate and bring the matter to a vote. Filibusters are so ubiquitous in the contemporary Senate that sixty votes, rather than a simple majority, are necessary to pass all legislation except for budget matters, which by Senate rules are exempt from the filibuster.

The result is that a minority of senators can block almost any legislation. It is estimated that forty senators representing 21 percent of the population can thwart legislation that the majority of Americans overwhelmingly favor.[1] As I explained in Chapter 2, the Senate was always profoundly anti-democratic, with every state having two senators regardless of population, a problem that has gotten radically worse as the difference between the most and least populous states has grown exponentially. An inherently undemocratic body has become even less representative. But the filibuster dramatically compounds the problem as a minority of a minority can stop virtually any legislation.

This situation is enormously troubling in terms of democracy, but it also contributes to the inability of the government to act, which furthers the public loss of confidence in government. The more polarized American politics becomes, the less likely it is that a bipartisan coalition can pass legislation and overcome the ability of the Senate minority party to block almost everything.

Again, the question must be: what has changed? Population shifts contribute, as the difference between large and small states has grown, as described in Chapter 2. But critically, in the 1970s the Senate rules concerning the filibuster were revised to make the practice far easier than it used to be. The result is a far greater paralysis in the Senate and a government that is ever less able to act effectively.

The Fascinating History of the Filibuster

Little is known about the prevalence of filibusters before the late nineteenth century.[2] Nevertheless, the strategic use of delay in debate is as old as the Senate itself. The first recorded episode of dilatory debate occurred in 1790, when senators from Virginia and South Carolina filibustered to prevent the location of the nation's capital in Philadelphia.[3] The issue had come to a vote once before; the House voted to locate it in Philadelphia, but the Senate voted against it. The Senate vote was so close that an ailing senator had to be carried in on his bed to cast the deciding vote. One rainy day, knowing that the ill senator could not be carried in, the Senate backers of the House proposal renewed their effort. To combat this move, Southern senators, who preferred a capital closer to home, made long speeches and dilatory motions that prevented the vote that day. Senator William Maclay, a supporter of the proposal for Philadelphia, reported in his memoir that "the design of the Virginians and the Carolina gentlemen was to talk away the time, so that we could not get the bill passed."[4] He complained that the "unreasonable delays" would erode "the confidence of the people" in the Senate.[5]

Standard histories of the Senate describe the early decades of the nineteenth century as the golden age of Senate debate.[6] Henry Clay, Daniel Webster, and John Calhoun were great orators and were prone to make lengthy speeches. Clay and Webster, however, were never accused of having used debate for dilatory purposes, and they actually favored restrictions on debate.[7] Calhoun, however, did not. He repeatedly used extended debate for the purpose of delay rather than exposition, in order to protect the interests of Southerners, as was consistent with his theory of minority rights. He was a leading proponent of an antimajoritarian theory of government that accommodated the views of the slaveholding white South, arguing that states were sovereign entities that could block federal government actions in their territory. Calhoun was second to none in his fierce protection of Southern states' ability retain slavery. The Senate's first serious controversies over "obstructive" uses of debate appear to have occurred in the 1820s, in the context of the sectional and party disputes.[8]

Interestingly, the precedents establishing a right of unlimited debate stemmed from the Senate's desire for independence from the executive branch rather than from a concern about minority rights.[9] The first such precedent dates from an 1826 conflict among President John Quincy Adams, Vice President Calhoun, and the voluble John Randolph, a senator from Virginia. Congress stymied President Adams early in his administration by ignoring the major recommendations of his ambitious legislative program. Randolph, an outspoken foe of Adams, made intemperate remarks on the Senate floor about the Adams administration, precipitating an issue of whether the vice president, as the presiding officer of the Senate, had the authority to call him to order.[10]

In the early and mid-nineteenth century, unlike today, the vice president was not the president's running mate, and Calhoun was no great friend of Adams. Calhoun ruled that the vice president lacked authority to call Senator Randolph to order, except at the request of a member of the Senate, thus reducing executive branch authority over the legislature in a fashion that was particularly galling to President Adams.[11] Two years later, the Senate overturned the Calhoun decision, reinstating the vice president's authority to call a senator to order and adding a right of appeal to the full Senate. This entire dispute, which occurred in the context of partisan rancor between the proto-Whig president and Jeffersonian senators, was fueled by long-standing animosity between Clay and Calhoun; it probably reflected the Senate's desire to be free of executive branch control more than its wish to permit unlimited debate. Thus, even this early restriction of debate and its subsequent repeal are not particularly indicative of the Senate's attitude toward unlimited debate.

Serious controversy about extended debate in the Senate dates from 1841, when President John Tyler attempted to enact the Whig legislative program.[12] The Whigs encountered stiff resistance from the Democratic minority. Senator Thomas H. Benton said the Democrats acted "on a system, and with a thorough organization, and on a perfect understanding. There were but twenty-two of us, but every one a speaker, and effective. We kept their measures upon the anvil, and hammered them continually; we impaled them against the wall, and stabbed them incessantly."[13]

The Democratic minority scoffed at the notion that extended debate wrongly prevented the majority from acting on legislation. "'Action, action, action,' cried Calhoun, 'means nothing but plunder, plunder, plunder!'" Frustrated by the delay, Henry Clay proposed to impose a one-hour limit on debate as a way to eliminate obstruction from the opposition.[14] But the Democrats, led by Calhoun, decided "to resist its introduction and trample upon the rule if voted."[15] Calhoun reportedly said in the Senate that he considered "an attempt to rule the Senate by the despotism of the gag as bad as introducing a band of soldiers into it to force measures through by pitching opposing senators out of the windows."[16]

This dispute between Calhoun and Clay, along with the sectional issues that underlay it, probably explains why the first significant strategic use of extended debate (which was not yet called filibustering) is said to have occurred in 1841. This early "filibuster"—over a bill appointing the publishers of the *Congressional Globe*—was a patronage dispute over partisan control of the Senate.[17] The Whig majority wanted to fire the publishers of the *Globe*, and the Democrats were determined to oppose it. The debate lasted ten days, but the effort to block the action was ultimately unsuccessful.

The second reported "filibuster" followed in the same year. It was an unsuccessful fourteen day talk-a-thon intended to block a bill that would establish a national bank. Thus, the origins of filibustering as an identifiable practice lie in the intense sectional and party crises of the 1830s and '40s. Filibustering represented the use of procedural rules in the battle for power along sectional and party lines. In this formative era of party politics, senators seized upon procedural rules as a weapon in the fight, at a time when Democrats and Whigs were both struggling (often against the cross-current of the everlasting sectional divide) to create party power.

The North-South sectional disputes of the 1850s gave filibustering its name. The term was borrowed from a form of mercenary warfare of the era and originally connoted piracy and brigandage. It derives from a Dutch word, *vrijbuiter*, or "free booter." From the Dutch, it passed into Spanish as *filibustero*, which referred to West Indian pirates who used a small swift ship known as a *filibot*.[18] In English, *filibusterers* were mercenary sailors who made war against the governments of Central and South America.[19] Although men of other countries engaged in such adventures, only the United States gained the reputation as a nation of filibusterers. This form of expansionism was a product of the breakdown of the Missouri Compromise (an effort to maintain parity between slave and free states) and a search for new territory where slavery might thrive.

The most notorious such filibusterer was William Walker, who before the Civil War led a group of Southern mercenaries to attack Nicaragua, hoping to establish a place hospitable to the expansion of the slavery economy.[20] Use of the term to refer to obstruction of Congress and thus connoted adventurism in an effort to thwart government, in which the perpetrator would be accused of "filibustering against the United States."[21]

Early filibusters were largely unsuccessful in blocking legislation; almost every filibustered measure before 1880 was eventually passed.[22] Because both the Senate and the scope of federal legislation were small by today's standards, the Senate had enough time to wait out the filibusters. Beginning about 1880, however, senators filibustered more often and more successfully. "Tactics remained essentially the same," observes the historian Franklin Burdette, "but boldness gave way to ruthlessness, and obstruction began to be bounded only by the daring ingenuity of its designers."[23] By the time the cloture rule was adopted in 1917, senators and the public alike perceived filibustering to be a serious problem.

Among the filibusters that gave rise to this perception were the seventy-five years of successful Southern filibusters against civil rights legislation, as well as several notorious Progressive and Republican filibusters. The heroism of being the determined minority was a key part of the political lore. Both the Southerners and the Progressives donned the mantle of the oppressed minority who were forced to filibuster to defend their principles. On many issues, their deeply held convictions were clearly at odds, but occasionally the two factions joined forces. For example, in 1890 a bill was introduced to provide federal supervision of Southern congressional elections to prevent intimidation of Black voters. The filibuster against it succeeded because Southern Democrats joined forces with Republicans who favored separate legislation, a silver bill. The Southerners appealed to the Republicans by persuading them to abandon the election bill in favor of the silver bill, thus aiding in the ultimate success of the filibuster.[24]

In 1893, senators waged another prolonged and spectacular filibuster against a bill to repeal a law that required the government to purchase 4.5 million ounces of silver each month. Farmer Democrats joined silver Republicans and silver Democrats to try to block the law. The endless speeches, quorum calls, roll calls, and maneuvering dominated the Senate calendar for forty-six days, but the filibuster ultimately failed.[25]

One of the most notorious cases was Progressive Senator Robert M. LaFollette's 1908 filibuster of a currency bill that he believed was a power grab by the rich. This filibuster set records for length, sophistication of procedural combat, and treachery, and it contributed significantly to the Senate's sense that something had to be done to limit debate. LaFollette held the Senate floor for eighteen hours in the stifling heat. A parliamentary ruling prohibited him from using quorum calls to get a moment's rest, so he spoke all night, sustaining himself with turkey sandwiches and eggnog from the Senate restaurant. After taking a large swallow from a particular glass of eggnog, he rejected it as adulterated. And indeed it was; the glass was laced with enough ptomaine to kill him.[26] The ptomaine he had swallowed made him quite ill, yet by forcing roll calls he managed to escape for a few minutes of respite, and he continued his speech for another eight hours.[27] He ultimately lost the filibuster when Senator Albert Gore, who was blind, yielded the floor as prearranged to a colleague, who, unknown to Gore, had just stepped out to the cloakroom.[28]

During World War I, President Wilson proposed to arm merchant ships against German U-boat attacks. The bill passed the House easily and came before the Senate on March 2. The day before, the so-called Zimmermann telegram was publicly released: it revealed a German invitation to Mexico to form an alliance against the United States in exchange for assistance in seizing Texas, New Mexico, and Arizona. Public outrage at Germany generated solid support for the bill, and an overwhelming majority of senators supported it.

But eleven (some count twelve) Progressives feared that arming merchant ships would lead the United States into war. They were determined to oppose the bill. LaFollette is now the best known of the "little group of willful men" who blocked it, but in fact he never had the opportunity to speak against it.[29] Initially, other members of the opposition spoke against it, but when the bill's supporters realized in the last few hours of the session that the bill could not be brought to a vote, supporters of the bill held the floor simply to prevent LaFollette from gaining the glory of speaking before the crowded galleries.[30] The bill died when Congress adjourned at noon on March 4, 1917.[31]

President Wilson issued a statement on March 5, attacking the opposition senators and calling for a change of the Senate rules. In response, Congress met in special session beginning that day, when Majority Leader Thomas Martin introduced a resolution to amend the Senate rules to provide for cloture. On March 8, the Senate adopted the Martin Resolution, a version of the current Rule XXII, by a vote of 76–3.[32] The rule provides that a cloture petition may be made at any time if signed by sixteen senators, and that "one hour after the Senate meets on the following calendar day but one," the Senate would vote on the motion. Once cloture is invoked, no senator is allowed to speak for more than one hour on the measure or its amendments, and further amendments can be offered only by unanimous consent. In addition, as originally written, Rule XXII required a vote of two-thirds of those present and voting to invoke cloture. The Martin Resolution reflected a compromise between those members of the Senate who favored simple majority cloture, and those who opposed it but were willing to accept some form of cloture. The senators who thought that discussion should end with a simple majority vote were outvoted, as they have been on many occasions since 1917.

For nearly fifty years after its adoption, Rule XXII served a purpose that was more symbolic than real. Between 1917 and 1927, cloture was voted on only ten times, and it was adopted only four times.[33] Between 1931 and the enactment of the Civil Rights Act of 1964, cloture was seldom sought and only twice obtained.[34] The reluctance to seek cloture and the difficulty of obtaining it resulted in large part from the battle over civil rights.

From the late 1920s until the late 1960s, the filibuster was almost entirely associated with the battle over civil rights. A coalition of Southern senators enjoyed extraordinary power in the Senate: they had the seniority that came from serving in safe seats representing one-party states, and they used the filibuster to block civil rights legislation. The Senate did not vote cloture a single time between 1927 and 1962,[35] partly because Southern senators refused to vote cloture on any issue, in order to be able to take a "principled" stand against cloture on civil rights issues. The conservative minority also chose to restrain its use of the filibuster for any issue except civil rights. The Senate's own debates about filibusters during this era were imbued with inflated rhetoric about an alleged Senate tradition of respecting minority rights and the value of extended debate on issues of great national importance.

Filibusters of civil rights legislation sparked controversy unequaled since 1917. Beginning during Reconstruction and continuing for nearly a century, anti–civil rights filibusters played a major role in blocking measures to prohibit lynching,[36] poll taxes,[37] and race discrimination in employment, housing, public accommodations, and voting.[38] Although the filibuster was not solely responsible for the delay of civil rights legislation—some responsibility must attach to

Franklin Roosevelt's reluctance to alienate the powerful Southerners whose support was crucial for the New Deal to survive[39]—the filibuster was indispensable in the Southerners' fight.

The filibuster against the Civil Rights Act of 1964 was unequaled in length and notoriety; it tied up the Senate for seventy-four days.[40] News coverage of it was also unprecedented: CBS News had Roger Mudd report on its progress from the steps of the Capitol during every newscast. The filibuster became such an epic event that news coverage itself became a news topic.

After the enactment of the Civil Rights Act, white supremacy filibusters finally began to fail, but they still made legislating excruciatingly difficult. A filibuster delayed the 1965 Voting Rights Act for a month. Conservatives unsuccessfully filibustered the Fair Housing Act of 1968, an extension of the Voting Rights Act in 1970, and an extension of Title VII in 1972. Not surprisingly, therefore, the debate about civil rights legislation became fused with the debate about filibusters and cloture: conservatives defended them and liberals opposed them.[41]

The Rules Change

In the 1970s, the rules concerning the filibuster changed to make it far easier for the minority party to block Senate action. This change was primarily the result of three factors. First, liberals came to join conservatives in the use of the filibuster. It lost its stigma of being the tool of segregationists. Previously, for a long time, the filibuster was used almost exclusively by the Southern Democrats as an anti–civil rights device. For decades, filibusters were almost always on only one issue, albeit one of great importance: civil rights. Moreover and quite important, during this time filibustering and cloture votes did not follow party lines. Opponents of cloture were conservative Southern Democrats joined by conservative small-state Republicans who either sympathized on the civil rights issue or saw the filibuster as a powerful tool to protect their constituents whose representatives were outnumbered in the House. But this coalition was unique to the civil rights era.

Because the filibuster was associated with blocking civil rights legislation, other senators eschewed using it. But after the enactment of civil rights laws in the mid-1960s, Senate liberals began resorting to filibusters to ward off conservative measures supported by the Nixon administration.[42] They filibustered to support environmental positions, to oppose the Vietnam War, and to defend busing for urban school desegregation. As result, liberal senators who previously favored easing the cloture requirements changed their position, while Southern senators who previously defended filibusters as fostering free debate began to vote for cloture.[43] The filibuster thus became much more common in the Senate.

The second factor in the development of the modern filibuster was the Senate's adoption of the "two-track system" in the 1970s. It was a new rule for handling floor debate in the Senate. In response to repeated civil rights filibusters, Senate Majority Leader Mike Mansfield developed a system whereby the Senate would spend the morning on the filibustered legislation and the afternoon on other business.[44] Mansfield wisely understood that this system would benefit both the Senate majority and the filibustering minority, which enabled him to obtain unanimous consent to changing the rules. On the one hand, the two-track system would strengthen the majority's ability to withstand a filibuster by allowing the Senate to enact other legislation. On the other hand, it would aid a filibustering minority by reducing the amount of time they must hold the floor. The only senators who might oppose the system would be those most anxious to enact the filibustered legislation. Yet even they consented to avoid alienating colleagues whose support they wanted, as the delay allows time to drum up additional votes. Since ending a filibuster is as exhausting to the majority as carrying it out is to the minority and success is not guaranteed, the majority leader was able to obtain unanimous consent for this new rule to allow the Senate to do other business while a filibuster was happening.

Although Mansfield devised the two-track system to deal with the exigencies of the civil rights debates, it then became a way of life in the Senate. Its adoption changed the game profoundly with a third change: the silent filibuster. A senator can filibuster a bill without uttering a word on the Senate floor. They merely have to make it known that they are filibustering, and the other senators must then muster sixty votes for cloture and bring the matter for a vote.

As filibustering crossed traditional ideological and party lines, many senators found the waste of valuable floor time simply intolerable. So they transformed the filibuster so that it could occur without any senator having to take and hold the floor at all. Jimmy Stewart could have done his filibuster in *Mr. Smith Goes to Washington* without having to say a word.

Throughout history, there have been periods in each congressional session when senators felt time was short; filibusters have been most effective during such moments. In the modern Senate, however, time is scarce for the entire congressional session. With an increased workload since the New Deal, senators could seldom afford to wait out a filibuster. Moreover, the Senate floor evolved from being the central forum for debate to being merely a location for casting votes and addressing the media. Most deliberation occurs, if at all, in committees. It is in committees where senators mark up bills, hold hearings, and informally negotiate over the content and scheduling of legislation. The Senate reserves the floor for voting, press coverage, and documenting its activities for the *Congressional Record*.

From 1917 to 1975, with a tweak in 1949, the Senate operated under a rule requiring a two-thirds vote for cloture, but aspects of the 1917 rule posed even larger constraints on filibustering. A cloture motion to end debate froze the Senate, forcing the body to vote on the motion before proceeding with any other business. Also, maintaining a "speaking" filibuster required a senator to hold the floor, individually or in relays. And importantly, supporters of the filibuster were required to ensure the presence of at least one-third of the senators in the chamber to head off a surprise two-thirds cloture vote. Once again, if opposition to a bill, especially civil rights legislation, was passionate enough, a filibuster could be maintained, but the triple costs of freezing the Senate, physically holding the floor, and physically maintaining a one-third presence in the chamber limited the number of times a filibuster could be successful.

In the early 1960s, when the Senate increased the time spent in session to more than nine months annually, the number of cloture votes rose sharply. Although early in the decade senators invoked cloture principally on civil rights legislation, later in the decade cloture votes increasingly addressed other issues.[45] In the 1970s and '80s the number of filibusters and the range of subjects they covered soared.[46] The Senate began to rely even more on Mansfield's two-track system, but that system too began to change. Ultimately, rather than dividing time between the filibustered measure and other matters, the Senate seldom even discusses an objectionable matter until the majority can muster sixty votes for cloture.

This modern incarnation of the two-track system, the "stealth filibuster," reduces the ability of a minority to hold other legislation hostage. Whereas the traditional filibuster prevented the Senate from accomplishing much, the stealth filibuster permits the Senate to consider anything but the objectionable legislation. The stealth filibuster is easier, both physically and politically, because it does not require a senator to hold the floor continuously. In contrast to the dilatory tactics of the past, modern filibusters virtually never involve the long speeches, all-night sessions, or parliamentary maneuvering that used to draw public attention. A credible threat that forty-one senators will refuse to vote for cloture on a bill is enough to keep that bill entirely off the floor. The Senate leadership simply delays consideration of the bill until it has the sixty votes necessary for cloture.

In effect, the stealth filibuster eliminates the distinction between a filibuster and a threat to filibuster; any credible threat to filibuster is a filibuster because the majority leader must regard it as such. Thus, the stealth filibuster is largely silent, invisible, and relatively painless for both the majority and minority.

The stealth filibuster has all but eliminated public accountability for senators who filibuster. Prior to the 1970s, the public could rely on detailed newspaper coverage to follow the high drama and outlandish comedy of a filibuster. In 1935, for example, the public read a newspaper log of Huey Long's famous filibuster against a provision of the New Deal; the story reported that at 4:32 p.m. one senator suggested Long sing rather than talk; at 6:50 p.m. Long recited recipes for frying oysters and making potlikker; at 12:50 a.m. he discussed the beauties of sleep; at 2:05 a.m. he asked the Senate's presiding officer what became of the sword that Frederick the Great sent to George Washington.[47] Now, of course, C-SPAN coverage of floor proceedings would make it even easier for the public to know about filibusters, which would substantially limit their use. In an era of public concern over

"gridlock" in Washington, most senators would not want their constituents to witness an old-fashioned filibuster.[48] In creating stealth
filibusters, the two-track system has substantially increased the use
(or abuse) of filibusters.

It all started in 1975, when the original "speaking filibuster" was
transformed into the modern virtual version. Southern senators agreed
to confine the filibuster to a short period in the morning session, while
allowing the Senate to move on to additional business in the afternoon
session. Then they agreed to a reduction in the cloture number from
two-thirds present and voting (a maximum of sixty-seven), to a fixed
sixty number of senators. All of a sudden, the three self-limiting factors that had kept the filibuster in check since 1806 disappeared. Maintaining a filibuster no longer presented an institutional cost, since the
Senate could conduct business as usual during most of the day. A filibustering senator no longer had to hold the floor physically for a long
period of time since the filibuster was confined to a short window in
the morning. And most important, supporters of the filibuster no longer had to worry about maintaining a one-third floor presence, since
it was now the job of opponents to marshal a fixed sixty votes to end
debate. Supporters of the filibuster could stay home in bed.

The net result was an explosion in the number of filibusters. Since
maintaining a filibuster no longer imposed costs on the Senate, the
filibuster, once a relatively rare device to protect the conscience of the
minority in a few deeply felt settings, morphed to a de facto supermajority voting rule requiring proponents of virtually all legislation to
secure sixty affirmative votes before it can be passed.

Filibustering has in effect created a supermajority requirement for
the enactment of most legislation. The filibuster has been abolished
for Supreme Court confirmations, Cabinet appointments, and lower
federal court nominations. In 2013, frustrated with Republicans using
the filibuster to block President Obama's judicial nominations, Senate
Democrats, under the direction of Senate Majority Leader Harry Reid,
changed the rules. They eliminated the filibuster for nominations to
federal district courts, federal appellate courts, and Cabinet positions.
In 2017, Senate Republicans overcame a Democratic filibuster of Neil
Gorsuch's nomination to the Supreme Court by changing Senate rules
to eliminate the filibuster for Supreme Court nominations.

One other major type of Senate business is exempt from filibuster threat: the budget process. Under the congressional legislation governing the budget, all budget reconciliation legislation is considered under procedural rules that strictly limit the time for debate and other procedural delays.[49] Reconciliation bills cannot be filibustered because the time for debate is strictly limited by statute. They cannot be delayed by excessive amendments because, when the time for debate expires, the Senate votes on all filed amendments without any debate and then immediately on the reconciliation bill itself. Because of the streamlined procedures for reconciliation bills, senators often try to draft proposed legislation as a reconciliation bill to prevent a filibuster. Indeed, a significant portion of the Senate's business is now being conducted as reconciliation bills.[50] President Biden's economic recovery legislation and his climate change bill were adopted through this approach.[51]

Thus, one rather technical consequence of the prevalence of stealth filibusters has been to prompt the Senate to consider a substantial part of its legislation under the rubric of the budget reconciliation process. It makes the Senate parliamentarian particularly important as the person who decides whether a bill fits within the budget framework. Several times, for example, the parliamentarian has denied permission to enact immigration reform legislation through the reconciliation process.[52]

The Senate, however, cannot prevent filibusters on all legislation simply by drafting everything as a reconciliation bill. Senate procedural rules require that reconciliation bills be germane to the federal budget.[53] Welfare and Medicaid bills obviously fit this category because they are relevant to federal expenditures. But a significant portion of the Senate's business cannot be shoehorned into the budget category, even through creative drafting.[54]

The bottom line is that the changes in the Senate rules with regard to the filibuster mean that all but some confirmations and budget matters requires sixty votes for passage. This is enormously significant when, as in the current Senate, neither party holds a sixty-seat majority, for it enables the minority party to exert substantial control over the legislation that reaches the floor. Nor, given the political polarization in the country, is it likely that either party will have sixty senators in the foreseeable future. The filibuster, especially in its current form, promises continued gridlock on Capitol Hill, at a time when the country urgently needs federal legislation to deal with many essential issues.

Implications

The anti-democratic nature of the Senate, with two senators for every state regardless of population, always should have been deeply troubling, but the shifts in population make it ever more disturbing, and the changes in the filibuster rules exacerbate the Senate's undemocratic nature. Senators representing a distinct minority of the population now have the ability to block almost any legislation. And they regularly do. The change in the Senate rules in the 1970s makes it far more likely that such filibusters will continue without constraint, obstructing the ability of the federal government to take essential action and heightening a widespread sense that the government is badly broken.

It is important to remember that the filibuster is created by Senate rules, not by the Constitution or even by a federal statute. The Senate could eliminate it by a majority vote. But both political parties know that they will sometimes be in the minority, and they do not want to give up this powerful tool. The result is that a tool that allows forty senators, representing a small percentage of the population, to block any legislation greatly exacerbates the anti-majoritarian nature of the Senate.

The effects are neither abstract nor theoretical. During the first two years of the Biden presidency, Democrats controlled both the House and the Senate. Important legislation to protect voting rights passed the House, only to die in the Senate because of a Republican filibuster. This is particularly notable because senators representing a minority of the popular vote were able to block legislation that would have protected voting rights throughout the country. Democracy has been further undermined and put at risk.

4

The 1980s and After
Partisan Gerrymandering Grows and Thwarts Democracy

A story, perhaps apocryphal, holds that in creating the first congressional maps in Virginia, Patrick Henry tried to draw district boundaries to thwart his rival James Madison's election to the House of Representatives.[1] Henry, who is most famous for saying, "Give me liberty or give me death," was an anti-federalist and a foe of the Federalist Madison. He got the Virginia legislature to specify that members of Congress would be elected from districts—and that to be elected, an individual had to be a resident of the district. He then drew the district around Madison's hometown, Orange, to include as many anti-federalists as possible. As the story goes, George Washington was pessimistic about the outcome of the election; Madison's defeat seemed to him "not at all improbable."[2]

Regardless of whether this actually happened, partisan gerrymandering has been part of American politics since its earliest days. It occurs when the political party that controls a legislature draws election districts to maximize safe seats for itself. It happens when a Republican-controlled state legislature draws districts to maximize safe seats for Republicans, or when a Democratic-controlled city council draws its districts to maximize seats for Democrats. Both political parties gerrymander when they can, though in recent years Republicans have done it more consciously and more successfully than Democrats.

The practice of gerrymandering takes its name from an early governor of Massachusetts, Elbridge Gerry. In 1812 he led the drawing of districts in Massachusetts to help his party gain seats. During this process, Gerry apparently remarked that one district looked like a salamander—and the name "gerrymandering" took hold.[3] In the March 26, 1812, edition of the Boston *Gazette*, the newspaper ran a cartoon of this district with the caption: "The Gerry-Mander: A new species of Monster."[4]

Gerrymandering has been carried out throughout American history, but how it is carried out has changed dramatically. For most of American history, those engaging in gerrymandering would choose between several possible maps based on their predictions of which would yield the greatest partisan advantage. Today the parties have computers generate thousands of maps, and they choose the one that provides the best chance of their own success. Intricate computer algorithms and detailed data about voters allow map drawers to engage in partisan gerrymandering with surgical precision. Nothing is left to chance.

Consider the case of North Carolina. It is basically a purple state: Obama carried it in 2008, then Romney won in 2012, and Trump came out ahead in 2016 and 2020. But all three won by close margins. For example, in 2020, Trump won over Biden by 1.34 percent.[5] After Republicans gained control of both houses of the North Carolina legislature in 2010, they redrew state legislative districts to ensure their continued control. They then set out to redraw the election map for North Carolina's thirteen congressional districts. One of the two Republicans chairing the redistricting committee stated, "I think electing Republicans is better than electing Democrats. So I drew this map to help foster what I think is better for the country."[6] He further explained that he drew the map with the aim of electing ten Republicans and three Democrats because he did "not believe it [would be] possible to draw a map with eleven Republicans and two Democrats." However, he was clear that if they could draw such a map, that is what they would do. The goal was clear and explicit: draw congressional districts to ensure as many safe seats for Republicans as possible.

The Republicans had the computer generate three thousand different maps and selected the one that gave them the best chance of controlling ten of the state's thirteen seats in the House of Representatives. It worked exactly as planned. In the North Carolina 2016 election, Republican congressional candidates received 53 percent of the vote, and Democratic candidates received 47 percent, but Republican congressional candidates won ten of North Carolina's thirteen House seats.[7] And in the 2018 midterm elections, Republican and Democratic candidates statewide each received 50 percent of the votes, but again Republicans won ten of thirteen congressional races.

This situation, of course, is not unique to North Carolina. In Pennsylvania, over several elections, the congressional elections in districts drawn by the Republican legislature resulted in Democrats receiving between 45 percent and 51 percent of the statewide vote, yet winning only five of eighteen House seats.[8] In Ohio, Democratic congressional candidates won between 39 and 47 percent of the statewide vote in four congressional elections, but they never won more than four of sixteen House seats.[9] Partisan gerrymandering always has existed, but never before with the precision and success that has developed in recent years.

Partisan gerrymandering undermines democracy for the only institution—the House of Representatives—created by the Constitution that was meant to be elected directly by the people. The president is chosen by the Electoral College; the Supreme Court justices and federal judges are chosen by the president; and senators were selected by state legislatures until 1913. Even today, by allocating two senators to each state regardless of its size and, as explained in Chapter 3, maintaining the filibuster makes the Senate profoundly anti-democratic. The House was always meant to be different and to be democratically chosen. That, however, is negated by partisan gerrymandering. And gerrymandering is not limited to congressional seats; it is common for state legislatures, city councils, and all other elected bodies with districts. It erodes democracy at all levels of government.

As computer programs have become ever more sophisticated, partisan gerrymandering has grown into an ever larger threat to the basic principles of democracy. As Justice Elena Kagan noted, "Gerrymanders will only get worse (or depending on your perspective, better) as time goes on—as data becomes ever more fine-grained and data analysis techniques continue to improve."[10] Unfortunately, in 2019, the Supreme Court slammed the door on any possibility of challenges to gerrymandering in federal court. As a result, gerrymandering with a vengeance has become the norm in much of the United States.

How Gerrymandering Occurs

Gerrymandering has a simple goal: the political party holding power wants to draw election districts so as to create as many as possible with a majority of likely voters from that party. There are an infinite variety of ways to draw maps allocating voters to districts.

Two techniques used to accomplish partisan gerrymandering are "packing" and "cracking." Packing occurs when the party in control of the legislature tries to pack voters from the opposing party into as few districts as possible. This allows the party to control the remainder of the districts. By contrast, cracking is when the party in control spreads the voters of the other party among many districts so that they are a majority in as few districts as possible. This dilutes the voting strength of the opposition and lessens its chances of winning seats.

Those engaging in gerrymandering utilize both strategies simultaneously to give their party control over as many districts as possible. Imagine a state with three congressional districts, with two-thirds Republican voters and one-third Democratic. If the Republicans gain control of the state legislature, they will attempt to draw three congressional districts each with two-thirds Republican voters, therefore controlling all the districts. Although unlikely, if the Democrats win the control of the state legislature, they could try to pack Republican voters into one district to give Democrats control of the other two. Either way, the representatives from that state will not reflect the political affiliations of the voters. In the former instance, Democrats have no representation in Congress at all, while in the latter Republicans are underrepresented relative to their numbers in the state.

The Constitution and the federal Voting Rights Act require that those engaged in districting must make sure that all districts are about equal in population and do not discriminate on the basis of race. But the latter can be circumvented: since Black voters cast their ballots for Democratic candidates about 90 percent of the time, those drawing districts can say they were focused on party, not on race, and the gerrymandering will be allowed despite the racially discriminatory effect. Within these constraints—having districts of about equal size and not discriminating based on race—partisan gerrymandering allows districts to be drawn to maximize the chances of one political party triumphing. The party drawing the districts then is virtually assured that it will remain in control of the legislature for elections to come. The evil of partisan gerrymandering becomes self-perpetuating: the party doing the districting will remain the majority indefinitely because it will keep drawing district lines to ensure that it stays in power.

The changes in partisan gerrymandering techniques—using computer algorithms and detailed voter information—make gerrymandering dramatically more effective than ever before. Justice Kagan expressed this well: "But big data and modern technology . . . make today's gerrymandering altogether different from the crude linedrawing of the past."[11] Before the availability of big data, those drawing districts had county-level data but not information about individual voters. In the past, with limited information and the need to draw maps by hand, only a few possible maps would be drawn. Now, as was done in North Carolina, a computer can draw thousands of possibilities, allowing politicians who control the process to choose the map that gives their party maximum advantage. As Justice Kagan observed: "The effect is to make gerrymanders far more effective and durable than before, insulating politicians against all but the most titanic shifts in the political tides. These are not your grandfather's—let alone the framers'—gerrymanders."[12]

No doubt gerrymandering succeeds, often brilliantly. After the Democrats' success in the 2008 national elections, Republicans devised a plan called the Redistricting Majority Project or REDMAP. The Republican State Leadership Council sponsored a $30 million effort to gain control over the redistricting process that would occur after the 2010 census. They targeted state legislative races in states where Republicans had the chance to tip political control of the legislature. Their central goal was to have Republicans in charge of as many states as possible for the redistricting following the 2010 census.

This plan was hugely successful. "All told, in 2010 Republicans gained nearly seven hundred state legislative seats. . . . [This] was a larger increase than either party has seen in modern history. The blue map was now red."[13] Republicans flipped nineteen state legislatures from Democratic to Republican control and held majorities in ten of the fifteen states that were set to gain or lose U.S. House seats.[14] Two years later nearly a million and a half more Americans voted for Democrats for Congress than for Republicans, but Republicans won a thirty-three-seat majority in Congress.[15] And once a party gains control of the state legislature, it can use gerrymandering to entrench that control and make it far more difficult for the other party to win in the future.

Consider Pennsylvania, another purple state, but one that leans blue. Republican gerrymandering after the 2010 census worked exactly as planned. In 2012 Barack Obama carried the presidential vote in Pennsylvania, and House Democratic candidates won 100,000 more votes statewide than Republican candidates. Nevertheless, Republicans won thirteen of Pennsylvania's eighteen seats in the House of Representatives.[16] Democrats received many more votes, yet Republicans won many more seats, the very antithesis of democratic rule.

The same occurred in Michigan, which Republicans had targeted in 2020 to gain control of the state legislature. In the 2012 election, Michigan voters preferred Obama over Romney by 10 points, and they reelected Democratic Senator Debbie Stabenow to a third term—she defeated the Republican candidate by a landslide 20.8 percent margin and nearly one million votes. But because of the gerrymandering, Republicans ended up with the lion's share of the state's congressional seats—nine, to the Democrats' five.[17]

A 2019 report from the Center for American Progress found that partisan gerrymandering of congressional districts shifted, on average, fifty-nine seats in the House during the 2012, 2014, and 2016 elections.[18] Put another way, without partisan gerrymandering, fifty-nine different people representing different parties likely would have been in Congress. Fifty-nine seats is more than the total number of Representatives from the twenty-two smallest states in population and more than the number of seats from California, the largest state. The report concluded that of those fifty-nine seats, twenty shifted in favor of Democrats while thirty-nine shifted in favor of Republicans.[19] "This means that from 2012 to 2016, the net two-party impact amounted to an average gain of 19 Republican seats per election."[20] In a closely divided House, nineteen seats can make a huge impact on which party is in control and what is possible to accomplish. The November 2022 elections gave Republicans a ten-vote majority in the House. Without partisan gerrymandering, Democrats almost surely would have controlled the chamber. Along with Democratic control of the White House and the Senate, the federal government could have done far more to tackle the huge problems facing the country and the world.

Why Partisan Gerrymandering Is Harmful and Inconsistent with Democracy

Gerrymandering rigs elections. The central precept of democracy is that voters choose their elected officials, but partisan gerrymandering means that elected officials are choosing their voters. As the Supreme Court itself once observed, the "core principle of republican government" is "that the voters should choose their representatives, not the other way around."[21] Partisan gerrymandering lets politicians cherry-pick voters to ensure their own reelection and to entrench themselves—and their party—in power for years to come.

This is inconsistent with democracy, and it also violates the constitutional rights of the voters. As a result of partisan gerrymandering, voters do not have an equal chance to influence the outcome of an election, which is antithetical to the requirements of equal protection. The Court first ruled on partisan gerrymandering in 1986, declaring it unconstitutional. Justice Lewis Powell observed that "unconstitutional gerrymandering" occurs when "the boundaries of the voting districts have been distorted deliberately" to deprive voters of "an equal opportunity to participate in the State's legislative processes."[22] Some voters will benefit and have more influence in choosing representatives, while others' votes will be diluted by partisan gerrymandering. That is a quintessential denial of equal protection of the laws. Partisan gerrymandering means that not all voters are treated the same. Voters for the party that is controlling the districting are much more likely to have representatives of their preferred party in power.

Partisan gerrymandering also infringes First Amendment freedoms. Voters for the minority party, solely by virtue of their party association, are at a significant disadvantage in electing representatives. In 2004 Justice Anthony Kennedy said that partisan gerrymandering is a "burden [on] a group's representational rights" of their "political association," "participation in the electoral process," "voting history," or "expression of political views."[23] Voters for the minority political party are enduringly handicapped solely because of how the districts were drawn.[24] After all, the very purpose and clear effect of partisan gerrymandering is to disadvantage the speech, association, and electoral efforts of an opposing political party.

A group of former members of the House of Representatives declared that the "overtly political [districting] process sows distrust among the electorate about the fairness of the districts as drawn and adds to the rancor between the political parties when one feels that the other is assigning lines that disadvantage their political opponents."[25] In this way, partisan gerrymandering contributes to loss of faith in government that lies at the root of the today's crisis in democracy. Partisan gerrymandering undermines the central purpose of the House of Representatives in the Constitution by frustrating democratic elections. Representatives with safe seats are likely to be more complacent and less responsive to constituents. Most of all, partisan gerrymandering thwarts the will of the voters in a state.

The Supreme Court Closes the Door on Challenges to Partisan Gerrymandering

As I've explained, partisan gerrymandering became more effective as computer technology advanced, and in recent years it has come to fruition in a major new way. Since politicians who benefit from partisan gerrymandering are not going to eliminate it, as it would reduce their influence and that of their political party, a solution from the Supreme Court is essential. In 1986 the Supreme Court held that partisan gerrymandering was unconstitutional,[26] but it abandoned that view in 2019 in *Rucho v. Common Cause*. There the Court held that federal courts can *never* hear challenges to partisan gerrymandering.[27] The case involved the partisan gerrymandering in North Carolina described earlier, where Republican gerrymandering awarded them ten of thirteen congressional seats. A companion case, briefed and argued at the same time, arose in Maryland, where a Democratic-controlled state legislature drew a district for a congressional seat to elect a Democrat.

Although the lower courts in both cases invalidated the partisan gerrymandering, the Supreme Court reversed and held 5–4 that the cases were "political questions" that cannot be decided by the courts.[28] Chief Justice John Roberts, writing the majority opinion, said that the ultimate question with partisan gerrymandering is how much is too much, but no judicially manageable standards for answering this question exist. Although many possible tests had been proposed for "evaluating partisan gerrymandering claims," he wrote, "... none meets the need for a limited and precise standard that is judicially discernible and manageable." Moreover "none provides a solid grounding for judges to take the extraordinary step of reallocating power and influence between political parties."[29] The Court threw up its hands and concluded that even if partisan gerrymandering violates the Constitution, as the lower courts held, the federal judiciary was not going to provide a remedy, concluding that "partisan gerrymandering claims present political questions beyond the reach of the federal courts. Federal judges have no license to reallocate political power between the two major political parties, with no plausible grant of authority in the Constitution, and no legal standards to limit and direct their decisions."[30]

Justice Elena Kagan wrote a vehement dissent, joined by Justices Ruth Bader Ginsburg, Stephen Breyer, and Sonia Sotomayor. Justice Kagan said that partisan gerrymandering undermines democracy: "Partisan gerrymandering of the kind before us not only subverts democracy (as if that weren't bad enough). It violates individuals' constitutional rights as well."[31] In answer to Chief Justice Roberts's argument that it is impossible to determine what is too much, Justice Kagan wrote that the Court should have concluded that wherever the line was to be drawn, North Carolina's gerrymandering was too much. Many possible legal tests might be used to determine when gerrymandering violates the Constitution, the dissent explained, but under any of them, the North Carolina Republicans violated the Constitution. Finally, the dissent concluded, "Of all times to abandon the Court's duty to declare the law, this was not the one. The practices challenged in these cases imperil our system of government. Part of the Court's role in that system is to defend its foundations. None is more important than free and fair elections."[32]

After the Supreme Court's decision in *Rucho v. Common Cause,* state legislatures drawing election districts after the 2020 census knew that they could engage in partisan gerrymandering without worrying that the federal courts would get involved and strike down their maps.

What Can Be Done?

Partisan gerrymandering can be prevented, despite the Supreme Court's decision in *Rucho v. Common Cause.* Voters in a state can create independent commissions to draw the election districts. In twelve states, commissions have primary responsibility for drawing congressional maps: Arizona, California, Colorado, Hawaii, Idaho, Michigan, Missouri, Montana, New Jersey, Utah, Virginia, and Washington.[33] And the idea seems to be catching on. In 2018 voters in four of these states—Colorado, Michigan, Missouri, and Utah—approved ballot measures creating independent district commissions.

Overall, these commissions have worked well and have succeeded in districting without regard to partisan considerations. Occasionally it has had unexpected results. When California adopted its commission, a former state senator told me that a truly independent commission would benefit Democrats. He said that when the legislators engaged in redistricting, the first thing they did was preserve safe seats for the incumbents of both parties. The Democratic majority gave their Republican colleagues safe seats for reelection. He predicted that, without that, Democrats would gain more seats. He was right. Ever since the independent commission drew the districts, Democrats have often had a super-majority of both houses of the California legislature.

But sometimes commissions have not worked well. New York's commission was created in a compromise between then-governor Andrew Cuomo, a Democrat, and Republican leaders. It was supposed to be bipartisan, with four Democrats, four Republicans, and two theoretically independent members. But when the two sides could not come to an agreement after the 2020 census, each gave its own districting plan to the New York legislature. Under the law, the legislature was supposed to send it back to the commission and tell them to try again. But the legislature simply adopted the Democrats' plan, which the New York Court of Appeals, in a split vote, then set aside.[34]

Federal legislation has been proposed to require independent districting commissions for House seats in all states.[35] Under the Constitution, federal law can set rules for the time, place, and manner of elections to Congress. The For the People Act would have outlawed both racial and political gerrymandering in drawing House districts. The bill passed the House in 2021 but was killed by a Republican filibuster in the Senate. Unfortunately, it seems to have little chance of passage in the foreseeable future.

There is another path to ending partisan gerrymandering: state courts can find that it violates state constitutions. The Supreme Court held only that *federal courts* may not hear challenges to partisan gerrymandering, but that does not preclude state courts from doing so. Indeed, state supreme courts in Pennsylvania, North Carolina, Ohio, and Wisconsin did exactly this and found that partisan gerrymandering violated their state constitutions.

But party politics plays a key role as to whether state courts are likely to stop partisan gerrymandering. Rarely does it happen when the state supreme court has a majority of justices who are from the same political party as the state legislature. The experience in North Carolina is telling. The North Carolina Supreme Court, with justices reflecting a 4–3 Democratic majority, found that the partisan gerrymandering by the Republican-controlled state legislature violated the state constitution.[36] It created a nonpartisan commission to draw districts for the 2022 congressional elections. Not surprisingly, in a state that is evenly divided between Democrats and Republicans, each party won seven of North Carolina's now fourteen congressional seats.

The November 2022 election also changed the composition of the North Carolina Supreme Court. It went from a 4–3 Democratic majority among the justices to a 5–2 Republican majority. In North Carolina, as in many states, justices are elected in partisan races. It then reversed the prior decision of its court and found that partisan gerrymandering does not violate the state constitution. The chance that opponents of gerrymandering can find a check based on the state constitution is now gone in North Carolina.

Because partisan gerrymandering has always existed, Americans tend to be complacent about it and not realize how malignant it has become. But it thwarts democracy and contributes to the current crisis in American government. It furthers political polarization. It undermines democratic accountability for the one branch of the federal government that was meant to be directly representative of the people.

5

The Twenty-First Century
The Supreme Court Undermines Democracy

On May 2, 2022, *Politico* published a draft opinion of the Supreme Court's decision in *Dobbs v. Jackson Women's Health Organization*, overruling *Roe v. Wade* and ending a constitutional right for women to choose to have an abortion. The Court prides itself on its secrecy; never before had an entire draft of an opinion leaked. Although the leak was shocking, the content of the decision should have been a surprise to no one. It was preordained once Justice Ruth Bader Ginsburg died and was replaced by Justice Amy Coney Barrett. At the oral argument on December 1, 2021, the five most conservative justices—Clarence Thomas, Samuel Alito, Neil Gorsuch, Brett Kavanaugh, and Amy Coney Barrett—left no doubt as to how they were going to vote.

Immediately after the draft opinion was leaked and published, the Court closed its building to the public and erected a large black fence outside its perimeter. It was chilling to see a crucial part of the seat of government closed in this way. After several months, the fence came down, but the building—the temple of justice in this country, if there is one—remained closed to the public.

On June 24 the Court released its final decision in *Dobbs*, which was remarkably unchanged from the leaked draft. Justice Alito, writing for the majority, declared that *Roe* was "egregiously wrong" and said that "its reasoning was exceedingly weak."[1] Rarely in American history has the Supreme Court taken away a constitutional right, but that is exactly what it did in *Dobbs*. For a half-century, conservatives had criticized *Roe*; they finally had the votes on the Court to overrule it, entirely because of the 2016 presidential election. Had Hillary Clinton, rather than Donald Trump, won and picked three justices, *Roe* would have been secure for decades to come. The Court's decision was not about legal principles; the basic maxim of *stare decisis*—respect for precedent—was shredded. The ruling in *Dobbs* was nothing but the raw power of the conservatives having five votes thanks to the three Trump-appointed justices.

A CNN poll showed that almost two-thirds of Americans disagreed with the Court's decision in *Dobbs*.[2] In one sense, that should not matter; the Court is not expected to follow public opinion and is meant to enforce the Constitution even when it goes against the will of the majority. But this ruling, one of a series during this century, heightens the sense that the Court has become ever more antidemocratic over time and has contributed to the crisis in American government. As explained in Chapter 4, the Court has blocked federal court challenges to the pernicious practice of partisan gerrymandering. Its rulings have gutted the Voting Rights Act and protected the right of corporations to spend unlimited amounts in election campaigns, contributing greatly to the problems plaguing our political system. And in rulings that attract much less public attention, the Court has made it much harder for federal courts to remedy illegal election practices in the days, weeks, and months before an election.

Simply put, at a time when our country is more politically polarized than at any time since Reconstruction, the Court has come down solidly on one side of that divide—far to the right on it. This, too, contributes to the crisis facing American government. Under these circumstances, the American people cannot regard the Court as a neutral umpire—as John Roberts tried to portray it at his confirmation hearings—or as having great legitimacy. They rightly see it as just another part of the partisan divide, and one that is likely to remain very conservative for a long time to come.

Here, too, bad choices were made in 1787 that haunt us to this day, whose effects recent events have only worsened.

The Initial Choices

The judicial branch of government was created by the Constitution—no federal courts existed under the Articles of Confederation. Although the framers at the Constitutional Convention disagreed substantially about the appropriate structure and authority of the federal courts, they agreed there should be a Supreme Court. As Max Farrand remarked in his authoritative history of the convention proceedings, "That there should be a national judiciary was readily accepted by all."[3]

In large part, the framers desired federal courts so they would effectively implement the powers of the national government. They feared that state courts might not fully enforce and implement federal policies, especially where federal and state interests conflicted. At a minimum, they thought a federal judiciary could provide a uniform interpretation of the Constitution and laws of the United States. They also agreed that a national tribunal was essential to resolve disputes between the states. A peaceful way to settle disagreements over matters such as borders was imperative, but the framers saw state courts as too parochial to perform this function. Additionally, some, such as James Madison, saw federal courts as necessary to ensure the protection of individual liberties.

A major dispute at the Constitutional Convention was whether lower federal courts should exist, or whether the judiciary should consist of just the Supreme Court and the state court systems. The Committee of the Whole, echoing resolutions offered by Edmund Randolph, proposed that there should be both a Supreme Court and inferior federal courts.[4] This proposal drew strong opposition from those who thought lower federal courts were unnecessary and undesirable and a superfluous expense because state courts, subject to review by the Supreme Court, were sufficient to protect the interests of the national government. Furthermore, lower courts could intrude on the sovereignty of the state governments. Having lower federal courts, Max Farrand explains, was "regarded as an encroachment upon the rights of the individual states. It was claimed that the state courts were perfectly competent for the work required, and that it would be quite sufficient to grant an appeal from them to the national supreme court."[5]

But others distrusted the ability and willingness of state courts to uphold federal law. James Madison stated, "Confidence cannot be put in the State Tribunals as guardians of the National authority and interests."[6] State judges were likely to be biased against federal law, Madison argued, especially in instances where state and federal interests conflicted.[7] Appeals to the Supreme Court were inadequate to protect federal interests because the number of such appeals would exceed the Court's limited capacity to hear and decide them.

The proposal to create lower federal courts was initially defeated at the Constitutional Convention, 5–4, with two states divided.[8] Madison and James Wilson then proposed a compromise: the Constitution would mandate the existence of the Supreme Court but leave it up to Congress to decide whether to create inferior federal courts. This obvious punt left the issue to others in the future. Their proposal was adopted by a vote of 8–2, with one state divided.[9] Thus, Article III of the Constitution says, "The judicial Power of the United States, shall be vested in one supreme Court, and in such inferior Courts as the Congress may from time to time ordain and establish." Congress, in its first judiciary act in 1789, established lower federal courts, and they have existed ever since.[10] Thus the question of whether state courts are equal to federal courts in their willingness and ability to uphold federal law—an issue that continues to be debated and that influences a great many aspects of the law of federal jurisdiction[11]—has its origins in the earliest discussions of the federal judicial power.

Once the framers decided to create a Supreme Court and to give Congress the option to create lower federal courts, the crucial question was how to select Supreme Court justices and federal judges and hold them accountable. In the American colonies, judges had been appointed by the king of England and served at his pleasure.[12] The colonists had been greatly dissatisfied with a court system that was beholden to the king and unresponsive to their needs. The enumeration of grievances in the Declaration of Independence stated that the king "made judges dependent upon his will alone for the tenure of their offices and payment of their salaries."

Seeking to insulate federal judges from such direct executive control, the drafters of Article III granted life tenure to federal judges, "during good Behaviour," and salaries that cannot be decreased during their time in office. A crucial lasting difference between federal and state court judges is the electoral accountability of the latter. In thirty-nine states, state court judges are subject to some form of electoral review.[13] In some states, judges run in partisan elections like all other politicians. In others, voters decide solely whether the particular judge should remain on the bench.

The life tenure of federal judges makes federal courts uniquely suited for the protection of constitutional rights.[14] For example, elected judges in Southern states would hardly have ordered desegregation when the Supreme Court finally ended the apartheid of Jim Crow laws. But others lament that life tenure creates a federal judiciary that is immune from any accountability.

Life tenure has a great virtue in providing judicial independence. It helps ensure that cases will be decided based on the judges' conclusions about the law and the facts of a case, not to please a constituency. It is easy to see why the framers, who lived in a regime where the king could summarily remove judges, wanted the protections of independence that were accorded by life tenure.

But life tenure comes at a cost, too: people remain in office even if they are no longer adequately performing the job or are severely out of touch with the country they are governing. This concern was less potent in 1787 because at that time the average life expectancy was thirty-eight years (though that number is somewhat misleading because of the high infant mortality at the time). Still, the framers did not expect that the average justice would serve for decades.

Before John Roberts became chief justice, he said, "The Framers adopted life tenure at a time when people simply did not live as long as they do now. A judge insulated from the normal currents of life for twenty-five or thirty years was a rarity then, but is becoming commonplace today."[15] From 1789 to 1970, the average Supreme Court justice served for 15.2 years.[16] By contrast, justices appointed after 1970 who have since left the bench have served an average of 27.6 years. Over the next hundred years, justices will average about thirty-five years on the Court, compared to seventeen years in the prior century.[17] Clarence Thomas was forty-three years old when he was confirmed for the Court in 1991. If he remains until he is ninety, the age at which John Paul Stevens retired, he will have been a justice for forty-seven years.

Amy Coney Barrett was forty-eight when she was confirmed. If she remains on the Court until she is eighty-seven, the age at which Ruth Bader Ginsburg retired, she will be a justice until the year 2059.

Such lengthened tenures are partly a result of presidents consciously picking younger individuals, but mostly it is about increased lifespans. The result is that life tenure greatly heightens the anti-democratic nature of the Court and risks justices who are seriously out of touch with the society they govern. To be sure, life tenure provides a benefit of stability and justices that are appointed by different presidents. But justices routinely serving for three or four decades is far different than could have been imagined in 1787. It is just too much power in a single person's hands for too long a period of time.

The independence of the judiciary, as well as its anti-majoritarian character, was enhanced by the way in which justices and all federal judges were to be chosen. The Constitution provides that the president nominates these individuals with the "advice and consent" of the Senate. This has been understood throughout American history to mean that the Senate must approve, by majority vote, a presidential nominee before that person can take office. And the Senate has exercised its power to reject nominees. In the nineteenth century, about 20 percent of presidential nominees to the Supreme Court were rejected. In the twentieth century, there were a handful of high-profile rejections: John Parker in 1930, Clement Haynsworth and Harold Carswell in 1969, and Robert Bork in 1987. In 2016 the Senate refused to even hold a hearing or a vote on the nomination of Merrick Garland, in a blatant effort to keep the seat open in case a Republican was elected 2016.

But life tenure and this selection method also pose a serious risk: a Court could become out of step with the country and in of itself pose a threat to the country. Lest this seem fanciful, between the 1890s and 1936, a very conservative Court struck down over two hundred progressive laws that were especially meant to protect workers and consumers.[18] This created a crisis of legitimacy for the Court especially as it struck down New Deal programs during the Depression. It led President Franklin Roosevelt to propose "Court packing," or expanding the size of the Court, and contributed to the Court dramatically changing course.

I believe that is where we are now, with a majority of the Court much more conservative than the overall American polity. Tension between judicial independence and judicial accountability is inevitable: justices and judges should not be deciding cases to please the voters. But life tenure for justices goes too far in creating a branch of government that is at odds with democracy. No other country in the world gives its judges life tenure, and that is for a good reason: individuals should not exercise such great power for such a long period of time.

Undermining Democracy

Not only is the Supreme Court less democratic because of the effects of life tenure and the manipulations of the appointment process, but its rulings in recent years have further undermined democracy and contributed to the current crisis. As discussed in Chapter 4, the Court, by blocking federal courts from hearing challenges to partisan gerrymandering, has prevented the judiciary from remedying a practice that is antithetical to democracy and that has undermined the House of Representatives as a representative body. Additionally, the Court has contributed greatly to the problems of democracy by nullifying key provisions of the Voting Rights Act of 1965, one of the most important federal laws ever adopted by Congress.

The United States has a long and disgraceful history of race discrimination with regard to voting. After the Civil War, the Fourteenth Amendment was ratified in 1868; it includes a provision that no state may deny any person equal protection of the laws. Two years later the Fifteenth Amendment was ratified to explicitly deal with the problem of race discrimination in voting. It states: "The right of citizens of the United States to vote shall not be denied or abridged by the United States or by any State on account of race, color, or previous condition of servitude." As a result of these amendments and of Reconstruction, more than a half-million Black men in the South became voters in the 1870s. (Women, of course, did not get the right to vote until the Nineteenth amendment was ratified in 1920.) This enfranchisement of Black men had a dramatic effect. In Mississippi, former slaves made up half of the state's population, and once they were allowed to vote, they exercised their political power. During Reconstruction, Mississippi elected two Black U.S. senators and several Black state officials, including a lieutenant governor.[19]

The compromise that decided the 1876 election ended Reconstruction, and Northern troops were withdrawn from the South. Southern states then adopted many laws designed to keep Black people from voting.[20] They created poll taxes, requiring that individuals pay a fee in order to vote. Georgia initiated the poll tax in 1871 and made it cumulative in 1877, requiring citizens to pay all back taxes before being permitted to vote. Every Southern state then enacted a poll tax. The Georgia poll tax probably reduced overall turnout by 16 to 28 percent, and turnout of Black voters by half.[21]

Southern states also adopted literacy tests, requiring a person seeking to register to vote to read a section of the state constitution to a county clerk and then explain its meaning. The clerk, who was always white, had discretion to decide whether the person was sufficiently literate. This excluded almost all Black men from voting because a significant percentage could not read, and for those that could, the clerk could deem their literacy inadequate.[22]

These states also enacted a "grandfather clause" that created an exception to the literacy tests for those whose grandfathers had qualified to vote before the Civil War. Obviously, this benefited only white citizens. These actions worked. In Mississippi alone, the percentage of Black voting-age men registered to vote fell from over 90 percent during Reconstruction to less than 6 percent in 1892.[23] Beyond the laws, white citizens directed intimidation at those who tried to register to vote. In 1940, as a result, just 3 percent of voting-age Black men and women in the South were registered to vote.[24] In Mississippi, under 1 percent were registered.

The civil rights movement worked to combat race discrimination in voting and to increase Black voter registration. Still, in 1964, only about 43 percent of adult Black men and women in the South were registered.[25] In Alabama, though, only 23 percent of African Americans were registered, and in Mississippi less than 7 percent of voting-age Black people were registered.[26]

The key change occurred when Congress passed the Voting Rights Act of 1965, one of the most important civil rights statutes adopted in American history. Section 2 of the Voting Rights Act prohibits voting practices or procedures that discriminate on the basis of race or against certain language minority groups. In 1982, Congress amended Section 2 to make clear that state and local laws that have the effect of disadvantaging minority voters violate the act. No proof is required that the government acted with the intent to discriminate against voters of color; lawsuits can be brought to challenge state or local actions that are alleged to violate Section 2.

But Congress, in adopting the Voting Rights Act, knew that allowing lawsuits to challenge election procedures was not adequate to stop discrimination in voting. Such litigation is expensive and time consuming. Congress also was aware that Southern states often invented new ways of disenfranchising minority voters. The arcade game Whac-a-Mole seems an apt analogy to what went on in many states: a state would adopt a law to limit voting by racial minorities, it would be challenged and struck down, then it would be replaced by a new voting restriction. Section 5 of the Voting Rights Act was adopted to prevent such actions.

Section 5 applied to jurisdictions that had a history of race discrimination in voting. It required that before any "covered jurisdiction" attempted to change "any voting qualification or prerequisite to voting, or standard, practice, or procedure with respect to voting," the state had to seek preapproval, termed "preclearance." Preclearance must come either from the U.S. attorney general, from the Department of Justice, or from a three-judge federal court in the District of Columbia.

In 1966 in *South Carolina v. Katzenbach*, the Supreme Court upheld the constitutionality of Section 5 of the Voting Rights Act and spoke of the "blight of racial discrimination in voting."[27] The Court found that Section 5 was a constitutional exercise of Congress's power to enforce the Fifteenth Amendment's prohibition of race discrimination in voting. Section 4(B) of the act determines which jurisdictions are required to get preclearance.

Congress repeatedly renewed Section 5 and its requirement that jurisdictions with a history of race discrimination get preclearance, including for five years in 1970, for seven years in 1975, and for twenty-five years in 1982. In 1982 Congress revised the formula in Section 4(B) for determining which jurisdictions were required to obtain preclearance before changing their election systems. After each reauthorization, the Supreme Court again upheld the constitutionality of Sections 4(B) and 5.[28] Preclearance was an effective and even essential way to prevent race discrimination in voting in jurisdictions that had a proven history of excluding voters of color.

These provisions were scheduled to expire again in 2007. In 2005–6, the House and Senate Judiciary Committees held twenty-one hearings, listened to ninety witnesses, and compiled a record of over fifteen thousand pages. Representative James Sensenbrenner, a Republican from Wisconsin who chaired the House Judiciary Committee, described this record as "one of the most extensive considerations of any piece of legislation that the United States Congress has dealt with in the 27½ years that I have been honored to serve as a Member of this body."[29]

Congress then voted overwhelmingly (98–0 in the Senate and 390–33 in the House) to extend Section 5 for twenty-five years. It did not change Section 4(B) or Section 5. Congress expressly concluded that voting discrimination persists in the covered jurisdictions, and that without Section 5, "minority citizens will be deprived of the opportunity to exercise their right to vote, or will have their votes diluted, undermining the significant gains made by minorities in the last 40 years."[30]

The record before Congress supported this conclusion. For example, between 1982 and 2006, the Section 5 preclearance requirement blocked 750 discriminatory changes in election systems in covered jurisdictions.[31] Another 205 discriminatory changes were withdrawn. Countless changes were not adopted because of the recognition that they were unlikely to receive preclearance. The continued discrimination in covered jurisdictions is further evidenced by 650 successful court challenges under Section 2 of the Voting Rights Act in these places. University of Michigan law professor Ellen Katz did extensive studies and found that covered jurisdictions had only 25 percent of the country's population but accounted for 56 percent of the successful suits under Section 2.[32] The evidence that Section 5 was needed and that it worked was overwhelming.

Nor is it over. Before the 2012 elections, of the twelve states with the largest Hispanic populations, seven adopted restrictive voting

laws.[33] Of the ten states with the largest African American populations, five adopted restrictive voting laws.[34] After the 2020 election,
nineteen states with Republican-controlled state legislatures adopted
new laws to restrict voting.

Despite this history, in *Shelby County, Alabama v. Holder* in 2013,
the Supreme Court declared Section 4(B) of the Voting Rights Act,
the provision that determines which jurisdictions have to get preclearance, unconstitutional.[35] Without Section 4(B), Section 5 is ren-
dered meaningless; *no jurisdictions have to get preclearance.* Thus, the
Supreme Court eliminated a crucial protection of voting.

Shelby County, Alabama, which is south of Selma, is a jurisdiction with a long history of race discrimination in voting. Because
of this history, it was a jurisdiction covered by Section 5; the county
thus challenged the constitutionality of this provision of the Voting
Rights Act. It lost both in the district court and in the federal court of
appeals. The U.S. Court of Appeals for the District of Columbia Circuit concluded that Congress found "widespread and persistent racial
discrimination in voting in covered jurisdictions" and that Section 5's
"disparate geographic coverage is sufficiently related to the problem
it targets."[36]

But the Supreme Court, 5–4, held that Section 4(B) was unconstitutional, effectively nullifying Section 5 because it applies only to
jurisdictions covered under Section 4(B). It was the first time since
the nineteenth century that the Court had declared unconstitutional a federal civil rights statute. Chief Justice Roberts, writing for
the Court, stressed that the formula in Section 4(B), last modified in
1982, rests on data from the 1960s and the '70s; the Court found that
this data no longer applies because "nearly 50 years later, things have
changed dramatically."[37]

The Court stressed that Section 4(B) intruded on the covered states
since they could not exercise their power to choose how to hold elections; under the provisions, the "States must beseech the Federal Government for permission to implement laws that they would otherwise
have the right to enact and execute on their own, subject of course
to any injunction in a § 2 action."[38] The Court also emphasized that
Sections 4(B) and 5, by requiring only some states to get preclearance,
violated the principle of equal state sovereignty: "Not only do States

retain sovereignty under the Constitution, there is also a 'fundamental principle of *equal* sovereignty' among the States. . . . Despite the tradition of equal sovereignty, the Act applies to only nine States (and several additional counties)."[39]

The puzzle of the Court's decision is what constitutional provision or principle was violated by the preclearance requirement. The fact that Congress relied on old data does not make the law unconstitutional, especially since Congress had more recently held exhaustive hearings finding continued discrimination in voting. Besides, the Constitution does not require that Congress provide data, let alone current data, to support its laws.

The Court said Section 4(B) was unconstitutional because it fails to treat all the states the same, violating what the Court termed the principle of "equal sovereignty." But the text of the Constitution mentions no such principle, and the Congress that ratified the Fourteenth and Fifteenth Amendments did not believe in it, as it imposed Reconstruction on the former rebel states in the South. Countless federal laws treat some states differently from others.[40] For the justices who believe in originalism, yet voted in the majority in *Shelby County*, this has to be wrong: the same Congress that ratified the Fourteenth Amendment also passed the Reconstruction Act, which created military rule over the South and prohibited these states from being readmitted to the union until they ratified the Fourteenth Amendment.

The Court's invalidation of the Voting Rights Act provisions had the predicted effect of making it harder for states to combat race discrimination in voting. Soon after it was adopted, Texas and North Carolina put into place election systems that had been denied preclearance because of their discriminatory effects against minority voters. Studies show that ending preclearance has had the predictable effect of allowing states to implement discriminatory laws and lessening voting by voters of color. Justice Kagan noted in 2021, that "although causation is hard to establish definitively," after the Court's decision in *Shelby County*, Black voter participation decreased in the areas covered by the statute. "The most comprehensive study available found that in areas freed from Section 5 review," she noted, "white turnout remained the same, but 'minority participation dropped by 2.1 percentage points'—a stark reversal in direction from prior elections. The results, said the scholar who crunched the numbers, 'provide early evidence that the Shelby ruling may jeopardize decades of voting rights progress.'"[41]

But the Court did not stop with ending preclearance. Eight years later, in 2021, it significantly weakened the other key provision of the Voting Rights Act, Section 2, which created liability for state and local governments that had election systems and practices that discriminated against minority voters.

In 1980, in *City of Mobile v. Bolden*, the Supreme Court held that proving race discrimination in voting—whether under the Fourteenth Amendment's Equal Protection Clause or the Fifteenth Amendment or Section 2 of the Voting Rights Act—requires proof of a discriminatory intent on the part of the government.[42] But intent is often very difficult to prove; government officials are unlikely to express their racism even when it motivates their actions. In 1982 Congress amended the Voting Rights Act to provide that proof of discriminatory impact was sufficient to show a violation of the law; no longer did there have to be discriminatory intent. Section 2 was revised so that a plaintiff could establish a violation of the law if the evidence established that, in the context of the "totality of the circumstance of the local electoral process," a standard, practice, or procedure had the result of denying a racial or language minority an equal opportunity to participate in the political process.

But in *Brnovich v. Democratic National Committee*, in 2021, the Court gutted Section 2 as a tool to combat race discrimination in the way elections are conducted. The case involved two provisions of Arizona law. One said that a ballot was not to be counted if it was cast by a person outside his or her precinct. The other prohibited "ballot harvesting," making it a felony to collect and deliver another person's completed ballot (with exceptions for family members, caregivers, mail carriers, and election officials). The Democratic National Committee and voters brought lawsuits challenging these provisions. They argued that these Arizona laws violated Section 2 of the Voting Rights Act because they had a discriminatory effect against minority voters. They also alleged a discriminatory intent behind the laws and claimed that they violated the Constitution as well as the Voting Rights Act.

The U.S. Court of Appeals for the Ninth Circuit ruled for the plaintiffs in a 7–4 decision. Judge William Fletcher, writing for the majority, found that the Arizona law would "have a discriminatory impact on American Indian, Hispanic, and African American voters in Arizona, in violation of the 'results test' of Section 2 of the VRA."[43] The Court also found that Arizona adopted the law with a racially discriminatory intent, thus violating the Voting Rights Act and the Constitution. The provision requiring voting in one's precinct for a ballot to be counted was discriminatory, the court explained, because polling places changed much more frequently in communities of color. The restriction on absentee ballots had a discriminatory effect on Native Americans, since access to postal services was far less on reservations.

However, the Supreme Court, in its 6–3 decision in *Brnovich*, reversed the Ninth Circuit and ruled in favor of Arizona. The Republican-appointed justices composed the majority, and the three Democratic-appointed justices all dissented. It surely was no coincidence that the restrictions had been adopted by a Republican legislature and signed by Arizona's Republican governor and would disproportionately help Republican candidates for office.

In a crucial part of the opinion, Justice Alito said that the model for identifying racial discrimination based on disparate impact that is used to interpret many other federal civil rights laws was "not useful" here."[44] He went on to list five factors that courts must consider when a voting rule is challenged under Section 2. Each of them will make it very difficult to find race discrimination in violation of Section 2. None are remotely hinted at in the Voting Rights Act.

- *The size of the burden imposed on voters.* Justice Alito wrote: "After all, every voting rule imposes a burden of some sort."[45] The Court requires a proof of a substantial burden on voting, but it never defines what is enough to meet this criterion. The federal court of appeals found a significant burden on voters of color from the Arizona law. But the Supreme Court said that was not sufficient, without explaining what was needed to prove a violation of the law.
- *The degree to which the rule deviates from the rule in effect in 1982, when Section 2 was last amended.*[46] This factor makes the untenable assumption that Congress meant to approve all

the election practices that existed in 1982. And it makes it easy to reject any challenges to current restrictions on voting. The Court just has to say that restrictions that existed in 1982 were worse than the current law being challenged and therefore uphold a discriminatory law with regard to voting.

- *The scale of any disparate racial impact.* The Court said there has to be substantial racial disparity for a violation of Section 2: "But the mere fact there is some disparity in impact does not necessarily mean that a system is not equally open or that it does not give everyone an equal opportunity to vote. What are at bottom very small differences should not be artificially magnified."[47] Again, the Court did not give any indication of what was enough to prove a racially discriminatory impact, but it clearly set a high threshold in order to prove a violation of the act.

- *The opportunities to vote provided by the state's overall system.* The Court said that if there are multiple ways to vote, it is unlikely that any restriction would be impermissible.[48] But this allows significant restrictions on methods of voting that are essential for some voters—such as absentee ballots—by allowing a court to point to other ways to vote however impractical and unhelpful they might be. The whole point of the 1982 amendments to the Voting Rights Act was to allow challenges when there is a racially disparate impact to a state election law. Now that is subordinate to the question of whether there are other ways to vote, even if they are unrealistic.

- *The strength of the state interests served by the rule, such as preventing fraud.* The Court said that "rules that are supported by strong state interests are less likely to violate Section 2. One strong and entirely legitimate state interest is the prevention of fraud." It is crucial to note that *nothing* in the Voting Rights Act says that discriminatory restrictions on voting are allowed if the government points to an interest in preventing fraud. Not one word in the law says that courts, in deciding whether the act has been violated, should look at the reasons for the restrictions on voting. This dramatically changes the analysis by giving courts latitude by approving discriminatory restrictions. It is all too easy for a government that wants to impose restrictions on voting that disproportionately affect voters of color to claim that it was acting to prevent fraud. The Court treats Section 2 of the Voting Rights Act as requiring a balancing test—weighing the discrimination against minority voters against the government's interests—in deciding whether there is a violation of the law. But that is not at all what the act says or what Congress intended.

The Court applied these five factors and concluded that the Arizona law did not violate Section 2 of the Voting Rights Act. Shockingly, none of these factors are stated or implied in the law. Conservative justices, who frequently proclaim a belief in textualism and in following the plain language of the statute, just made it all up. The ruling makes no mention in the Voting Rights Act or its legislative history that suggests that courts should consider whether discriminatory restrictions on voting are justified if the state claims an interest in preventing fraud.

Justice Kagan wrote a vehement dissent. The factors identified by the Court had no basis in the statute, she said: "What is tragic here is that the Court has (yet again) rewritten—in order to weaken—a statute that stands as a monument to America's greatness, and protects against its basest impulses. What is tragic is that the Court has damaged a statute designed to bring about the end of discrimination in voting."[49]

No doubt the Court's decision will make it much harder to use Section 2 of the Voting Rights Act to challenge state laws imposing restrictions on voting. The five factors articulated by Justice Alito all point in one direction: making it far more difficult to find a violation of Section 2 of the Voting Rights Act. This is particularly important now because many states have adopted new laws that restrict voting and that likely will have a discriminatory impact against minority voters. In 2021, nineteen states adopted thirty-three new laws restricting voting. As Justice Kagan noted: "In recent months, State after State has taken up or enacted legislation erecting new barriers to voting. Those laws shorten the time polls are open, both on Election Day and before. They impose new prerequisites to voting by mail, and shorten the windows to apply for and return mail ballots. They make it harder to register to vote, and easier to purge voters from the rolls. Two laws even ban handing out food or water to voters standing in line."[50]

The laws all have been adopted in states with Republican legislatures, and all are designed to make voting harder in counties, districts, and precincts that vote for Democratic candidates. Because Black Americans vote for Democratic candidates about 90 percent of the time, many of these restrictions undoubtedly will have a discriminatory impact. The Court's decision in *Brnovich* will make successful challenges far more difficult and further undermine the democratic process and voter confidence in it.[51]

Invalidating Campaign Finance Restrictions

Few Supreme Court decisions in history have had as strong an effect on our political system as *Citizens United v. Federal Election Commission*. In 2010 the Court held that the First Amendment protects the right of corporations to spend unlimited amounts of money in election campaigns to have candidates elected or defeated.[52] *Citizens United* was a 5–4 decision split along ideological lines, with five conservative justices appointed by Republican presidents in the majority. Democracy is undermined when the wealthiest—including corporations out of their treasury—have such disproportionate influence in elections.

The Bipartisan Campaign Finance Reform Act of 2002 was the result of years of hearings and debate. Congress sought to close loopholes and solve problems that had developed with regard to campaign finance. Over a century earlier, Congress prohibited corporations from contributing money directly to candidates for federal office, and the Court extended this to unions more than a half-century ago. These laws reflected the widely supported view that the wealth of corporations and unions should not decide elections, as well as the reality that large contributions inevitably create the appearance of elected officials beholden to those who got them elected.

But corporations and unions found ways to circumvent these restrictions, including by taking out advertisements about the issues that did not expressly endorse or oppose candidates by name. As a result, the limits could be circumvented just by omitting the magic words "Elect Jane Doe," or "Vote for John Smith." The corporations' ad could say, Jane Doe supports releasing dangerous criminals, as long as it did not contain an explicit endorsement as to how to vote. No one, though, would have doubt as to the intended message. As the Court noted, "Corporations and unions spent hundreds of millions of dollars of their general funds to pay for these ads, and those expenditures, like soft-money donations to the political parties, were unregulated."[53]

The Bipartisan Campaign Reform Act—often called the McCain-Feingold Act after its bipartisan Senate sponsors, Republican John McCain and Democrat Russell Feingold—regulated broadcast advertisements by corporations and unions. It prevented corporations and unions from using money from their treasuries for broadcast advertisements to support the election or defeat of a candidate for federal office within thirty days of a primary election or sixty days of a general election. Additionally, the law provided that coordinated electioneering communication—where corporations or unions worked together with a candidate on their ads—be treated as contributions to candidates or parties.

In 2003 the Supreme Court in *McConnell v. Federal Election Commission* upheld these provisions as constitutionally permissible ways of preventing circumvention of federal law by issue advertisements. In a 5–4 decision, Justices Sandra Day O'Connor and John Paul Stevens—both appointees of Republican presidents—wrote of the government's important interests in limiting corporate and union spending in election campaigns. The decision was based on precedents that had established the government's great interest in preventing corporate and union treasuries from drowning out other voices and deciding elections.

However, seven years later, in *Citizens United v. Federal Election Commission*, the Supreme Court overruled *McConnell* and held that the restrictions on independent expenditures by corporations violated the First Amendment.[54] What had changed in this short time? Had the Court found a musty history of the First Amendment that led it to believe it was mistaken earlier? Had problems emerged under the law? No, all that had changed was the composition of the Court, and specifically the replacement of Justice O'Connor with Justice Alito.

A 5–4 majority to uphold the law became a 5–4 decision to strike it down. Again, it wasn't about legal principles, but about the raw power of new, more conservative justices overruling a very recent precedent.

With Justice Anthony Kennedy writing for the majority, the Court held that corporations have free speech rights and that limits on their expenditures are unconstitutional restrictions of core political speech. Limits on independent expenditures by corporations and unions, the Court concluded, violated the First Amendment: "The censorship we now confront is vast in its reach. The Government has 'muffle[d] the voices that best represent the most significant segments of the economy.' And 'the electorate [has been] deprived of information, knowledge and opinion vital to its function.' "[55] The Court declared: "The Government may not suppress political speech on the basis of the speaker's corporate identity. No sufficient governmental interest justifies limits on the political speech of nonprofit or for-profit corporations."[56] Simply put, corporations can spend as much as they want from their corporate treasuries to get the candidates they want elected or defeated.

Justice Stevens wrote a lengthy, vehement dissent that was joined by Justices Ginsburg, Breyer, and Sotomayor.[57] The dissent rejected the majority's premise that corporations are entitled to the same First Amendment rights as individuals, writing that the First Amendment was never intended to protect corporate speech.[58] "In the context of election to public office," Justice Stevens stated, "the distinction between corporate and human speakers is significant. Although they make enormous contributions to our society, corporations are not actually members of it. They cannot vote or run for office."[59]

Furthermore, the dissent stressed that even under the restrictions of the Bipartisan Campaign Finance Reform Act, corporations and unions could engage in campaign spending through political action committees. Justice Stevens argued that the limits on spending directly from corporate and union treasuries was justified to prevent corruption and the appearance of corruption, the distorting effects of corporate wealth in elections, and the protection of corporate shareholders from having their funds spent against their beliefs. Justice Stevens concluded his dissent by declaring: "At bottom, the Court's opinion is thus a rejection of the common sense of the American people, who have recognized a need to prevent corporations from undermining self-government since the founding, and who have fought against the distinctive corrupting potential of corporate electioneering since the days of Theodore Roosevelt."[60]

The Court's decision in *Citizens United* has had a profound effect on our democracy as corporations can now spend unlimited money to get candidates elected or defeated. As one report noted: "It has also become a growing problem as each respective election cycle has seen record-breaking amounts of spending. Campaign spending by corporations and other outside groups increased by nearly 900 percent between 2008 and 2016. In 2020, total election spending was $14.4 billion, up from $5.7 billion in 2018, and more than $1 billion in dark money was spent."[61] Dark money is money that organizations spend without having to disclose its donors. As election law expert Richard Hasen states, *Citizens United* "helped to usher in a sea change in American elections, and its influence on the decade that followed is hard to overstate."[62] The result has been an explosion of undisclosed money, super PACS, and foreign influence in American elections.

The Court's decision in *Citizens United* further undermines democracy and the legitimacy of our political system. Chief Justice Roberts, in a later opinion striking down a federal campaign finance law, declared, "There is no right more basic in our democracy than the right to participate in electing our political leaders."[63] It is tragically perverse that Chief Justice Roberts and the Court's conservative majority used this right to strike down laws limiting the ability of corporations and the wealthy to spend money in election campaigns, but are untroubled when those who are kept from participating are the poor and racial minorities.

By empowering corporations, while at the same time gutting the Voting Rights Act, conservative justices have had an enormous political effect. One need not be a cynic to see it as Republican justices helping elect Republican candidates at every level of government. The loser in all this is our democracy.

The *Purcell* Principle

Although the Supreme Court rulings gutting the Voting Rights Act and protecting corporate campaign spending received much attention, another significant development has largely been ignored. The Court's ruling in *Merrill v. Milligan*, on February 7, 2022, makes it harder for federal courts to enjoin illegal voting practices.[64] The Court's decision means that many illegal restrictions on voting will have to be used for one election before they can be challenged.

Under the Constitution, every state must redraw its election districts, including those for congressional seats, every ten years after the census is conducted. After the 2020 census, the Alabama legislature did this in such a way as to reduce the likelihood that voters would elect Blacks to the House of Representatives. Alabama's population is 27 percent Black, but the legislature drew the districts so that Black voters were a majority in only one congressional district. To dilute their voting power, most Black voters were packed into that one district, and the rest were spread among the remaining six districts.[65]

The federal district court in Alabama heard seven days of testimony, read over one thousand pages of briefing, and concluded that the map drawn by the Alabama legislature for congressional seats was discriminatory. The three-judge panel—which included two judges appointed by President Donald Trump and one appointed by President Bill Clinton—found that the map likely violated the Voting Rights Act.[66] But the Supreme Court, in a 5–4 ruling (with Chief Justice Roberts joining the three liberal justices in dissent), stayed the lower court ruling and allowed the discriminatory map to be used in the 2022 elections. Strikingly, none of the nine justices, including those in the majority, disagreed with the lower court's conclusion about the map's discriminatory effect. In fact, in June 2023, the Supreme Court ultimately found that the lower court was right and that Alabama had indeed violated the Voting Rights Act.[67] Nonetheless, the Court allowed the discriminatory map to be used for the 2022 primary and general elections.

One of the most basic rules of appellate procedure is that the appeals court should grant a stay of a lower court decision only if there is a substantial likelihood that the party seeking the relief will ultimately prevail on the merits. But in this case, none of the five conservative justices pointed to any error of law or fact made by the three-judge district court. Nor did any of the justices claim that the district court misapplied the law in finding a violation of the Voting Rights

Act. As Chief Justice Roberts explained in his dissent, "The District Court properly applied existing law in an extensive opinion with no apparent errors for our correction."[68]

Why, then, did the conservative justices stay the ruling by the district court? The Court offered no opinion, but Justice Brett Kavanaugh, who was in the majority, wrote an opinion explaining the rationale behind the Court's order. He invoked the principle that federal courts should not mandate changes to state and local election practices soon before an election: "The stay order follows this Court's election-law precedents, which establish that federal district courts ordinarily should not enjoin state election laws in the period close to an election."[69]

Kavanaugh then invoked *Purcell v. Gonzalez*, a Supreme Court order that was also handed down without briefing or oral argument. In *Purcell*, the federal court of appeals had found that an Arizona law requiring photo identification for voting violated the Constitution and stopped the law from going into effect.[70] But the Supreme Court allowed the Arizona law to go into effect for the election, saying, "Given the imminence of the election and the inadequate time to resolve the factual disputes, our action today shall of necessity allow the election to proceed without an injunction suspending the voter identification rules."[71]

The Court has never explained the constitutional basis for this ruling. Why should unconstitutional or illegal restrictions on voting be acceptable just because the challenge is being heard soon before an election? Nonetheless, the Court has invoked *Purcell v. Gonzalez* many times as establishing that federal courts cannot enjoin state and local election laws soon before an election, even when the judges conclude that the Constitution is being violated. For example, in *Republican National Committee v. Democratic National Committee* (2020), a federal district court in Wisconsin issued an order, five days before the scheduled election, that absentee ballots mailed and postmarked after election day, April 7, would still be counted as long as they were received by April 13.[72] The judge issued this order because of the dramatic increase in absentee ballots in April 2020 at the height of concern over the COVID-19 pandemic. Wisconsin law had previously required that ballots be received by election day.[73] The federal judge's order made great sense because otherwise many ballots would not be received in time to be counted, through absolutely no fault of the voter.

The Supreme Court, though, overturned this order and said that extending the date by which voters may cast ballots for an additional six days after the scheduled election day "fundamentally alters the nature of the election."[74] The Court invoked *Purcell v. Gonzalez* and said, "This Court has repeatedly emphasized that lower federal courts should ordinarily not alter the election rules on the eve of an election."[75] This meant that people—and this was in the earliest days of the pandemic—had to choose between refraining from voting or standing close together in long lines.

The Court has never explained what interval of time before an election justifies the application of *Purcell*. In the Alabama case, the situation was not one in which the federal court acted days or even weeks before the election; the district court issued its order in February for the Alabama primary in May and the general election in November.

The threat to fair elections is that the Court's approach in the Alabama election case will make challenges to election districting almost impossible for the first election after districts are drawn. New districts cannot be drawn until after the census, and completing the districting process inevitably takes a good deal of negotiating and time. If a legislature delays districting long enough, then no federal court can hear a challenge in enough time before the next election. Under Justice Kavanaugh's reasoning, if Alabama had drawn districts that made it unlikely that any Black representative could have been elected, then the federal court could have not provided relief before the election. In fact, no matter how blatantly discriminatory the maps, courts could not stop them from being used if the challenge was soon before the election, even if there was no opportunity for an earlier challenge.

The Court's order put in place an electoral map that a three-judge federal court found to be discriminatory. The result of the ruling was that the map drawn by the Alabama legislature, which diminished the voting strength of Black voters and therefore violates the Voting Rights Act, was used in the 2022 primary and general election. As a result, Alabama gained an additional Republican seat in the House of Representatives. This is particularly inexplicable because the Supreme Court ultimately affirmed the lower court and found that the districting in Alabama violated the Voting Rights Act.[76] The Supreme Court harmed democracy and created a principle that will do so again and again in the future.

What It Means

I support having a Supreme Court that is largely insulated from majoritarian politics interpret and enforce the Constitution. But I am deeply troubled by justices who will routinely serve three or four decades on the Court. No individual—let alone individuals who are unaccountable—should have that kind of power for so long. The decisions of the Court over the last decade have undermined democracy by preventing challenges to partisan gerrymandering, gutting the Voting Rights Act, protecting the right of corporations to spend unlimited money in election campaigns, and stopping lower court rulings from protecting voting rights. All this undermines democracy. The Supreme Court must be seen as part of the problem to be overcome. It is unlikely, given its current composition, to be a solution to the crisis in governance now facing the United States.

6

Yesterday and Today

Racial Inequalities Unabated and Their Threat to Democracy

In 1987, as Americans celebrated the bicentennial of the ratification of the U.S. Constitution, Supreme Court Justice Thurgood Marshall sounded a discordant note. In a speech before the San Francisco Patent and Trademark Law Association, which was later published as an article in the *Vanderbilt Law Review*, Justice Marshall said that the Constitution as originally written was profoundly racist.[1] Marshall, who spent his career as a lawyer at the NAACP, argued thirty-two cases before the Supreme Court and won twenty-nine of them, including *Brown v. Board of Education*.[2] He had served as a federal court of appeals judge and as solicitor general of the United States, the federal government's top lawyer in the Supreme Court, before President Lyndon Johnson in 1967 nominated him to be the first Black person to serve on the Supreme Court. Marshall, in his powerful speech, said that "the government [that the framers] devised was defective from the start."[3]

He noted that "we need look no further than the first three words of the document's Preamble: 'We the People,'" to see that it excluded enslaved people.[4] He stated the plain reality: the Constitution protected the institution of slavery because Southern states would not otherwise have ratified it. Justice Marshall wrote: "No doubt it will be said, when the unpleasant truth of the history of slavery in America is mentioned during this Bicentennial year, that the Constitution was a product of its times, and embodied a compromise which, under other circumstances, would not have been made. But the effects of the Framers' compromise have remained for generations. They arose from the contradiction between guaranteeing liberty and justice to all, and denying both to Negroes."[5]

Justice Thurgood Marshall was exactly right. The unequal treatment of citizens of African descent has been a devastating flaw in the United States since its inception. The delegates at the Constitutional Convention were sharply divided over the issue of slavery, and their choice to protect the institution of slavery has plagued the country ever since and had a tragic impact on those of African descent throughout American history.

Northerners at the Constitutional Convention knew that those from the South never would agree to a constitution that limited slavery. They deliberately chose to concede to the Southerners on this issue in order to obtain a constitution. The bargain has had calamitous consequences ever since, as our society continues to be profoundly and increasingly separate and unequal. Can a democracy survive if these inequalities continue unabated and even grow?

Early American History

The enslavement of those of African descent preceded British North America. It is estimated that from 1514 to 1866, more than 12.5 million individuals in Africa were kidnapped and brought forcibly to Europe and the Americas.[6] Human beings were captured like animals and taken from their homes by force. They were put on ships in conditions that were horrible beyond imagination. The men were chained with leg irons in overcrowded spaces. Many died en route.

An estimated 645,000 enslaved people were brought to North America. The first known enslaved individuals were brought to St. Augustine, Florida, in 1565 by the Spanish admiral Pedro Menéndez de Avilés.[7] 1619 is the date most frequently mentioned as the beginning of slavery in England's mainland American colonies, marking the arrival of the first recorded Africans on these shores.[8] That year the privateer *White Lion* brought twenty enslaved Africans who had been seized from the Portuguese slave ship *Sao Jao Bautista* ashore in the English colony of Jamestown, Virginia.

By the time of the Constitutional Convention, slavery had been deeply entrenched in colonial America. It officially began in Virginia with a law adopted in 1661. African slave labor was central to the operation of plantations in Virginia and other Southern states, which relied on enslaved people for their crops, such as tobacco, indigo, and rice. In Virginia, which had the most enslaved individuals, almost 40 percent of its population were enslaved people. South Carolina had the largest percentage, 43 percent, of its population enslaved. Among all the states, about 18 percent of the population—700,000 out of 3.8 million people—were enslaved.[9]

Although slavery existed to a limited extent in most Northern states, by the end of the Revolutionary War, this part of the country developed strong opposition to slavery and was beginning to adopt abolition laws. By the time of the Constitutional Convention in 1787, an enormous gulf had opened between the Northern and the Southern states over slavery.

At the convention, many Northern delegates—such as John Jay, Oliver Ellsworth, and Gouverneur Morris—expressed strong opposition to slavery. But Southern delegates, such as Charles Pinckney and John Rutledge, who owned slaves, were clear that they would not support a constitution that abolished it. Rutledge, whose plantations in South Carolina had made him rich and who later would be appointed to the Supreme Court (though he never served), said the people of South Carolina "would never be such fools as to give up so important an interest."[10] Twenty-five of the fifty-five delegates to the Constitutional Convention were slave owners, including George Washington, who presided, and James Madison, who played a crucial role and took the official notes of the proceedings. They shaped the convention discussions and were not about to champion restricting slavery or to allow a constitution that did so.

Why, if some of the framers were so strongly against slavery, did they not fight to abolish it? Today, when we rightly understand that slavery is abhorrent and violates the most elemental aspects of humanity, it is hard to understand why they didn't try harder to end this terrible practice. In fact, there is no indication that they agonized over the issue at the convention or seriously debated whether the Constitution would abolish slavery.

This silence likely reflected the framers' general understanding, as Justice Thurgood Marshall observed, that the Southern states, which saw slavery as essential to their agricultural economies, would not agree to a constitution that ended slavery. The delegates who owned slaves did not see the immorality of slavery and would not be persuaded of it. Implicit in their ownership of slaves as property to be bought and sold was their view that those of African descent were less than human beings. No argument from Northern non-slave owners was going to change that view. This was true at the Constitutional Convention, and it would have been so at the state ratifying conventions that had to approve the document. Even those who opposed slavery likely did not see all people as created equal. Racism was endemic then in perceptions of those of African descent, and it has been part of this country ever since.

Those framers who opposed slavery at the convention likely rationalized accepting the document that protected it by thinking that slavery was not likely to have an economic future and would slowly disappear. Some said so explicitly during the deliberations.[11] This assumption, of course, proved tragically wrong: slavery continued until the Thirteenth Amendment abolished it in 1865. For the first seventy-eight years of American history—*almost a third of this country's entire existence*—slavery existed and was expressly protected by law, including the U.S. Constitution.

Constitutional Choices

If the framers did not contemplate that the new constitution would eliminate slavery, they still had to make choices about how the new governing document would treat slavery as it was. A crucial question was how to count enslaved people in determining a state's representation in the House of Representatives and in apportioning taxes among the states. Under the Articles of Confederation, taxes were apportioned not according to population but based on land values. But the states consistently undervalued their land in order to reduce their tax burden.

In 1783 the Continental Congress considered amending the Articles of Confederation to apportion taxes by population. The issue arose as to how enslaved individuals should count in this calculation. Northerners wanted enslaved slaved people to count almost the same as free individuals and proposed a ratio of four to three. Southern states did not want slaves to be calculated in the taxes they owed and proposed a ratio of four to one. James Madison proposed a compromise: a ratio of five to three. Only two states objected, New Hampshire and Rhode Island. But changing the Articles of Confederation required unanimous agreement, so the proposal was defeated.

At the Constitutional Convention, this compromise, which had previously been rejected, was revived. Northern states did not want enslaved individuals to be counted in allocating seats in the House of Representatives. Enslaved people, they reasoned, did not get to vote and were obviously not a part of the political process. Also, counting those who were enslaved would benefit the Southern states in the House and correspondingly decrease the power of Northern states. As would be expected, Southern states vehemently disagreed and wanted their enslaved population to count fully in allocating House seats.

The debate was contentious. A liberal northern delegate, James Wilson of Pennsylvania, revived Madison's idea and proposed the Three-Fifths Compromise: each enslaved person would count as three-fifths of a person in allocating seats in the House of Representatives and in determining taxation. Hence the Constitution says: "Representatives and direct Taxes shall be apportioned among the several States which may be included within this Union, according to their respective Numbers, which shall be determined by adding to the whole Number of free Persons, including those bound to Service for a Term of Years, and excluding Indians not taxed, *three fifths of all other Persons.*"

The word *slave* is not mentioned in this provision. Indeed, it appears nowhere in the Constitution. One wonders if this omission reflects shame about slavery even in a document that strongly protected it. But slavery is entirely what this clause is about. Southern states were willing to pay the higher taxes that came from including slaves in that apportionment in exchange for having greater political representation in the House of Representatives. But the clause also provided that slaves would count less than others in calculating the taxes that these states had to pay. Still, the Three-Fifths Clause gave Southern states more influence in choosing the president because each state receives the number of electors equal to the sum of its senators and representatives. Counting the enslaved population not only augmented the number of representatives that a state sent to the House but also increased its allocated electors in the Electoral College.

The political implications were huge. Four of the first five presidents were slave owners from Virginia. Indeed, in twelve of the first sixteen presidential elections, a Southern slave owner won.

The Three-Fifths Clause gave Southern states disproportionate influence in the House of Representatives, which mattered greatly in the efforts to restrict slavery by legislation. In 1793 Southern slave states held forty-seven of the 105 seats, but they would have had only thirty-three seats had they been assigned based solely on free populations. In 1812, slave states had seventy-six seats out of 143 instead of the fifty-nine they would otherwise have had.[12]

The Three-Fifths Clause was a key reason that the abolitionist William Lloyd Garrison called the Constitution a "covenant with death and an agreement with hell." It was a compromise essential to approval of the Constitution, but its bargain plagued the country until after the Civil War, when slavery was finally eliminated and the Three-Fifths Clause became irrelevant.

At the Constitutional Convention, a second major issue arose about slavery: what to do about the slave trade. Ten of the thirteen states already had abolished importing additional slaves into the United States. To be clear, that did not mean that they abolished slavery. States with slavery already had substantial enslaved populations and were just limiting the importation of additional slaves. But three states still allowed this importation: Georgia, North Carolina, and South Carolina. Their delegates were emphatic that if the new constitution prohibited the importation of additional slaves, they would leave the convention.[13] They wanted a provision in limiting Congress's power to restrict importing slaves and another to forbid Congress from taxing exports because their economies benefited greatly from agricultural exports.

The debates over these issues were fierce. Several delegates argued strongly that Congress should have the power to ban the importation of slaves. Luther Martin of Maryland said that forbidding Congress to ban the importation of slaves was "inconsistent with the principles of the revolution and dishonorable to the American character."[14] Gouverneur Morris of Pennsylvania said that slavery was a "nefarious institution" and a "curse of heaven on the states where it prevailed."[15] George Mason of Virginia spoke at length about the horrors of slavery and criticized slave owners, calling them "petty tyrants," while slave traders, he said, "from a lust of gain embarked on this nefarious traffic."[16] Delegates from Northern states also objected to placing limits on Congress taxing exports and the loss of revenue to the federal government that this would entail.

But the Southern delegates strongly defended slavery and opposed a ban on importing slaves. Charles Pinckney, a slave owner from South Carolina, said: "If slavery be wrong, it is justified by the example of the world. . . . In all ages one half of mankind have been slaves."[17] Oliver Ellsworth of Connecticut, who was to become the second chief justice of the United States, said that banning the slave trade would "be unjust towards South Carolina and Georgia."[18]

Ultimately, the delegates reached a compromise: Congress could not ban the importation of slaves for twenty years. Article I, Section 9 of the Constitution declares: "The Migration or Importation of such Persons as any of the States now existing shall think proper to admit, shall not be prohibited by the Congress prior to the Year one thousand eight hundred and eight, but a Tax or duty may be imposed on such Importation, not exceeding ten dollars for each Person." Again, the word *slave* is not used, but this provision is undoubtedly about slavery. Article V of the Constitution, which provides for amending the document, makes this provision one of only two that cannot be changed by amendment.[19]

Why did the Northern delegates who regarded slavery as immoral and abhorrent agree to this compromise? Wanting a new constitution that would be passed by the convention and ratified by the states, they saw no alternative. Without this compromise, several southern states would most likely have abandoned the entire project of drafting a new constitution. We certainly can debate whether the Northern delegates made a bad choice and whether it would have been better to have no Constitution than one that protected the importing of enslaved individuals. Simply put, the Northern delegates' desire for a new constitution was more important to them than their desire to protect enslaved persons of African descent.

They rationalized their choice by asserting that slavery would ultimately disappear on its own. "As population increases," said Oliver Ellsworth, "poor laborers will be so plenty as to render slaves useless. Slavery in time will not be a speck in our Country."[20]

That hope was unfounded. Between 1788 and 1808, the number of African slaves imported into the United States exceeded 200,000, which was only about 50,000 fewer than the total number imported in the preceding 170 years. In 1800 Congress passed a law banning the importation of slaves into the United States. It was to go into effect in 1808, the earliest that the Constitution allows.

The Three-Fifths Clause and the ban on slave importation until 1808 reflected compromises among the delegates to the Constitutional Convention. But a third provision flat-out protected the rights of slave owners: the Fugitive Slave Clause, which required that escaped enslaved individuals be returned to their owners.

In 1772, fifteen years before the Constitutional Convention, a judge in England, Lord Mansfield, had ruled that an enslaved person from Massachusetts who reached England was a free person who could not be legally returned to his American owners.[21] Although the decision had no binding effect in the United States, it was well known to slave owners. As the historian Steven Lubet observes, "Nonetheless, the *Somerset* precedent was frightening to southern slaveholders. It had been widely published in America, and often over-interpreted as having completely abolished slavery under British law. News of the ruling had spread by word of mouth among slaves, which of course was troubling to their masters."[22]

On July 13, 1787, while the Constitutional Convention was underway, the Confederation Congress, acting under the authority of the Articles of Confederation, adopted one of its most important laws, the Northwest Ordinance, with the precedent of the *Somerset* case very much in mind. This statute chartered a government for the territory north of Ohio, and it provided a method for admitting new states to the Union from this area. Although the Northwest Ordinance prohibited slavery in the new territory, it required that any escaped slave be returned to its owner. Article VI of the Northwest Ordinance prevented those in this territory from giving refuge to an escaped slave, and it authorized a slaveholder to capture a runaway who had made it safely to that territory.

Almost simultaneously, the Constitutional Convention put a similar provision into the U.S. Constitution. It engendered much less debate than the Three-Fifths Clause or Congress's ability to ban the importation of slaves. Pierce Butler and Charles Pinckney of South Carolina—both slave owners—introduced the Fugitive Slave Clause during the deliberations. James Wilson of Pennsylvania opposed it because it "would oblige the Executive of the State to [return fugitive slaves] at the public expence."[23]

Butler and Pinckney then withdrew their proposal, but reintroduced it the following day, and it was adopted without dispute. Article IV, Section 3 of the Constitution states: "No person held to Service or Labour in one State, under the Laws thereof, escaping into another, shall, in Consequence of any Law or Regulation therein, be discharged from such Service or Labour, but shall be delivered up on Claim of the Party to whom such Service or Labour may be due." In other words, an enslaved person who escaped to a free state had to be returned to his or her owner. The Fugitive Slave Clause was a blatant and crucial protection of the rights of slave owners and a further denial of freedom to enslaved individuals.

Again, the provision does not mention "slavery," but there was no question what it was about. General Cotesworth Pinckney, a slave-owning delegate at the convention, remarked, "We have obtained a right to recover our slaves in whatever part of America they may take refuge, which is a right we had not before."[24]

After the ratification of the Constitution, in 1793 and 1850, Congress adopted laws that allowed escaped enslaved individuals to be pursued, captured, and returned. Under these laws, thousands of enslaved people were kidnapped and taken back to their owners. The judiciary consistently enforced the institution of slavery by ruling in favor of slave owners and against enslaved individuals.[25]

In 1793 the second Congress passed the Fugitive Slave Act, implementing the Fugitive Slave Clause: it required that judges return escaped slaves. The Supreme Court also implemented the Fugitive

Slave Clause aggressively and prevented Northern states from protecting escaped slaves. In Pennsylvania, a law had prevented the use of force or violence to remove any person from the state to return that individual to slavery. The law did not forbid the return of enslaved individuals—it just prohibited the use of force or violence, a crucial interest that states always can pursue. Nonetheless, in *Prigg v. Pennsylvania*, the Supreme Court declared the Pennsylvania law unconstitutional,[26] relying on the Fugitive Slave Act and the Fugitive Slave Clause.

Justice Joseph Story, writing for the Court, noted that "few questions which have ever come before this court involve more delicate and important considerations; and few upon which the public at large may be presumed to feel a more profound and pervading interest."[27] Story was the youngest person ever to sit on the Supreme Court, being nominated in 1811 at age thirty-two. He is regarded as one of the most important justices in history, partly because he wrote a treatise on constitutional law, *Commentaries on the Constitution of the United States*, that is still cited to this day. He is widely venerated and celebrated, and a building is named after him at Harvard Law School. But he was a product of his times and wrote one of the most important Supreme Court decisions—*Prigg v. Pennsylvania*—protecting the rights of slave owners.

His opinion held that the Constitution prohibited states from interfering with the return of fugitive slaves. He wrote that the "object of [the Fugitive Slave Clause] was to secure to the citizens of the slaveholding states the complete right and title of ownership in their slaves, as property, in every state in the Union into which they might escape from the state where they were held in servitude."[28] Indeed, the Court said that the clause "was so vital . . . that it cannot be doubted, that it constituted a fundamental article, without the adoption of which the Union could not have been formed."[29] Thus, the Court concluded that "we have not the slightest hesitation in holding, that under and in virtue of the constitution, the owner of a slave is clothed with entire authority, in every state in the Union, to seize and recapture his slave."[30] Likewise, the Court held that states could punish those who harbored fugitive slaves.[31]

These three provisions of the Constitution—the Three-Fifths Clause, the limit on the importation of slaves for twenty years, and the Fugitive Slave Clause—all made clear that the document protected slavery. Not a word in the Constitution suggested otherwise. Northerners who opposed slavery made a deal with the devil: they got a constitution and a single nation, but at the expense of the human beings who were and would be enslaved. As the historian Donald Robinson explains, "There is no evidence that any framer thought that the Constitution contained power to abolish slavery. . . . The framers, as of 1787, agreed unanimously to place the institution of slavery, as it existed within the South, not 'in the course of ultimate extinction,' as Lincoln argued, but beyond national regulation."[32]

It was not surprising, then, that seventy years after the Constitution was adopted, in *Dred Scott v. Sanford*, the Supreme Court found attempts by Congress to limit slavery to be an unconstitutional taking of property.[33] *Dred Scott*, decided in 1857, is one of the most infamous decisions in American history. Sadly it seemed preordained by the choices that the framers made at the Constitutional Convention seventy years earlier.

In 1819 a major national controversy erupted over the admission of Missouri to the Union. Would Missouri, and other states coming from the Louisiana Purchase, be a free state or a slave state? To resolve the issue, Congress reached an agreement known as the Missouri Compromise: it admitted Missouri as a slave state but prohibited slavery north of latitude 36' 30". Territories below this line could decide whether to allow slavery and could make that choice when admitted as states.

In *Dred Scott v. Sandford*, the Supreme Court declared the Missouri Compromise unconstitutional and broadly held that slaves were property, not citizens. Dred Scott, a slave in Missouri owned by John Emerson, was taken into Illinois, a free state. After Emerson died, his estate was administered by John Sandford, a resident of New York.[34] Scott sued Sandford in federal court, basing jurisdiction on diversity of citizenship, and claimed that his residence in Illinois made him a free person.

The Supreme Court ruled against Scott in a decision that fills over two hundred pages in *United States Reports*. Chief Justice Roger B. Taney, who himself had once owned slaves, began by stating: "The question is simply this: Can a negro, whose ancestors were imported into this country, and sold as slaves, become a member of the political community formed and brought into existence by the Constitution of the United States, and as such become entitled to all the rights, and privileges, and immunities, guarantied by that instrument to the citizen?"[35]

The Court held that enslaved individuals were not citizens and thus could not invoke federal court diversity of citizenship jurisdiction. At the time when the Constitution was ratified, the Court explained, enslaved people were considered "as a subordinate and inferior class of beings, who had been subjugated by the dominant race, and, whether emancipated or not, yet remained subject to their authority, and had no rights or privileges but such as those who held the power and the Government might choose to grant them."[36] The Court reviewed the laws that existed in 1787 and concluded that a "perpetual and impassable barrier was intended to be erected between the white race and the one which they had reduced to slavery."[37] Slaves were not citizens, the Court said, and so could not sue as citizens in the federal courts.

Even though the Supreme Court concluded that it lacked jurisdiction to hear Scott's suit, it went further and declared the Missouri Compromise unconstitutional. One of the most basic principles of law—then and now—is that a court without jurisdiction must dismiss a case without deciding its merits. Among its other tragic mistakes, the Court ignored this in its desire to protect the rights of slave owners. It ruled that Congress could not grant citizenship to enslaved people or their descendants, because it would be a taking of property from slave owners without due process or just compensation: "The right of property in a slave is distinctly and expressly affirmed in the Constitution."[38]

As a result, the Court said that the Missouri Compromise, in limiting slavery in some of the territories acquired by the United States, was unconstitutional. Scott was not made free by being taken into Illinois. Enslaved individuals were the property of their owners, and it was unconstitutional for Congress to change this. The Court was aggressively enforcing the terrible choices made at the Constitutional Convention almost three-quarters of a century earlier.

Undoubtedly the Supreme Court thought that in *Dred Scott v. Sandford*, it was resolving the controversy over slavery, but the decision had exactly the opposite effect. It became the focal point in the debate over slavery and, by striking down the Missouri Compromise, helped to precipitate the Civil War.[39]

Implications of These Choices

The bargains that the framers struck to institutionalize slavery in the Constitution had consequences that have lasted to this day. After the Constitution was adopted, slavery continued to exist for over three-quarters of a century. Its existence sent a powerful message that those of African descent were less than human, in that they could be held in captivity and bought and sold as chattel. As Thurgood Marshall observed, racism was written into the Constitution from the outset. The enormous racial inequalities, in every aspect of life and by every measure, that have existed throughout American history and that continue largely unabated, must be seen as a direct result of the choices made in 1787.

Not surprisingly, a constitution that protected slavery did not include any mention of equal protection. The Preamble, which so eloquently states the core values of the Constitution—democratic government, effective governance, liberty, justice—notably does not include equality as one of those values.[40] Not until 1868, eighty-one years after the Constitution was drafted, was an Equal Protection Clause added to the Constitution with the adoption of the Fourteenth Amendment. It says no state can deny any person equal protection of the law. To this day, the Constitution contains no provision that says that the federal government cannot deny equal protection, though the Supreme Court, on its own, has applied the guarantee of equal protection to the federal government.[41] But it remains an embarrassment that nowhere does the Constitution even hint that the federal government must require equal protection under the law.

Slavery and the race discrimination that followed it made a tremendous lasting impact on American history. Even after the adoption of the Equal Protection Clause, little was done to enforce it for almost a century. Quite the contrary: laws in every Southern state and in many other parts of the country required separation of the races, under the doctrine of "separate but equal"—even though separate facilities were never equal. In 1896, in *Plessy v. Ferguson*, the Court approved those laws.[42] Not for fifty-eight years, until *Brown v. Board of Education*, did the Court begin declaring that laws that imposed apartheid in every aspect of life were unconstitutional.

The United States experiences the effects of this history to this day. In 2022, according to the Economic Policy Institute, a typical Black worker earned 13 percent less than a typical white worker of the same age and gender, the same amount of education, and in the same region.[43]

And the racial wealth gap is even larger than the wage gap. A Brookings Institution study of wealth in the United States found "staggering racial disparities."[44] In 2016 the net worth of a typical white family, at $171,000, was nearly ten times greater than that of a Black family, at $17,150. The difference is growing, not shrinking: the ratio of white to Black family wealth is higher today than in 2000.[45] As a Harvard study found, "The wealth gap between Black and white Americans has been persistent and extreme. It represents the accumulated effects of four centuries of institutional and systemic racism and bears major responsibility for disparities in income, health, education, and opportunity that continue to this day."[46]

A study by the Federal Reserve Bank found that in the United States, "the average Black and Hispanic or Latino households earn about half as much as the average white household and own only about 15 to 20 percent as much net wealth. . . . [T]his wealth gap has widened notably over the past few decades."[47] Put another way, white households hold 86.8 percent of the country's overall wealth, buy they account for only 68.1 percent of the number of households; by comparison, Black households hold only 2.9 percent of the wealth, though they compose 15.6 percent of the country's households.[48]

Wealth inequality in the United States is enormous. It is estimated that the top 1 percent of households and nonprofit organizations hold 31.2 percent of all the country's net worth.[49] This gap is larger than that of virtually all other developed countries. And a Stanford University study found much less economic mobility in the United States than in other wealthy countries, including Australia, Canada, France, Germany, and Japan.[50]

It is hard to know what this will mean for American democracy over the long term. A United Nations report found that in democratic societies, wealth inequality generally erodes trust and paves the way for authoritarian and nativist regimes to take root.[51] The relationship between the tremendous U.S. wealth gap and the authoritarian and nativist appeals made by Republicans cannot be ignored. Nor, in thinking about the future of the country, can we ignore the vast racial disparities, which spring from the tragic choices made in drafting the Constitution.

7

The 2010s and Beyond
The Internet and Social Media
Endanger Democracy

Two days before a close presidential election, a video of one candidate taking a large bribe to do something awful while in office appears on social media. It goes viral on the internet. Viewers have no doubt as to what the candidate did; they can see it with their own eyes and hear it with their own ears. Mainstream media quickly report it, and there are immediate calls for the candidate to withdraw from the race. But it turns out that the video was a deepfake, a computer-generated clip that looks and sounds real but is not. And it was inserted into social media by Russia to try and throw the election in favor of its preferred candidate.

No one should doubt that this could happen. The technology exists, as does the motivation to use it, whether by Russia or by some other actor. As many suspect, Russia helped to make Donald Trump president of the United States in 2016. Indisputably, the Russian government deliberately used the internet and social media to help Trump defeat Hillary Clinton. It utilized every major social media platform—Facebook, Twitter, YouTube, Tumblr, Instagram, and PayPal—to try to influence the election outcome. Russian information operatives working for the Internet Research Agency (IRA) targeted conservatives with posts on immigration, race, and gun rights. The Russians also sought to undermine participation by Black voters—a core part of the Democratic constituency—by extensively spreading misinformation about the electoral process in media sites that were especially used by African Americans. Given how very close the election was, we cannot know if Russia ultimately decided the presidential election.

Russian involvement in the 2016 election is not the idle speculation of conspiracy theorists. Special Counsel Robert Mueller's later report documented the Russian effort,[1] as did the report of a Senate committee with a Republican majority.[2] The Senate report found that the IRA sought to harm Clinton and support Trump "at the direction of the Kremlin."[3] It concluded that the IRA focused on socially divisive issues like race in order to pit Americans against one another.[4] Senate Intelligence Committee chairman Richard Burr, a Republican from North Carolina, said in a written statement, "By flooding social media with false reports, conspiracy theories, and trolls, and by exploiting existing divisions, Russia is trying to breed distrust of our democratic institutions and our fellow Americans."[5]

Since 2016, the technology for false speech, such as deepfakes, has grown exponentially, as have tensions with Russia and polarization within the United States. What happened that year will likely be minor compared to future efforts. Nor will the problem of false speech, including deepfakes, be limited to presidential elections.

The internet and social media are relatively new communication tools that powerfully advance democracy by allowing for more speech and more access to information, but they also undermine democracy in profound ways. In the 2020 presidential election, the internet and social media were flooded with the false information that Donald Trump had won the presidential election and was cheated out of the presidency, despite the absence of any evidence to support this assertion.

The claim had a pernicious effect. It led to the insurrection at the Capitol on January 6, 2021. More than two years after the 2020 presidential election, about 70 percent of Republicans still say they believe that the election was stolen from Trump.[6] In fact, Trump and his agents had fomented this belief online: they mobilized social media to propagate baseless election fraud allegations that persist to this day.[7] Astoundingly, about half of 2022 Republican candidates for federal office spread the lie that Trump was cheated out of the presidency.[8]

What does it mean for the legitimacy of government when a significant portion of the population believes, without foundation, that an election was stolen from their candidate?

Even Trump's former attorney general, William Barr, called claims of a stolen election "bullshit."[9] Supporters of Trump brought dozens of lawsuits on his behalf, alleging that election improprieties had cost him the election. But *every* judge who heard one of those cases—state and federal, Democratic- and Republican-appointed—rejected the existence of election fraud.[10] Still the internet and social media continue to spread the lies, Republican candidates still espouse them, and a great many Americans still believe them. The internet, and social media in particular, make it easier for disinformation and falsehoods to be broadly disseminated and to gain acceptance. It is hard to imagine the Trump election lie taking hold without these tools.

Up to now I have focused on the flaws in the Constitution that have contributed to today's crisis in American democracy. But one of the Constitution's greatest virtues—the First Amendment and its protection of freedom of speech—is now contributing too, and the dangers only will grow. An examination of the current threat to democracy must consider the role of these media and their impacts on our political process, both positive and negative. To be sure, the internet and social media advance democracy. And any solution that attempts to regulate expression potentially harms speech more than it helps. Regulating speech over the internet, even false speech, raises serious First Amendment issues. Yet it would be a mistake to ignore the role of technology in the forces that threaten democracy.

How the Internet and Social Media Have Changed Speech

The internet and social media are the most important developments concerning expression since the creation of the printing press. That statement is not hyperbole. Throughout history, a central problem with speech was the scarcity of opportunities for its expression. Even when newspapers were far more prevalent than they are now, they were limited in number, and a person had to be fairly rich to own one. And when broadcasting developed, first radio and then television, the limited number of frequencies on the spectrum created scarcity. A half-century ago the Supreme Court held unanimously that because of the inherent scarcity of spectrum space, the federal government could regulate the broadcast media and impose a fairness doctrine.[11] But over time, the number of newspapers being published has precipitously decreased.[12] Ironically, the internet and social media—which so increase the availability of speech—have contributed to this decline.[13] As people can get information for free, it is harder for newspapers to sell subscriptions, and their advertising revenue then falls. Few newspapers have found a way to successfully monetize their content over the internet.

With the internet and social media, scarcity is no longer an issue. Anyone can speak and potentially reach a mass audience instantly. And everyone has access to virtually unlimited information. A half-century ago, if free speech advocates had engaged in science fiction and tried to devise media to maximize expression, the Web and Twitter and Facebook and YouTube would have been beyond their imagination.

A quarter-century ago, before the advent of social media, UCLA law professor Eugene Volokh wrote a prescient article, "Cheap Speech and What It Will Do." He predicted that online communication would promote democracy by making publishing and receiving a vast amount and variety of information easily available to a wide range of individuals.[14] He made this prediction before Facebook or Snapchat or Twitter existed. What he described has come to fruition in an exponential way: in June 2017, Justice Anthony Kennedy noted: "Seven in ten American adults use at least one Internet social networking service. . . . According to sources cited to the Court in this case, Facebook has 1.79 billion active users. This is about three times the population of North America."[15] In the years since 2017, these numbers have surely grown dramatically.

Three characteristics of the internet and social media are particularly important for free speech, though they all pose a threat to expression as well. First, the internet has democratized any individual's ability to reach a mass audience. It used to be that to reach a large audience, a person had to be rich enough to own a newspaper or to get a broadcast license. Now anyone with a smartphone—or even access to a library with a modem—can reach a huge audience instantaneously. No longer are people dependent on a relatively small number of news sources.

Moreover, the internet and social media empower individuals who would otherwise be voiceless to express their opinions, and they give them a place to do so.[16] The internet provides a platform for those who cannot physically gather and organize.[17] Previously silenced or marginalized individuals now have access to a method to disseminate their political ideas.[18]

But empowerment and access also allow an almost infinite number of sources to quickly spread false information. Confidential information can also be quickly disseminated[19] by *doxing*, or publishing private information about a person on the internet, often with malicious intent to harm them.[20] The internet and social media can be used to harass.[21] A study by the Pew Research Center found that "40 percent of adult Internet users have experienced harassment online, with young women enduring particularly severe forms of it."[22]

In the past, newspapers generally acted as an important filter, excluding false and other types of harmful information. They have an editorial process, and if not journalistic ethics, then at least they have a fear of liability. Sometimes newspapers' filters failed, and they did harm. But at least there were filters. But none exist for the internet and social media. Anyone can post anything for the world to see.

Second, the internet has dramatically increased the dissemination and permanence of information, or to phrase it differently, our ability to access information. It provides us all with truly unprecedented access to information, surely a benefit. Lawyers and law students can do all their research online, reading cases and treatises that previously would have required a trip to the law library. We can visit the great museums of the world online anywhere, at any time. We have access to virtually unlimited information from nearly infinite sources.

But easy access and permanence have a downside. Take defamation as an example. Imagine that before the internet, a local newspaper published false information about a person that harmed their reputation. Readers of that issue could learn the information and circulate it by word of mouth, causing great harm to the person's reputation. But that printed issue of the newspaper would all but disappear, except on microfilm or microfiche.

Now, though, the defamatory newspaper story, in electronic form, can be quickly spread across the internet, be accessed from anywhere, and will likely remain there forever. It is enormously difficult, if not impossible, to erase something from the internet. Back when newspapers were local, harms to a person's reputation, even if great, were likely limited to that geographic area. Now even local newspapers are published on the internet for all the world to see, and media sources quickly copy from one another, allowing a local story to go viral and international quickly.

To pick an easy example: in September 2023, the *Jewish Journal*—a relatively limited-circulation newspaper—published an inflammatory article about my law school. It reported that a student group, Law Students for Justice in Palestine, had called for barring speakers who supported Israel. The article was misleadingly headlined "Berkeley Creates Jewish Free Zones." The next day Barbra Streisand tweeted the story to 800,000 people, and it quickly attracted national and international media attention. The furor lasted for weeks, and the story even was covered in a front-page story in *The New York Times*. A single story online, misleading in its headline and content, can spread with astounding speed. Members of Congress, the state legislature, and Jewish organizations around the world were soon condemning me and my law school, with no sense of what had actually happened.

Finally, the internet does not respect national boundaries. Again, this can have great benefits. Totalitarian governments cannot easily cut off information to their citizens. When the 2011 revolution began in Egypt, the government tried to halt internet access, but people with satellite phones could maintain it and disseminate what they learned.[23] The Supreme Court has estimated that 40 percent of pornography on the internet comes from foreign countries, making any attempt to control it within a country impossible.[24] And as we saw in the 2016 presidential election, foreign countries and actors now have a vehicle to try to influence the outcome of U.S. elections.[25]

Simply put, the First Amendment generally assumes that more speech is better. But that is not always so: if the speech is child pornography or false advertising, more is not better. But overall, the premise of the First Amendment has long been that we should try to increase opportunities for expression. In that respect, the internet and social media have brought us, in many ways, a golden age of free speech.

The Threat to Democracy

The same virtues of the internet and social media for advancing democracy also make it a serious threat. We are still in the relative infancy of these media: Facebook began in 2006 and Instagram in 2010. So the dangers only will grow, especially with the development of artificial intelligence to generate and direct messages. The ability to create totally believable deepfakes is a frightening, relatively new development.

False speech. False information can cause great harm, and social media facilitates its rapid dissemination.[26] A 2018 MIT study found that "false news spreads faster and to more people than true stories, reaching more people than any other type of information."[27] The unprecedented speed and scale of digital communication have simplified the dissemination of false information as never before, frequently outrunning efforts to debunk it.[28]

Social media algorithms can prioritize content that is more likely to generate user engagement regardless of its veracity.[29] Facebook, and other media, are sending people specific content based on its assessment of their interests, but with little regard for the truth or falsehood of the information. In the political realm, widely disseminated falsehoods can change the outcome of elections, especially if they are dropped soon before election day, when little time remains to refute them. The spread of disinformation and misinformation can prevent voters from making well-informed decisions regarding candidates.[30] A false accusation that is quickly and widely circulated can make the difference between who wins and who loses. False speech has enormous implications for politics, public health, elections, and other domains where the accuracy of information is vital.

Additionally and quite importantly, false information instills doubt in reliable sources and credible news.[31] The First Amendment is predicated on the romantic notion—articulated by John Stuart Mill and Oliver Wendell Holmes—that a marketplace of ideas exists and that allowing all speech will lead to the triumph of truth over falsehoods. But many studies show that people do not often give up their false beliefs when confronted with true information.[32] False information has permanent effects. When 70 percent of Republican voters believe that Trump was cheated out of the presidency in 2020, it's hard to have faith that in the world of the internet and social media, truth will triumph over falsity.

This problem will grow as technology becomes more sophisticated. It is all too easy to imagine that in the days before an election, unscrupulous persons could circulate a deepfake of an opposing candidate saying something repulsive. What we see and hear for ourselves seems true, even if it is created by bots and artificial intelligence. A deepfake showing a politician taking a bribe will create lingering doubts for many, and some will continue to believe it even after it has been shown to be fictitious.

A solution to the problem of false speech over the internet and social media is elusive, especially because of the First Amendment. The law is, and likely always will be, inconsistent on whether the Constitution protects false speech. In some areas, the Court has found that false expression is protected, but in other instances, it has upheld the ability of the government to punish it. It's tempting to say that the government should just ban false speech. But sometimes the First Amendment protects—and should protect—false speech so that true speech is not unduly chilled. Also, who is going to be the arbiter of what is true and what is false, especially in the political realm?

The Supreme Court, rightly, has emphatically declared the importance of protecting false speech. The most important case in this regard—and one of the most important free speech decisions of all time—is the 1964 case *New York Times Co. v. Sullivan*.[33] L. B. Sullivan, an elected commissioner of Montgomery, Alabama, successfully sued *The New York Times* and four African American clergy members for defamation for an advertisement that had been published in the newspaper on March 29, 1960. The ad criticized police in Montgomery for mistreating civil rights demonstrators.

The ad indisputably contained some minor false statements. It said the demonstrators sang "My Country 'Tis of Thee," when they actually sang the national anthem; it said that Dr. Martin Luther King, Jr., had been arrested seven times, but in reality it was only four; it said

that nine students were expelled for the demonstration, but their sus-
pension was for a different protest at lunch counters; and it mistakenly
said that the dining hall had been padlocked. Pursuant to a judge's
instructions that the statements were libelous, the jury awarded a
$500,000 verdict to Sullivan.

The Supreme Court held that allowing liability for *The New York
Times* violated the First Amendment. Justice William Brennan, writing for the Court, explained that criticism of government and government officials was at the core of speech protected by the First
Amendment.[34] The fact that some of the statements were false was
not sufficient grounds to deny the speech First Amendment protection.[35] A false "statement is inevitable in free debate and [it] must be
protected if the freedoms of expression are to have the 'breathing
space' that they 'need ... to survive.'"[36] These points are surely correct. If any false statement about a government official, no matter how
minor, were a basis for liability, speech about our government would
be chilled and lost.

Subsequently, in a very different context, the Court again recognized the importance of judicial protection of false speech in *United
States v. Alvarez*.[37] A federal law had made it a crime for a person to
falsely claim to have received military honors or decorations.[38] Xavier
Alvarez spoke at a public meeting and boasted of having won the Congressional Medal of Honor. He was prosecuted under the Stolen Valor
Act, but he won in the Supreme Court.[39]

Most important, Justice Kennedy expressly rejected the government's argument that false speech is inherently outside the scope of
the First Amendment.[40] He denied that there is "any general exception
to the First Amendment for false statements." He stressed that "some
false statements are inevitable if there is to be an open and vigorous
expression of views in public and private conversation, expression the
First Amendment seeks to guarantee."[41] He further explained that
"the Court has been careful to instruct that falsity alone may not suf-
fice to bring the speech outside the First Amendment."[42]

Why does false speech, given its harms, enjoy First Amendment
protection? In large part, it is because giving anyone, including (or
maybe especially) the government, the power to decide what is true
and what is false would be dangerous. Would Democrats want the

Trump administration, or Republicans the Biden administration, to have the power to scour the internet and social media and remove what it deems false? It is so much easier to put faith in the marketplace of ideas to refute falsehoods, even when we know that it is likely to fail in many instances. In doing so, though, we must be cognizant of the likelihood that false speech can inflict great harm on our democracy.

But the First Amendment does allow some restrictions on false speech. In some contexts the Supreme Court has refused to protect false speech and has allowed it to be prohibited and punished. For example, false and deceptive advertisements are clearly unprotected by the First Amendment.[43] The government can constitutionally prohibit making false statements under oath (perjury) or to law enforcement officials. But these areas where false speech can be punished are limited. The Court has generally treated commercial speech as being of lower value than political speech, which may make it easier to say that false advertising is entitled to no constitutional protection. As for perjury, prosecuting it requires proving that the person told a falsehood knowingly and intentionally.

The Court's inconsistent statements about false speech may reflect the competing interests inherent in First Amendment analysis. On the one hand, false speech can create harm, even great harm. While speech is protected especially because of its importance for the democratic process, false speech can distort that process. Speech is safeguarded, too, because of the belief that the marketplace of ideas is the best way for truth to emerge. But false speech can infect that marketplace, and we have no reason to believe that truth will triumph. False speech can hurt reputations, and it is fanciful to think that more speech can undo that harm. The Supreme Court has recognized this problem and declared that "false statements of fact are particularly valueless [because] they interfere with the truth-seeking function of the marketplace of ideas."[44]

At the same time, allowing the government to prohibit and punish false speech would be greatly concerning. *New York Times Co. v. Sullivan* was unquestionably correct when it said that false "statement is inevitable in free debate, and . . . it must be protected if the freedoms of expression are to have the 'breathing space' that they 'need . . . to survive.'"[45] Also, allowing the government to prohibit false speech places it in the role of being the arbiter of truth. As Justice Kennedy explained, "Our constitutional tradition stands against the idea that we need Oceania's Ministry of Truth."[46]

A great deal of the problem is that the quantity of speech over social media is so enormous that it makes content moderation difficult. A staggering quantity of information is posted daily, and social media companies already conduct an enormous amount of content moderation. For example, from October to December 2021, Facebook says it took action against terrorism content 7.7 million times, bullying and harassment 8.2 million times, and child sexual exploitation material 19.8 million times.[47] In the last quarter of 2020, Facebook took action on over 1.1 million pieces of content *per day*.[48] Designing a system to exclude false speech—even if it could be decided what is false and even if mandating it would not violate the First Amendment—seems an insurmountable task.

But no one should have illusions. Future elections will be decided because of false speech circulated over social media, especially in the days just before the voting. The threat to democracy is real and will grow.

Foreign interference with elections. Another way the internet and social media threaten democracy is that they enable foreign nations and entities to attempt to change the outcome of elections. As we have seen, Russia engaged in a concerted effort to use speech, including false speech, to influence the outcome of the 2016 presidential election.[49] It was suspected during the campaign season, and American intelligence agencies confirmed it soon after the election.[50] In February 2018, Special Counsel Mueller issued a thirty-seven-page indictment charging thirteen Russians and three companies with executing a scheme to subvert the 2016 election and to help elect Donald Trump president.[51] The indictment details "how the Russians repeatedly turned to Facebook and Instagram, often using stolen identities to pose as Americans, to sow discord among the electorate by creating Facebook groups, distributing divisive ads and posting inflammatory images."[52]

The fact that Russia attempted to influence an American election outcome understandably stirs outrage. Yet we must remember that the United States has long done exactly that, using speech—including false

speech—to try to influence the outcomes of elections in other countries. Dov Levin of Carnegie Mellon University has identified eighty-
one instances between 1946 and 2000 when the United States did so.[53]
As one report introduced the concept: "Bags of cash delivered to a
Rome hotel for favored Italian candidates. Scandalous stories leaked
to foreign newspapers to swing an election in Nicaragua. Millions of
pamphlets, posters and stickers printed to defeat an incumbent in Ser-
bia. The long arm of Vladimir Putin? No, just a small sample of the
United States' history of intervention in foreign elections."[54]

It's easy to condemn Russian meddling in the American election, but the underlying First Amendment issue is difficult to grapple
with. Obviously illegal conduct, such as hacking into the Democratic
National Committee headquarters and subsequently disseminating
unlawfully gained information,[55] is not constitutionally protected.
But what about foreign speech that is legal and that expresses an
opinion—or is even false?

The Supreme Court has repeatedly said that for First Amendment
purposes, the source of information does not matter. In *First National
Bank of Boston v. Bellotti*, in 1978, the Supreme Court declared unconstitutional a Massachusetts law that prohibited banks or businesses
from making contributions or expenditures in connection with ballot
initiatives and referenda.[56] Justice Lewis Powell, writing for the Court,
concluded that the value of speech is in informing the audience. Any
restriction on speech, regardless of its source, therefore undermines
the First Amendment. "The inherent worth of the speech in terms of
its capacity for informing the public," Justice Powell explained, "does
not depend upon the identity of its source, whether corporation, association, union, or individual."[57]

The Court relied heavily on this principle in *Citizens United v.
Federal Election Commission*, where it held that corporations have the
constitutional right to spend unlimited amounts of money directly
from their treasuries to elect or defeat candidates for political office.[58]
The value of the speech, the Court stressed, does not depend on the
speaker's identity, and corporate speech is protected not because of
the inherent rights of corporations but because all expression contributes to the marketplace of ideas. The Court wrote that "the First
Amendment bars regulatory distinctions based on a speaker's iden-

tity"[59] On other occasions, too, the Court has declared that "the identity of the speaker is not decisive in determining whether speech is protected."[60]

But then why should it matter whether the speaker is a foreign government or individual? Federal law prohibits foreign governments, individuals, and corporations from contributing money to candidates for federal office.[61] A federal court upheld this restriction on foreign speech, declaring, "It is fundamental to the definition of our national political community that foreign citizens do not have a constitutional right to participate in, and thus may be excluded from, activities of democratic self-government." As a result, "the United States has a compelling interest for purposes of First Amendment analysis in limiting the participation of foreign citizens in activities of American democratic self-government, and in thereby preventing foreign influence over the U.S. political process."[62] But can this statement be reconciled with the Supreme Court's declaration that the speaker's identity should not matter in First Amendment analysis? Although my answer is not comfortable, I do not see how to exclude foreign speakers in a way that is consistent with the Court's premise that the speaker's identity cannot be the basis for regulation. The First Amendment assumes that more speech is better, regardless of whether the speaker is foreign or domestic.

At the very least, it would be desirable to disclose speakers' identities so that people can know when speech comes from a foreign government or other foreign source. But this, too, raises First Amendment issues as the Supreme Court has held that people have a First Amendment right to speak anonymously. In *McIntyre v. Ohio Elections Commission*, the Court declared unconstitutional a law prohibiting the distribution of anonymous campaign literature.[63] Justice Stevens, writing for the Court, stated that "an author's decision to remain anonymous, like other decisions concerning omissions or additions to the content of a publication, is an aspect of the freedom of speech protected by the First Amendment."[64] Moreover, Justice Stevens said that anonymity provides a way for a speaker "who may be personally unpopular to ensure that readers will not prejudge her message simply because they do not like its proponent."[65]

All that said, society has a compelling interest in preventing speakers from masking their identity and deceiving voters. It is one thing to speak anonymously but another to present oneself falsely, especially to deceive and manipulate voters. Whether the speaker is domestic or foreign, false self-presentation should be regarded as a form of fraud that is unprotected by the First Amendment. At the very least, we should implement laws that prohibit it and pass stronger disclosure laws, especially for foreign speakers. The Supreme Court has consistently upheld the constitutionality of laws that require disclosure of the identity of those spending money in election campaigns. These requirements must be significantly strengthened.

But the transnational nature of the internet makes even constitutional controls elusive. As we saw in 2016, foreign governments can use the internet and social media to influence American elections without their officials or agents ever physically entering the United States. It is unclear how American law can be successfully applied to them. The internet allows them to engage in false speech (and all other kinds of expression) with relatively little fear of legal sanctions. And whether meaningful international sanctions could be imposed is at best uncertain.

Increasing political polarization. The internet and social media also threaten democracy by increasing political polarization, which is greater now than at any time since Reconstruction or perhaps the Civil War. The tremendous proliferation of sources of information—which unquestionably has many benefits—allows people to easily choose the messages that they want to hear. In fact, internet and social media companies use algorithms that direct people to information based on their existing beliefs. Many people thus read and hear only information that reinforces their beliefs, increasing polarization.

Social media help create the phenomenon of echo chambers,[66] virtual environments where individuals are surrounded by information and opinions that validate their existing beliefs and attitudes.[67] Within an echo chamber, individuals are more likely to encounter information that aligns with their preexisting biases than information that challenges them.[68] This enhancement can make individuals more extreme in their perspectives and less inclined to engage with alternative viewpoints.[69] Consequently, people may become more entrenched in their views and less open to considering alternative perspectives.

Echo chambers also make it easier for people to access extremist positions, which poses its own dangers to democracy.

Echo chambers and the resulting polarization detrimentally affect democratic discourse. They hinder communication among groups and make consensus on important issues difficult to reach.[70] Furthermore, they can impede problem-solving efforts and contribute to the spread of misinformation and conspiracy theories.[71] Echo chambers filled with misinformation are extremely harmful to constructive public discourse and democracy.

Americans have always had sharp disagreements. They were present at the Constitutional Convention in 1787, and they have been here ever since. But the development of nationwide media—first movies, then radio, and then television—helped to unify the country. As for news, for years, there were three television networks, and many people got their news from them and the trusted voices of Walter Cronkite, Chet Huntley, and David Brinkley. Today, though, we have no commonly shared authoritative voices. We have a great multiplicity of voices, and people choose the ones they want to hear from. Not surprisingly, this multiplicity contributes significantly to our deep and growing polarization.

There are no easy or even apparent solutions to these problems. It is too soon even to know whether the net benefits of the internet and social media outweigh their harms. But any discussion of threats to democracy must address their role. The question—and no one has suggested persuasive answers yet—is how to deal with false political speech and with foreign influence in elections in a manner that is consistent with the First Amendment. These crucial challenges for democracy are unlike anything the country or the world has faced before.

Two hundred thousand Americans participated in the civil rights movement's Freedom March on Washington, pouring down Constitution Avenue on their way to the Lincoln Memorial, where they would hear and be moved by the Rev. Martin Luther King, Jr's pivotal "I Have a Dream" speech, August 28, 1963. *(Photograph by Ed Clarity / NY Daily News Archive via Getty Images)*

PART III

———

CAN THE *UNITED* STATES BE SAVED?

8

What Can Be Done Without Changing the Constitution?

What Needs to Be Done?

The mistakes made in 1787 are haunting us in the twenty-first century. It is not hyperbole to say that they are putting American democracy at risk. A few years ago, Harvard professors Steven Levitsky and Daniel Ziblatt wrote a compelling book, *How Democracies Die*, that described, by many measures, the "reasons for alarm" for the future of our democracy.[1] They explained that the guardrails are failing and that the country is following a pattern that has led many other nations to authoritarian rule.

They began by observing that they never imagined that they would feel "dread" for the future of American democracy.[2] I feel exactly the same way. It's tempting to believe that a form of government that has worked relatively well since 1787, at least in avoiding authoritarian rule, will continue even without major change. But over the last half-century, American public trust in the government declined from 77 percent in 1964 (the year of the Civil Rights Act's passage) to our contemporary 20 percent.[3] Can a government survive without the confidence of the people? Think of Donald Trump's unprecedented election denial and the Capitol attack on January 6, 2021.

Ultimately, I reluctantly conclude that to restore public confidence and to make government much more effective, we must make fundamental changes in American government—we must fix the bad bones of the Constitution. Crucial changes must include:

The Electoral College must be eliminated, and voters must elect the president directly. Twice in this century alone, the loser of the popular vote became president, and it almost happened twice more. No other country in the world has anything like the Electoral College. The current partisan alignment and demographics make it likely that ever more election losers will become president. Government will then forfeit the trust and confidence of the people.

Representation in the Senate must be allocated based on population. Two senators per state, regardless of their population, is inconsistent with the most basic premise of a democracy: one-person, one-vote. No conception of democracy can justify the fact that California and Wyoming have the same number of senators, when California has seventy times more people. The Senate that was elected in November 2020 had fifty Democrats and fifty Republicans, but the Democratic senators represented 60 percent of the population and the Republicans only 40 percent.

The filibuster must be eliminated. The filibuster effectively requires sixty senators to pass virtually any piece of legislation. It allows forty senators representing as little as 22 percent of the population to block virtually any law from being enacted. For much of twentieth century, it prevented the passage of civil rights laws. In recent years, it precluded essential voting rights legislation that had been passed by the House of Representatives from even coming to a vote in the Senate.

Partisan gerrymandering must be abolished. Sophisticated computer algorithms and detailed population data now make it possible for partisan gerrymandering to occur with far more precision than ever before. They allow the political party that controls a legislature to increase and entrench its dominance. Members of the other political party do not get nearly their fair share of representation or the chance to change that in the future.

The size of the House of Representatives must be increased. The House of Representatives was set at 435 members in 1929 and it has not changed since. Yet the country's population has grown enormously since then. The size of congressional districts has tripled over the last century from an average of roughly 212,000 inhabitants per district after the 1910 Census to about 710,000 inhabitants following the 2010 Census.[4] By 2050, it is projected, each member of Congress will represent a million or more people.[5] Expanding the size of the House of Representatives would mean that each representative served a smaller constituency. Also, House districts currently vary greatly in size because small states are assured of at least one representative. Expanding the number of districts would lessen the influence of these states in the Electoral College. It would also decrease the likelihood that an election loser would become president, as more populous states would have more representation in the Electoral College; since the number of each state's electors is the sum of its representatives and senators. There is no magic number of representatives, and obviously having too many would interfere with the ability of the House to function (though at times it is hard to see how it could get worse). But the number could certainly be expanded without harming its operation.[6]

Life tenure for Supreme Court justices must be eliminated, in favor of term limits. Today Supreme Court vacancies occur due to accidents of history. Our longer life expectancies have meant that justices remain on the bench for increasingly long tenures. From 1787 until 1970, a justice served an average of fifteen years. For those appointed since 1970 who are no longer on the bench, the average has been twenty-seven years, and that is growing. Justices appointed in their forties and early fifties—like Clarence Thomas (age forty-three when appointed), Amy Coney Barrett (age forty-eight when appointed), John Roberts and Elena Kagan (both fifty when appointed)—may serve forty years or more. That is too much power for one person to have for too long a period of time.

Supreme Court rulings that have undermined democracy must be overruled, especially those allowing corporations to spend unlimited money on elections and those gutting the Voting Rights Act. The original flaws in the Constitution that undermine democracy have been exacerbated by a Court that has empowered the wealthy and disempowered racial minorities that were already long disenfranchised.

Profound racial inequalities, traceable to the tragic choices made concerning slavery in 1787, must be addressed. The "staggering racial disparities" in wealth and income—which are growing—must be reduced.[7] More effective civil rights laws and better enforcement are essential.

The threats that the internet and social media pose for democracy must be addressed. The new communication tools have the ability to spread false speech, to facilitate foreign interference in American elections, and to foment an echo chamber and polarization. We must solve these problems in ways that do not undermine freedom of speech. There are no easy answers, but we cannot ignore the threat that these media pose for the future of democracy. At the very least, we should ban deepfakes in the weeks before an election.[8] We need stricter disclosure laws as to speakers' identities; this is crucial with regard to foreign speakers, but also for those spending money on campaign advertisements. The Supreme Court has generally upheld disclosure requirements.[9] The law could go much further in this regard—especially to deal with the problems of foreign spending and dark money—than it currently does.

If somehow people could be polled on these reforms without knowing whether their political party would be helped or hurt by them, they would likely have widespread support. The Harvard philosophy professor John Rawls once suggested imagining that people lived behind a "veil of ignorance" and, without knowing their own situation, had to make choices about what was best for the country. Suppose they did not know whether they were from a large state or a small state, Republican or Democrat, and had to decide on the best structure of government. In that case, they would widely support the changes I describe above. But we do not live behind a veil of ignorance, and every one of the changes outlined above would politically benefit some and disadvantage others, and which would do which is easy to recognize.

Are these changes possible to make without amending the Constitution? What can be done now by either judicial or legislative action?

The Problems Can Be Solved Without Constitutional Change

Surprisingly, most of the reforms I've detailed could, in one way or another, be instituted without amending or replacing the Constitution. The most important exception is that equal representation of states in the Senate cannot be altered even by constitutional amendment. Article V of the Constitution, which covers the amendment process, explicitly disallows it.

But other changes that I propose could be done without having to amend or replace the Constitution.

Electoral College. The Electoral College is arguably unconstitutional and could be invalidated by the Supreme Court. This may sound strange at first. The Electoral College is created by the Constitution, so how can a provision of the Constitution be unconstitutional? The answer is that it is unconstitutional if it violates any of the subsequent amendments to the Constitution. Amendments, by definition, modify the text that was adopted in 1787. For example, Article I authorizes Congress to regulate interstate commerce, and this would allow federal licensing of the press, except that the First Amendment unquestionably makes that unconstitutional. Article III permits a federal court to hear a suit against a state by citizens of other states. But the Eleventh Amendment was adopted to preclude such litigation and has been interpreted broadly by the Supreme Court to prohibit state governments from being sued in federal court. The whole point of constitutional amendments is to modify the text of the Constitution.

Simply put, the Electoral College is unconstitutional if it violates an amendment that has been added since 1787. The Supreme Court has long held that the Fifth Amendment assurance of due process of law includes a requirement that the federal government not deny any person equal protection of the laws.[10] And for over a half-century, the Court has ruled that a core aspect of equal protection is one-person, one-vote; every person must have an equal ability to influence the outcome of an election. In *Wesberry v. Sanders* in 1964, the Court announced that as much as is practicable, the Constitution requires that "one man's vote . . . is to be worth as much as another's."[11] In *Bush v. Gore* in 2000, the Court stated, "Having once granted the right to vote on equal terms, the State may not . . . value one person's vote over that of another."[12]

The Electoral College is inconsistent with the basic democratic principle of one-person, one-vote. Because every state has two senators, smaller states have disproportionate influence in choosing the president. Wyoming has a population of 581,381 and has three electoral votes, which means that each Wyoming elector represents roughly 193,793 voters. California has a population of 39,029,342 and has fifty-five electoral votes, so each elector represents roughly 709,624 voters. A presidential vote in Wyoming is worth 3.7 times more than a vote in California. Courts thus can and should declare that the guarantee of equal protection found in the Fifth Amendment modifies Article II of the Constitution and requires that electors be allocated strictly on the basis of population.

At first blush, many will likely feel discomfort at the prospect of the courts fundamentally changing the system for the election of president by declaring unconstitutional the method of choosing the president outlined in Article II. But the judicial role is most important when the political system is incapable of reforming itself to comply with the Constitution.[13] This is exactly why the Court's decisions concerning apportionment were so crucial. Prior to the 1960s, many state legislatures and congressional districts were badly malapportioned; within a state, districts varied widely in population. Those who benefited from this inequity were not about to redraw legislative districts to vote themselves out of power. The Court articulated the one-person, one-vote rule: for any legislative body, all electoral districts must have about the same population.[14] Chief Justice Earl Warren once remarked that the most important decisions during his tenure on the Court were those ordering reapportionment, precisely because the political process was never going to solve the constitutional problem.[15]

The same is true with regard to the Electoral College. Amending the Constitution requires the approval of two-thirds of both houses of Congress and then three-quarters of the states. The smaller states that benefit greatly from the Electoral College will never approve a constitutional amendment to eliminate it. Constitutional amendments to change the Electoral College have been repeatedly proposed; one commentator estimated that "nearly one-tenth of all constitutional amendments proposed in Congress have sought electoral college reform."[16] None has ever come close to adoption, and none ever will. Because the political process never will deal with the clear unconstitutionality of the Electoral College, it is especially important for the Court to act.

As I've explained earlier, the problem of the Electoral College is compounded by state laws that provide that electoral votes are awarded on a winner-take-all basis. In all states except Nebraska and Maine, the candidate who wins the state's popular vote—even by the narrowest margin—gets all the electoral votes from that state. This, too, greatly increases the chances of the Electoral College choosing a president who has lost the popular vote.

Effectively, winner-take-all meant that in 2020 a vote for Donald Trump in California or for Joe Biden in Texas had absolutely no effect. Nebraska and Maine allocate electoral votes by congressional district: the elector for each congressional district votes for the candidate who got the majority of the votes there, while the remaining electors are chosen statewide. So Nebraska and Maine have a much more proportional allocation of electoral votes than states where the principle is winner-take-all.

At the very least, the courts should hold that winner-take-all, which is provided by state law and not by the Constitution, is unconstitutional. This would not entail declaring the Electoral College unconstitutional, just state laws that allocate electors. Such holdings would greatly increase the chances that the winner of the popular vote would be chosen president, as should happen in a democracy.

Moreover, winner-take-all has a significant racially discriminatory effect against minority voters and thus violates Section 2 of the Voting Rights Act, which prohibits electoral systems that limit or dilute the ability of racial and language minorities to elect candidates of their choice. As Matthew Hoffman explained: "Voting in presidential elections is highly polarized along racial lines. Consequently, choosing presidential electors through the winner-take-all system results in a paradigmatic example of the kind of discrimination that section 2 was meant to eliminate."[17] In states like Alabama and Texas, voters of color realistically have no voice in choosing the president because of the winner-take-all approach.

Eliminating winner-take-all requires judicial action. Individual states are not going to unilaterally disarm. California is not going to abolish winner-take-all and give some of its electors to the Republican candidate for president unless it knows Texas is going to do the same and give some of its electors to the Democratic candidate. But a court could invalidate winner-take-all for all states simultaneously and thereby create a far better election system, one that is less likely to put the popular vote loser in the White House.

The filibuster. The filibuster—and all aspects of it—was created by Senate rules, not by the Constitution or even by a federal statute. The Senate could abolish it by a majority vote of its members. It already has done this for some matters. During the presidency of Barack Obama, when Republicans were using filibusters to block some of his judicial nominees, Senate Democrats changed the rules to abolish the filibuster for nominations to federal district courts, to federal courts of appeals, and to cabinet posts. During the Trump presidency, when Democrats filibustered the nomination of Neil Gorsuch to the Supreme Court, Senate Republicans changed the rules to eliminate the possibility of a filibuster for a Supreme Court nomination.

The other exception where filibusters are not allowed is the budget process. Under the congressional legislation governing the budget that was adopted in 1974, all budget reconciliation legislation is considered under procedural rules that strictly limit the time for debate and other procedural delay.[18] Reconciliation bills cannot be filibustered because the time for debate is strictly limited by statute. They cannot be delayed by excessive amendments because, when the time for debate expires, the Senate votes on all filed amendments without any further discussion and then immediately on the reconciliation bill itself. But this restriction on Senate debate is limited to budget matters. Senate procedural rules require that reconciliation bills be germane to the federal budget.[19] The Senate parliamentarian decides if a bill meets this requirement and thus cannot be subject to a filibuster.

The Senate could, if it chose, further modify its rules to end the filibuster altogether, or to create more exceptions to it. Or it could change the rules to return the filibuster to how it used to operate, including rules requiring that those filibustering actually hold the floor, as Jimmy Stewart did in *Mr. Smith Goes to Washington*. Eliminating the stealth filibuster at least would reduce its use.

Alternatively, the filibuster could be ended by being declared unconstitutional. The argument that the filibuster is unconstitutional is based on the text and original intent of the Constitution, which strongly suggest that a majority vote in each house of Congress is sufficient to adopt a bill. The Constitution is specific about the situations where more than a simple majority is required for Congress, or a house of Congress, to act. The Constitution explicitly requires a supermajority in only seven situations,[20] such as ratifying a treaty, which requires two-thirds approval of the Senate.

The careful enumeration of the situations where a two-thirds vote is required is consistent with the framers' belief that majority vote would be sufficient for legislative action and the assumption that Congress would generally operate by majority rule.[21] But with the filibuster, adopting a law requires 60 percent approval of the senators, rather than a simple majority. Thus, it is unconstitutional.

Other constitutional provisions further support the argument that the Constitution makes a majority vote sufficient for action by the Senate. Article I, Section 3, Clause 4 provides that the "Vice President . . . shall be President of the Senate, but shall have no Vote, unless they be equally divided." The vice president's role as a tiebreaker would occur only if the Senate utilizes a majority vote, creating a situation where the Senate could be equally divided.

Article I, Section 5 provides that "a Majority of each [House] shall constitute a quorum to do Business." The Supreme Court in 1891, in *United States v. Ballin*, held that "the act of a majority of the quorum is the act of the body. This has been the rule for all time."[22]

Article I, Section 7 provides that if the president vetoes a bill, Congress can override the veto by a two-thirds vote of each House. The requirement for a supermajority to override a veto implies that less than two-thirds is necessary to adopt the law initially. Presumably the framers thought that a simple majority vote of each House would pass a bill and then a two-thirds vote would be needed if to override a presidential veto.

All these textual provisions arguably establish that the Senate must follow a majority vote rule, except in those instances where the Constitution specifies otherwise. Senate Rule XXII, which governs filibusters, thus would be unconstitutional in that it requires a supermajority of sixty votes to end debate and in practical effect requires sixty votes to adopt legislation any time a filibuster is in effect.

But I don't want to overstate the strength of this argument. There are counterarguments. The Constitution, in Article I, Section 5, specifically provides: "Each House may determine the Rules of its

Proceedings." Therefore textual authority exists for Congress to make rules concerning matters such as the length of debate. Moreover, Rule XXII does not require sixty votes to adopt a law; it only requires sixty votes to end debate. Passing a bill still requires only a simple majority.

Also, because the text is silent about the vote needed to stop debate or pass a law, one could argue, Congress has the option to set the voting requirement. The enumeration of seven instances where a supermajority vote is required does not mean that these seven instances are the only situations where such a supermajority vote is permissible. It is equally consistent to read the text as requiring supermajority votes in the enumerated instances, but leaving it to Congress in other situations to decide the required voting margin. Where the text enumerates a requirement, it must be followed, but otherwise, Congress may decide the voting rule.

My point is simply that the filibuster could be eliminated without constitutional amendment by either the Senate changing its rules or by the courts declaring it unconstitutional.

Ending partisan gerrymandering. Congress, by legislation, could end partisan gerrymandering for elections to the House of Representatives. Article I, Section 4 of the Constitution says that states determine the time, place, and manner of elections to Congress, "but Congress may at any time make or alter such regulations." Congress therefore could, by federal legislation, require that all districts for Congress be drawn by independent commissions.

Even without congressional action, state governments can end partisan gerrymandering for federal and state elections. State courts can find that partisan gerrymandering violates state constitutions. And as some have done, states can create independent, nonpartisan commissions to draw election district lines.

Expanding the size of the House of Representatives. Congress can do this by statute. No constitutional change is needed.

Establishing term limits for Supreme Court justices. The idea of term limiting Supreme Court justices has overwhelming public support. A recent poll showed that over 77 percent of people favor such restrictions on justices' length of service.[23] Liberals and conservatives alike have advocated this change. Texas governor Rick Perry, when running for the Republican presidential nomination, argued for eighteen-year nonrenewable terms for those on the high court.[24]

The United States is the only country that bestows life tenure on its judges. In Germany, justices of the Federal Constitutional Court are appointed for a single, nonrenewable twelve-year term. South Africa has the same provision. And in Colombia and Taiwan, constitutional justices are appointed for an eight-year term.

We have always assumed that the Constitution grants life tenure to federal judges and that changing that would require a constitutional amendment. Every person confirmed for the Court since 1787 has remained a justice until resignation or death.

But arguably Congress, by statute, could impose term limits without violating the Constitution.[25] Article III of the Constitution says, "The judges, both of the supreme and inferior courts, shall hold their offices during good behaviour, and shall, at stated times, receive for their services, a compensation, which shall not be diminished during their continuance in office." But what does "hold their offices" mean? Congress could provide, some have argued, that after eighteen years, a Supreme Court justice could take senior status, continue to receive the same salary, serve as a federal court of appeals judge, and sit on the Supreme Court only when needed because of a recusal or vacancy.[26] The justices thus would continue to "hold their office," they just wouldn't be sitting on the Supreme Court on a regular basis.

Bills have been introduced in Congress to impose these term limits. The Supreme Court Tenure Establishment and Retirement Modernization Act (Term), sets eighteen-year terms for Supreme Court justices and establishes a process for the president to appoint a new justice every two years.[27]

The statutory approach to term limits has prominent advocates, but I am skeptical of its constitutionality, especially as applied to current justices. Can the justices really be said to hold their office if they are not serving on the Supreme Court? The "office" for which they were appointed and confirmed is being a justice on the U.S. Supreme Court. Certainly. All the current justices took office with the expectation that it would be a lifetime position because it always has been. Changing it by statute while they are serving seems suspect. And if term limits were to take effect only for future justices, it would be a long time before they had any impact. Justices Barrett, Gorsuch, Jackson, and Kavanaugh all are in their fifties and will likely be on the Court for decades to come.

Overturning Supreme Court decisions that undermine the democratic process. The Supreme Court can overturn anything it previously decided. Throughout American history and especially in recent years, the Supreme Court has overruled its precedents. *Roe v. Wade* protected a constitutional right to abortion until it was overturned by *Dobbs v. Jackson Women's Health Organization.*[28] The Court allowed affirmative action by colleges and universities for decades until it reversed those decisions and held that such efforts deny equal protection and violate the Constitution.[29]

Some of the major Supreme Court decisions that undermine the democratic process could be overruled. The Court could overturn its decision in *Citizens United v. Federal Election Commission* (which held that corporations can spend unlimited amounts of money in election campaigns) and again allow restrictions on funds from corporate treasuries.[30] Similarly, the Court could conclude that it was wrong in *Rucho v. Common Cause* and that federal courts can hear challenges to the constitutionality of partisan gerrymandering.[31] It could revisit its rulings on the Voting Rights Act to give it a much broader scope and even restore the provisions that it declared unconstitutional.[32]

Congress, by statute, cannot overrule Supreme Court cases. But the Court on its own can do so.

Racial justice. No easy path exists to create racial justice and overcome the country's legacy of slavery and its long history of racial discrimination. But if I could make one change in constitutional law to advance equal protection, it would be to eliminate the requirement of proof of discriminatory intent in order to show the existence of discrimination. Proof that a law or government policy has a racially disparate impact should be sufficient. Over the last forty years, the Supreme Court has continually held that demonstrating a discriminatory impact of a government action is not enough to show that it constitutes racial discrimination. Proving discrimination requires proving that the action has a discriminatory purpose.[33] Requiring proof of discriminatory purpose in order to demonstrate an equal protection violation has dramatically lessened our ability to use the

Constitution to create a more just society. All this could be changed if the Court were to recognize its error and overrule these precedents.

Showing that a government action has a discriminatory impact is crucial for determining the reach of the Equal Protection Clause. In many instances, laws that do not mention race are administered in a manner that discriminates against minorities or that has a disproportionate impact against them, but evidence is insufficient to prove that the government acted with a discriminatory purpose.[34] Current law means that the government need not offer a racially neutral explanation for these effects and, indeed, generally need do no more than show that its action is reasonable.[35] To prove the existence of a racial classification—or at least to shift the burden to the government to prove a nonrace explanation for its action—requires proving discriminatory intent.[36]

Washington v. Davis was a key case in establishing this requirement.[37] Applicants for the police force in Washington, D.C., were required to take a test, and statistics revealed that blacks failed the examination much more often than whites. The Supreme Court, however, held that proof of a discriminatory impact is insufficient, by itself, to prove the existence of racial discrimination. Justice Byron White, writing for the majority, said that there has to be proof of a "racially discriminatory purpose" in order to deem that a law violates equal protection, even if it has—like the Washington law—a significant discriminatory effect against people of color.[38] The Court explained that discriminatory impact, "standing alone, . . . does not trigger the rule that racial classifications are to be subjected to the strictest scrutiny and are justifiable only by the weightiest of considerations."[39] In other words, laws that are facially neutral as to race (they don't explicitly mention race) will receive more than rational basis review—under which they are sure to be upheld—only if there is proof of a discriminatory purpose.

The Supreme Court has reaffirmed this principle, that discriminatory impact is insufficient to prove a racial classification, many times. For example, in *McCleskey v. Kemp*, the Court held that proof of discriminatory impact in the administration of the death penalty was insufficient to show an equal protection violation.[40] Statistics powerfully demonstrated racial inequality in the imposition of capital punishment,[41] but the Court said that for the defendant to demonstrate an equal protection violation, he "must prove that the decisionmakers in *his* case acted with discriminatory purpose."[42] Because the defendant could not prove that the prosecutor or jury in his case was biased, no equal protection violation existed. Moreover, the Court said that to challenge the law authorizing capital punishment, the defendant "would have to prove that the Georgia Legislature enacted or maintained the death penalty statute *because of an* anticipated racially discriminatory effect."[43] These burdens are impossible to meet.

The law is clear that proof of a discriminatory impact is not sufficient by itself to prove an equal protection violation; there also must be proof of a discriminatory purpose.[44] What is wrong with the Court's requirement for proof of discriminatory purpose? First, it misunderstands the goal of equal protection. Equal protection should be concerned with the results of government actions and not just with their underlying motivations. The government should not be able to act in a manner that harms racial minorities, regardless of why it took the action.

In *Washington v. Davis*, the Court, in imposing a requirement for proof of discriminatory intent, said that the purpose of the Equal Protection Clause "is the prevention of official conduct discriminating on the basis of race."[45] But the Court never has justified this premise that the focus should be solely on the government's motives and not the effects of its actions. Quite the contrary, equal protection should be concerned with, and measured by, outcomes as well as intentions. A crucial question should be whether the government's action is creating inequalities on the basis of race (or other protected classifications). If so, at the very least, the government should have to offer a sufficient nondiscriminatory explanation for its actions. Laurence Tribe explained this well when he stated: "The goal of the equal protection clause is not to stamp out impure thoughts, but to guarantee a full measure of human dignity for all. . . . [M]inorities can also be injured when the government is 'only' indifferent to their suffering or 'merely' blind to how prior official discrimination contributed to it and how current official acts will perpetuate it."[46]

Second, the Court's requirement for proof of a discriminatory purpose ignores the reality of unconscious bias. Rarely will legislators or government officials express a discriminatory motivation; benign purposes can be articulated for most laws.[47] Therefore many laws with both a discriminatory purpose and a discriminatory effect will be upheld simply because of evidentiary problems inherent in requiring proof of such a purpose. Scholars such as Charles Lawrence argue that this is especially true because racism is often unconscious, and such "unconscious racism . . . underlies much of the disproportionate impact of governmental policy."[48]

Since *Washington v. Davis* in 1976, a large body of psychological literature has documented the reality of implicit bias and explained its significance for the legal system.[49] The science of implicit bias shows that "actors do not always have conscious, intentional control over the processes of social perception, impression formation, and judgment that motivate their actions."[50] Research has shown that we all have biases at an unconscious level and that these biases may influence our decision-making processes in ways of which we are completely unaware.[51]

A crucial problem with requiring proof of discriminatory intent is that it focuses solely on biases that are expressed; it ignores unconscious biases.[52] The requirement to show a discriminatory purpose in order to prove the existence of a racial classification fails to account for the reality of implicit bias. As Christine Jolls and Cass Sunstein have explained: "Ordinary antidiscrimination law will often face grave difficulties in ferreting out implicit bias even when this bias produces unequal treatment."[53]

Implicit bias research creates a basis for believing that laws with a racially disparate impact do not result from coincidence but rather reflect unstated—and perhaps unrealized—discriminatory intentions. Put another way, in a society with a long history of discrimination, we can presume that many laws that have a discriminatory impact likely were motivated by a discriminatory purpose.[54]

In every area of law, the requirement for proof of discriminatory intent has frustrated the ability to use equal protection to remedy race discrimination. Consider a few examples.

In the 1990s and 2000s, sentences for users of crack cocaine were as much as one hundred times greater than those for users of powder cocaine, even though the drug is the same. This had a huge racial discriminatory impact. As the Sentencing Project explained: "Defendants convicted of crack possession in 1994 were 84.5 percent black,

10.3 percent white, and 5.2 percent Hispanic. . . . Defendants convicted of simple possession of cocaine powder were 58 percent white, 26.7 percent black, and 15 percent Hispanic. . . . The result of the combined difference in sentencing laws and racial disparity is that black men and women are serving longer prison sentences than white men and women."[55]

In California, people of color account for over 98 percent of those sent to state prisons for possession of crack cocaine for sale. From 2005 to 2010, blacks accounted for 77.4 percent of state prison commitments for crack possession for sale, although they made up just 6.6 percent of the state's population. Latinos account for 18.1 percent of those convicted of crack cocaine offenses, while whites are 1.8 percent of those in prison for such charges. By contrast, those convicted for powder cocaine offenses are overwhelmingly white.

Yet efforts to challenge this disparity as violating equal protection failed because the courts said that there was no proof of discriminatory intent for the sentencing disparity.[56] The law had an enormously discriminatory effect—many more African Americans and Hispanics were in prison—but the courts provided no remedy. As David Sklansky noted, "The federal crack penalties provide a paradigmatic case of unconscious racism."[57] In 2010 Congress lessened this disparity, though did not eliminate it, with the Fair Sentencing Act, which reduced the statutory penalties for crack cocaine offenses to produce an 18-to-1 crack-to-powder drug quantity ratio and eliminated the mandatory minimum sentence for simple possession of crack cocaine.

Another disparity created by requiring proof of discriminatory intent is in the application of the death penalty. In *McCleskey v. Kemp*, the Supreme Court held that proof of discriminatory impact in the administration of the death penalty was insufficient to show an equal protection violation.[58] Countless studies have proved racial inequality in the imposition of capital punishment.[59] The national death-row population is roughly 42 percent Black, while the U.S. population overall is only 13.6 percent Black.[60] Undoubtedly, these statistics reflect the biases, often unconscious, of prosecutors as to when to seek the death penalty, or of juries as to when to impose it. But *McCleskey v. Kemp* and the requirement for proof of a discriminatory intent makes it impossible to challenge on equal protection grounds.

I choose these examples—cocaine sentencing and the death penalty—because they are areas where there are no statutes allowing recovery based on disparate impact. Thus they have enormous consequences for the Supreme Court's requirement for proof of discriminatory purpose. In fact, the areas where statutes exist that allow for proof of discrimination by a showing of disparate impact—Title VII for employment discrimination,[61] the Fair Housing Act,[62] and the Voting Rights Act Amendments of 1982[63]—demonstrate the great difference when there can be liability without proof of discriminatory intent.

Combating false speech over the internet and social media. As I explained in Chapter 7, false speech poses a serious threat to democracy, a danger that will grow with artificial intelligence and deepfakes. The First Amendment rightly creates an obstacle to regulating speech, even false speech. But some things can be done. As a first step, Congress and state legislatures can ban deepfakes created by artificial intelligence from being used in the weeks before an election. The harm of deepfakes far outweighs any First Amendment value, and prohibited expression can be defined in a way that does not risk chilling other speech.[64] Also, Congress and state legislatures should adopt much stricter disclosure requirements so that people can know who is speaking and spending money in election campaigns. The First Amendment value of this additional speech far outweighs any rights that speakers have to remain anonymous.

Can It Really Happen?

I have intentionally separated the questions of whether these changes *can* be made from whether they are *likely to be made*. Few of these changes are likely to happen in the foreseeable future. It is far-fetched to imagine the Supreme Court declaring that the Electoral College or even winner-take-all violates equal protection. Any justice would find it difficult after almost 240 years of the country using it to choose the president. Conservative justices appointed by Republican presidents are especially unlikely to take an action that would reduce the likelihood that a Republican would ever again be elected to the White House.

The Senate shows no signs of being inclined to eliminate the filibuster, even for specific types of legislation, such as bills to protect voting rights. It might do it in the future, but whatever political party is
in the majority wants to preserve the filibuster knowing that one day
it will be in the minority, and it does not want to give up that tool. Nor
is it likely that the courts will declare the filibuster unconstitutional.
Several lawsuits have been brought, and they have gone nowhere.[65]

The House of Representatives is unlikely to pass legislation to end
partisan gerrymandering for congressional elections by mandating
independent commissions to draw district lines. Too many members
of Congress benefit from partisan gerrymandering for such legislation
to have a realistic chance of adoption.

Legislation to impose term limits on Supreme Court justices may
be more realistic, especially as the Court's approval ratings shrink and
frustration with the Court grows. But, as I've explained, the constitutionality of such legislation, especially as applied to current justices, is
at best uncertain.

Finally, the Court could overrule its precedents about campaign
finance, the Voting Rights Act, and partisan gerrymandering, but
that seems far-fetched for the foreseeable future. It could also reverse
decades of precedents and allow proof of racial discrimination by
demonstrating a disparate impact, but no one imagines this Court
doing that. Had Hillary Clinton won the presidency in 2016, all these
precedents likely would have been reconsidered. But now that won't
be realistic for a long time to come, as a conservative majority on the
Court is likely to remain for years and even decades.

Still, it is important for us to remember that most of the essential
changes in government can happen without a constitutional amendment or a new constitution. What seems implausible today might
become more likely over time, especially if the sense of a crisis of
democracy grows. When calls to reform government emerge in a serious way—and I expect that our current path will take us there—it will
be crucial to know it can be done.

But if the major changes needed to protect American democracy
are not going to happen by legislation or judicial decisions, are there
other paths to these reforms?

9

Can the Constitution Be Fixed?

I f federal statutes and judicial decisions do not fix the flaws in the
Constitution, then our focus must shift to the possibility of constitutional amendment. Every defect in the Constitution, except
for one, can be solved by amendment. The exception is that every state
must have the same number of senators. Article V makes this one of
two constitutional provisions that cannot be amended. At the Constitutional Convention, the representatives of smaller states insisted
on equal representation in the Senate as a condition for agreeing to
the Constitution, and they made sure that provision could never
be changed.[1]

In theory, we might circumvent this exception by breaking large
states like California into smaller states, with each then having two
senators. But political realities make this idea far-fetched. Granting
statehood to the District of Columbia and Puerto Rico, so residents in
these areas have representation in Congress, has proved impossible.
Republicans believe this move would add more Democratic senators,
so they do all they can to block it. Moreover, the small states that currently benefit from equal representation in the Senate have sufficient
political strength that they will not approve of adding more states and
diminishing their own influence. If nothing else, their senators can
stage a filibuster to ensure that such legislation is not enacted.

Every other problem with the Constitution, even Supreme Court
interpretations of it, can be solved by constitutional amendment.

But the Constitution that was adopted in 1787 creates a huge obstacle: amendments are enormously difficult and likely impossible for the reforms that are essential to save democracy. A crucial flaw in the Constitution is that it is so difficult to change. To be sure, the essence of a constitution, compared to all other laws, is that it is harder to revise. But the framers of the Constitution went too far in preventing amendments. As University of Chicago law professor Eric Posner has declared, "The founders blundered. They made passing an amendment too hard."[2]

Article V of the Constitution, which details the amendment process, provides two possible paths for revisions. One method is for both the House and the Senate, by a two-thirds vote, to propose a constitutional amendment.[3] If it is then approved by three-quarters of the states, it is deemed adopted.[4] This process has been used for all twenty-seven amendments that have been adopted since 1787.

Article V offers another path for amendment that has never been used. Two-thirds of the state legislatures can call for a constitutional convention.[5] Congress then convenes one, and its proposals are adopted if three-quarters of the states approve them.[6] It's unclear how this process would work. How would the delegates be selected? Would the convention's scope be limited to specific topics, or would it able to reconsider the whole document? Would states vote, as they did in Philadelphia in 1787, or would delegates vote as individuals? But those questions could be answered if enough states were to call for a constitutional convention.

History shows that the amendment process, at best, is daunting and often impossible. Since 1789, approximately 11,848 amendments have been proposed, but only thirty-three have been ratified by two-thirds of both houses of Congress, and only twenty-seven have been ratified by the states.[7] Of those twenty-seven amendments, over almost 240 years, ten were adopted in 1791 as the Bill of Rights.[8] Two others were to impose and then repeal Prohibition.[9] Apart from Prohibition, there have been only fifteen amendments since 1791.[10]

Therefore a defining characteristic of the American Constitution is that it is very difficult to alter. It is worth thinking about why and how it came to be this way and whether it is a virtue or, as I think, a flaw.

Why should a society that is generally committed to majority rule choose to be governed by a document that is very difficult to change? Harvard professor Laurence Tribe puts the question succinctly: "Why would a nation that rests legality on the consent of the governed choose to constitute its political life in terms of commitments to an original agreement—made by the people, binding on their children, and deliberately structured so as to be difficult to change?"[11]

The framers deliberately made changing the constitution difficult in order to prevent a tyranny of the majority. A government that had a structure based on statutes might have an overwhelming tendency to create dictatorial powers in a time of crisis. If individual liberties were protected only by statutes, a tyrannical government could overrule them. If terms of office were specified in a statute rather than in the Constitution, those in power could alter it to remain in power.

Thus, a constitution represents society's attempt to protect the values it most cherishes. A powerful analogy is the story from ancient Greek mythology of Ulysses and the Sirens.[12] Ulysses, fearing the Sirens' seductive and deadly song, bound himself to the ship's mast so that he could resist temptation. His sailors plugged their ears with wax to be immune to the Sirens' call, whereas Ulysses, tied to the mast, heard the Sirens' song but remained unscathed. Despite Ulysses's pleas for release, his sailors followed his earlier instructions, keeping him bound and unable to heed the Sirens' song. His life was saved because he recognized his own weakness and protected himself from it.

A constitution is a society's attempt to tie its own hands, to limit its ability to succumb to weaknesses that might harm or undermine its cherished values. History teaches that passions of the moment can cause people to sacrifice even the most basic principles of liberty and justice. The Constitution is society's attempt to protect itself from itself. The Constitution enumerates basic values—regular elections, separation of powers, individual rights, equality—and makes changes very difficult.

The analogy between the Constitution and Ulysses is appealing but inexact: Ulysses tied his own hands, whereas a constitution binds future generations. The analogy is even more imperfect when one considers that the framers of the Constitution were all white male property owners, hardly representative of their society or ours. The problem is not just that no one alive today approved the Constitution.

Most of us did not even have ancestors in the country at the time, and the ancestors of those who did likely could not participate in its drafting and ratification. Thus we must understand the Constitution as an intentionally and profoundly anti-majoritarian document.

I am not questioning the framers' decision to entrench the Constitution and make it difficult to change. That is in the nature of constitutions and is a good thing. But how easy or difficult should amendment be? Yale law professor Stephen Carter has observed that "Article V is very nearly a dead letter."[13] Making amendment difficult makes sense, but the current Constitution makes it almost impossible.

A close examination of the debates of 1787 reveals that the framers meant for the Constitution to be hard to amend but not this difficult.[14] Amendment was never meant to be almost impossible. In fact, some of the framers thought the Constitution would be *too easy* to amend.[15] Others, including Alexander Hamilton, used the word *easy* to describe a desirable method of amendment.[16] Thomas Jefferson, who was not present at the convention, disagreed with veneration of the Constitution out of fear that it would reinforce "the view that the Constitution was a sacred jewel to be kept as close as possible to its original form," thus making "Americans reluctant to revise their Constitution, even in the case of sensible constitutional amendments that time and experience might reveal were necessary."[17]

The Constitution was very much a reaction to the failure of the Articles of Confederation that preceded it: the Articles required unanimous approval of the states for amendment, a process that never took place.[18] The delegates to the Constitutional Convention saw this as a significant flaw and did not want to replicate it.[19] They thought that they were creating easier paths to revision.

The framers also were motivated by the self-interest of wanting to protect their handiwork. They feared that if change required unanimous consent of the states, "another convention might someday throw out the whole (as they were doing with the Articles), whereas an operable amending might leave most of the structure intact."[20] By providing two methods for proposal and two for ratification, the new constitution provided easier paths to amendment than the Articles of Confederation.

The story of how the framers adopted the amendment process at the Constitutional Convention is fascinating. The convention "took for granted the need for a mechanism to allow for future amendments to the Constitution," so debate focused on best procedures and the limitations on what amendments could accomplish.[21] The delegates agreed early in their deliberations to consider permitting the states to amend the Constitution without congressional approval.

But after agreeing to these basic premises, the framers paid little attention to designing the amendment process. Indeed, they largely ignored the amendment process, giving it the shortest amount of time for discussion of any major issue.[22] Months into the convention, at the end of July, the delegates still "were unconcerned with issues related to the process of amendment ratification."

When the amendment process finally was discussed, some argued that the process was necessary as a way of increasing the new government's stability while protecting states from potential abuse by the national legislature.[23] Massachusetts delegate Elbridge Gerry (whose name would be immortalized as the architect of gerrymandering) stated that the "novelty & difficulty of the experiment requires periodical revision. The prospect of such a revision would also give intermediate stability to the Govt."[24] Likewise, Virginia delegate George Mason said that it would be "better to provide for [amendments] in an easy, regular and Constitutional way than to trust [alterations] to chance and violence."[25] After agreeing to include an amendment process, the framers did not go back to consider a draft of provisions about it until late August, near the end of the convention. The first draft included only the option for two-thirds of the states to call a convention for proposing amendments.[26]

But some delegates believed this approach made amendments too difficult and advocated that Congress have a greater role in proposing them. For instance, Alexander Hamilton noted the great obstacles to amending the Articles of Confederation.[27] He suggested that Congress, acting on its own initiative, should have the power to call a convention to propose amendments.[28] In his view, Congress would perceive the need for amendments before the states did.[29]

Roger Sherman took Hamilton's proposal a step further, moving to authorize Congress itself to propose amendments that would become part of the Constitution upon ratification by all states.[30] James Wilson then moved to modify Sherman's proposal to require approval of three-quarters of the states for an amendment's ratification.[31] James Madison offered substitute language that permitted two-thirds of both houses of Congress to propose amendments *and* that required Congress to propose an amendment after two-thirds of the states had applied for one.[32] This language passed with nine states voting aye, one divided, and one voting no.[33]

The framers also debated whether Article V should prohibit amendments on specific subjects. Some delegates from the southern states, including John Rutledge of South Carolina, opposed allowing amendments that would limit Congress's power to restrict the importation of slaves or to levy taxes on land or slaves.[34] To preserve the compromise on the issue of slavery, the delegates added a sentence to the draft of Article V prohibiting amendments on these subjects before 1808.[35] At a later convention meeting, Roger Sherman and Gouverneur Morris proposed that no state should, without its consent, be deprived of equal suffrage in the Senate.[36] This proposal, which sought to safeguard state sovereignty and the delegates' delicate compromise on the structure of the national legislature, was agreed to without debate and appended to the end of the draft text.[37]

Finally, as the convention drew to a close, the delegates agreed to include a means for the states to propose constitutional amendments. George Mason expressed concern that as drafted, Article V would permit Congress to block constitutional amendments favored by the states.[38] Gouverneur Morris and Elbridge Gerry proposed to remedy this perceived problem by requiring Congress to call a convention of the states for proposing amendments upon the application of two-thirds of the states.[39] James Madison did not see the need for this convention mechanism.[40] He argued that Congress would be bound to propose amendments legislatively upon the request of two-thirds of the states.[41] Nevertheless, Madison did not oppose including a provision allowing for a constitutional convention.[42] The motion passed unanimously.[43]

After the convention, the state ratifying conventions, in debating the Constitution, touched briefly on the amendment process. Federalists argued that the high vote thresholds for proposal and ratification would protect the Constitution from harmful changes but leave room for amendments to deal with major flaws. In *Federalist* 43, Madison praised the draft process: "The mode preferred by the Convention seems to be stamped with every mark of propriety. It guards equally against that extreme facility, which would render the Constitution too mutable; and that extreme difficulty, which might perpetuate its discovered faults."[44] Hamilton concurred in *Federalist* 22, criticizing the old Articles' unanimity requirement to praise the proposed process.[45]

Anti-federalists who opposed ratification of the Constitution were concerned that the amendment process was too difficult. They wanted to add amendments to the document before ratification. Federalists countered that amendment was premature and that the Constitution must be given a fair trial first.[46] In *Federalist* 85, Hamilton specifically addressed the demand for amendment prior to ratification.[47] He explained that it would jeopardize the entire project of writing a new constitution to "prolong the precarious state of our national affairs, and to expose the Union to the jeopardy of successive experiments, in the chimerical pursuit of a perfect plan."[48] He found it unlikely that any document that the framers produced would be perfect or that another convention with similar conditions could occur. As a practical matter, supporters of the Constitution felt that permitting later amendments to an imperfect document would be easier than trying to satisfy all states during the drafting and ratification process. Hamilton argued that it would be better to consider one amendment at a time than to consider changes when the whole document was open to renegotiation and when each proposed alteration had to go through every state.

Anti-federalists were also concerned that the national government would try to retain its power by disallowing amendments proposed by the states.[49] In response, Hamilton emphasized that Article V allowed for two-thirds of states to call a convention and that "future amendments will likely deal with 'the organization of the government, not . . . the mass of its powers.'"[50] Hamilton's arguments were persuasive, and the states ratified the Constitution, but many expressly stated the goal of adding amendments quickly.[51] Several states wanted to fix the problems they saw through a second convention and suggested that one be called immediately. Undoubtedly, they saw this as a way of revising some of the choices that had been made that they didn't like.

But a second convention would have risked a "wholesale revision" of the Constitution by a group of delegates with the same authority as the original.[52] The idea of an immediate second convention was rejected and instead the first Congress proposed amendments, which became the Bill of Rights.

The framers wanted to strike a balance between stability for the Constitution and flexibility to allow change. They erred on the side of the former by creating high hurdles for amendments; they could not have foreseen how difficult the amendment process would be in practice. The mechanism of states calling for a constitutional convention was key to reassuring doubters that there was a path to amendment, but it has never been used.

Also quite crucially, our society's veneration of the Constitution and the widespread belief in its non-amendability became a self-fulfilling prophecy. This homage, too, can be traced back to choices made at the outset. Madison encouraged veneration of the Constitution; "he wanted Americans to revere the document because this would, in his view, generate a stable regime reinforced by a long-enduring constitutional text."[53] Early Americans celebrated those who had created the country, and myths were developed to further exalt them. George Washington never chopped down a cherry tree. Betsy Ross likely didn't sew the American flag. Over time the Constitution became, as some have called it, a "civic religion," and the populace developed a strong disposition against amendment.[54]

Can Amendments Fix the Problems?

Both in its text and its traditions, the Constitution is enormously difficult to amend. It was much easier for Ulysses to find his way home than it is for us to fix the flaws in the Constitution. The simple reality is that amendment is possible only if Americas share a widespread consensus that the change is desirable. Even when amendments are plausible, the constituency for them must care enough to do the arduous work to get approval of two-thirds of both houses of Congress and three-quarters of the states.

The Electoral College will never be abolished by constitutional amendment. The small states that benefit from it will not adopt an amendment to abolish it, and without them, there is no path to getting three-quarters of states to approve it. Also, at this time, the Electoral College is rightly seen as favoring Republicans over Democrats. Both George W. Bush in 2000 and Donald Trump in 2016 won the presidency despite losing the popular vote. The smaller, more rural states are overwhelmingly Republican, and they are not going to ratify an amendment that decreases their influence in choosing the president.

In theory, constitutional amendments could abolish the filibuster, eliminate partisan gerrymandering, impose term limits on Supreme Court justices, and overturn decisions such as *Citizens United v. Federal Election Commission*.[55] I believe that such amendments would have significant support. And perhaps the best strategy for reform would be to work for some of these changes by constitutional amendment. But we must recognize that every one of them will be a daunting challenge. It is hard to imagine two-thirds of the Senate passing an amendment to eliminate the filibuster. If eliminating the filibuster had that kind of support, the Senate already has the power to get rid of it by majority vote. Likewise, so many members of the House of Representatives benefit from partisan gerrymandering that it will be hard to get two-thirds of them to approve an amendment to end the practice, even though it is inconsistent with the most basic principles of democracy. In fact, Congress already has the power to pass legislation to eliminate partisan gerrymandering for elections to the House of Representatives under its power to regulate the time, place, and manner of these elections.

A constitutional amendment for term limits for Supreme Court justices may be the most realistic change because it has strong bipartisan support. But what constituency will care enough to do the substantial work to make a constitutional amendment happen? More fundamentally, term limits that apply to the current justices likely cannot pass because Republicans in Congress and state legislatures would not approve it. They know they have a conservative majority on the Court for a long time. Imposing prospective term limits—for justices who are yet to be appointed—seems much more realistic. The downside is that it will be a long time before they have an effect.

Many proposals have been made to amend the Constitution to overrule *Citizens United*.[56] None have gotten much traction, largely because many politicians benefit from the decision and do not want to surrender corporate campaign money. Also, the corporate interests that secure influence through their campaign spending would work very hard to block such an amendment in Congress and in the states. The presumption against amending the Constitution, and amending the First Amendment in particular, is a huge obstacle too, even though most people—both Democrats and Republicans—disagree with the Court's ruling that corporations can spend unlimited amounts of money in election campaigns.

Addressing the pervasive continuing racial inequalities also seems unlikely through the amendment process. To be sure, the Supreme Court's restrictive decisions with regard to race—striking down a key provision of the Voting Rights Act, requiring proof of racially discriminatory intent for a violation of equal protection, and eliminating affirmative action by colleges and universities—could be overcome by constitutional amendments. And there is precedent for amending the Constitution to combat racial discrimination. After the Civil War, three amendments were adopted that focused on race. The Thirteenth Amendment, which was ratified in 1865, abolished slavery and involuntary servitude. Three years later the Fourteenth Amendment was adopted, which among other things ensured that state governments could not deny equal protection of the laws. And in 1870 the Fifteenth Amendment was added to the Constitution, providing that the right to vote could not be denied on account of race or previous condition of servitude.

These amendments are vitally important, but they did not go nearly far enough. They did not outlaw racial segregation or create a duty of the government to address racial inequalities. Moreover, for far too long, little was done to realize the promise of the Fourteenth and Fifteenth Amendments. The Supreme Court did not fulfill their mandate until 1954, almost a century later, when for the first time it found a law mandating racial segregation to be unconstitutional.

No subsequent constitutional amendment in over 150 years has addressed the issue of race. This fact should not be surprising. Protection of a minority is unlikely to come from a process requiring a supermajority's actions—two-thirds of both houses of Congress and three-quarters of the states. The Republican filibuster made it tremendously difficult for Congress to pass civil rights legislation. The civil rights movement of the 1950s and '60s created the pressure that ultimately led to the passage of historic civil rights acts, and the political situation briefly changed enough to allow landmark civil rights laws to be passed in 1964 and 1965. It took the political clout of President Lyndon Johnson who brilliantly urged adoption of the Civil Rights Act as a tribute to a slain president. The Civil Rights Act of 1964 prohibits hotels and restaurants from discriminating based on race, forbids recipients of federal funds from discriminating based on race, and outlaws employment discrimination based on race, sex, or religion. The Voting Rights Act of 1965, though it has since been greatly weakened by the Supreme Court, was an enormous advance in safeguarding voting rights.

But the last major civil rights act was adopted in 1991, largely to overturn several Supreme Court decisions that had narrowly interpreted the Civil Rights Act of 1964. Many new statutes to advance civil rights have been proposed since 1991, but Congress has passed none. That speaks volumes about the difficulty of getting two-thirds of both houses of Congress and then three-quarters of the states to approve a constitutional amendment advancing racial equality.

But It Is Possible

I worry that the difficulty of the amendment process means that people don't even try. It has been a long time since amendments have been proposed to abolish the Electoral College or to overcome *Citizens United*. A self-fulfilling prophecy has developed: because amendments seem difficult, no efforts are made to propose them, and then the conclusion becomes that it is impossible to amend the Constitution.

But at other times in American history, constitutional amendments have been made with some frequency. From 1913 to 1920, the Constitution was amended four times, and from 1913 to 1933, six times. Admittedly two of those were to create and then repeal Prohibition, but others made crucial changes, including allowing for a federal income tax, providing for direct election of senators, guaranteeing women the right to vote, and moving the inauguration of the president from March 4 to January 20, to shorten the lame duck period.

My optimistic hope is that the frustration, and even despair, over American government will fuel a new effort to amend the Constitution and fix its flaws. Some changes by amendment may be unlikely, but others—such as ending partisan gerrymandering and creating term limits for Supreme Court justices—have widespread public support and could come about if people were to organize and work for them.

10

Is It Time for a New Constitution?

Every year I ask my students whether it is time to have a new constitution for the United States. Why should our country be governed by a document that was written long ago for a very different world? I ask. Overall, they are resistant to the idea of a new constitution. Those who grew up in the United States have been instilled with reverence for the constitution ever since primary school. When they speak about James Madison and Alexander Hamilton, they do so with such awe that they almost seem to believe that the framers were divinely inspired and that our current generation could not possibly do as well. But some of the skepticism about a new constitution arises from fear of what might replace it. They easily see the flaws in the current Constitution, but they understandably worry that a new constitution would lose what works in the current document and that it would create a governing structure that could be much worse. They understandably fear that their political foes would capture the process and create a new document that embodies values they loathe.

I share their fears, but the time will come when Americans will realize that the Constitution itself is endangering democracy and they will start thinking of replacing it. No constitution lasts forever. Someday the United States will be governed by a different Constitution, hopefully one better than the current one. With trepidation, I think the time to start that conversation is now, knowing that the process will likely take many years to come to fruition. Rather than pursue several individual amendments to fix what is broken in the current Constitution, it might be better to start over and adopt a new constitution.

I understand the skepticism that will greet this suggestion. If the other reforms are unlikely to come about, readers will ask, isn't drafting a new constitution even less plausible? If states won't ratify amendments to fix the Constitution, why believe they would adopt a new one? And does it make sense to contemplate drafting and adopting a new constitution when our country is so deeply divided?

All these questions are crucial. Creating a new constitution will be a daunting task, but I want to argue that it is possible if there is a serious effort to make it happen. Actually, it might be easier to adopt a new constitution than to pass several separate amendments. At its best, the process of drafting a new constitution might engage the country and produce an impetus for change. Most of all, I want to suggest that it is time to begin thinking and talking about it.

What Would Have to Happen for the Country to Consider a New Constitution?

First, the American people would have to recognize that our current Constitution is failing. Opinion polls show a dramatic loss of faith in American democracy and government on both the left and the right. Americans must see that these failures stem from the Constitution itself. Eventually, this recognition might lead to a sufficient consensus to make a new constitution realistic, but it will take sustained advocacy. The basic question for the American people will be whether it makes sense for them to continue to be governed by a document written in 1787 for an agrarian slave society.

Ironically, the Supreme Court's increasing embrace of originalism helps explain the rationale for a new constitution. In 2022, in *New York State Rifle and Pistol Association v. Bruen*,[1] the Supreme Court held that the Second Amendment prohibits gun regulations except for the types that existed in 1791 or maybe 1868. Since then, lower courts have struck down a federal law prohibiting those who are under a restraining order from having guns,[2] a federal law prohibiting the sale or possession of guns without serial numbers,[3] and prohibitions of semi-assault weapons that are used in mass shootings.[4] The courts have said these types of regulations are impermissible because they did not exist in 1791 when the Second Amendment was ratified. Of course, in 1791, there was also virtually no protection of women against domestic violence, ghost guns didn't exist, and there was no such thing as an AR-15. Opinion polls show that most people reject the Court's rigid limits on needed gun regulations. The more the Supreme Court limits the Constitution to what was thought in 1787 or 1791 or 1868, the more people will realize that we need a new constitution for the world we live in today.

Second, pursuant to Article V of the Constitution, states can call for a constitutional convention that Congress must convene. This procedure has never been used, but as described earlier in this chapter, the Constitution explicitly provides for it. Alternatively, Congress can call a constitutional convention on its own, as it did in 1787. That history is instructive as to how a constitutional convention can be held.

A crucial question will be how representatives are allocated and chosen. The temptation will be to follow the experience of 1787 and allow each state to send a delegation. But I think that would be a huge mistake. It would, as it did in 1787, encourage delegates to think of themselves as representing their states' interests. Indeed, many of the flaws in the document came from exactly that state orientation: Southern delegates fought to protect slavery, delegates from small states wanted a Senate with equal representation, and state legislatures chose senators. If representation at a constitutional convention were allocated to the states, the new constitution would likely replicate some of the worst features of the existing document, such as keeping the Electoral College and equal state representation in the Senate.

What would be the alternative? I suggest that in calling a constitutional convention, Congress specify that the president will appoint its delegates, with an equal number of Democrats and Republicans. Or perhaps several individuals—the president, the Speaker of the House, and the majority leader of the Senate—could all appoint delegates. It even is possible to imagine electing delegates to the Constitutional Convention. There is no magic number but I suggest fifty-five, the number of delegates in 1787. Using that number offers a tie to the past. It is small enough to be workable and large enough to allow diversity. Its mandate should be to propose a new constitution within two years. Any deadline would be arbitrary, but the time allocated should be long enough to allow for careful deliberation, but not so long that it stretches on and on. The new framers will have to make very difficult choices, and at some point they will have to make decisions.

The mandate and the focus of a new constitutional convention should be on making the American government more democratic. We can keep much in the current Constitution, although the provisions on slavery should obviously be deleted. Many aspects of the Constitution have worked well, including the basic framework for the separation of powers and the protection of many rights. We should continue to have a legislature, an executive, and a judiciary. We should replicate many of the rights found in the constitution's amendments. We should fill in gaps, such as the current Constitution's failure to grant express authority for judicial review and its failure to mention a right to privacy. But above all, the convention's focus should be on curing the flaws in the current Constitution that threaten American democracy.

Once the document is drafted, the ratification process will begin. Here my proposal is more radical: we should conduct a national popular vote, as other countries have done, on whether to approve the new document. Leaving approval to the states would limit the opportunities for reform. States that benefit from the Electoral College and from equal representation in the Senate would never ratify a document that decreases their political power, however fair and worthy it would be to do so. The Constitution, which exalts states' rights, will not be changed by states that benefit from it.

The current Constitution provides no mechanism for a national popular vote. Article V says that changes in the Constitution require the approval of three-quarters of the states. I am proposing—and I believe it is essential—that ratification be carried out by the people in a national referendum, not by the state governments. There is precedent for revising or replacing the Constitution without following the procedures for change that it specifies. The Articles of Confederation, which preceded the Constitution, required unanimous consent of the states for change, but the Constitution, in Article VII, said it could be adopted if three-quarters of the states approved it.[5] The new constitution should provide that it will be adopted if a majority of the voters in the United States approve it.

Lest this proposal seem far-fetched, the Yale law professor Akhil Amar has powerfully argued that the Constitution should be read to grant the people an unenumerated right to amend it.[6] A simple majority of the American electorate, he contends, could amend the Constitution through something like a national referendum. He bases his argument primarily on the language of Article V itself. In his view, Article V enumerates the only modes by which the government can change the Constitution, but it does not otherwise hinder the people's right to amend the Constitution. Harvard law professor Richard Fallon has argued that the American people have a moral right to amend the Constitution without following the procedures prescribed in Article V.[7]

Ultimately, we must remember that the current Constitution was adopted without complying with the Articles of Confederation. Therefore adopting a new constitution does not necessitate complying with the existing document.

Readers may react instinctively that attempting to replace the Constitution is unthinkable at a time when the country is so profoundly polarized. But the country was polarized in 1787 as well. New York ratified the Constitution by three votes, 30–27.[8] Virginia ratified it by ten votes, 89–79.[9] Rhode Island, the last state to ratify the Constitution, passed it by just two votes.[10] Waiting for a time when the country is not ideologically divided would mean never engaging in essential reform.

I recognize that the new constitution, like the existing one, will require compromises on most major issues. Perhaps it will turn out to be impossible to abolish the Electoral College and two senators per state and so make a meaningful difference in advancing equality. But we must try.

The danger exists that the new constitution could be worse than the existing one. Liberals surely fear a document that enshrines the current conservative agenda, while conservatives obviously fear the reverse. How will the constitutional convention deal with the most divisive issues, like abortion and gun rights? Both sides of the divide on these issues will try to have the document embody its views. Both sides also know that their work will be for naught unless the document can be passed by the convention and ultimately ratified by the people. That will be a tremendous force to keep it from going too far in either ideological direction. The need for popular ratification will be the ultimate check. It is hard to imagine the American people ratifying a new constitution that was extreme in either political direction.

We have reason to believe, or at least to hope, that the new framers will rise to the occasion, as did those who gathered in Philadelphia in 1787. They surely will understand the stakes and their potential role in history. They have a chance to draft the document that will govern the country for decades and maybe centuries to come. They will all know that they have the potential to be the next James Madisons and Alexander Hamiltons.

The drafting of a new constitution might fail. Or the voters might reject it. Or they might ratify a document that is worse than the current one. But if one begins, as I do, with the premise that the current Constitution is leading us down a path to destruction, then we have a strong impetus to begin a conversation about drafting a new one.

Ultimately, at some point, the American people will realize that the age of the U.S. Constitution is a liability, not a strength. The world of 1787 is too different from the world of the twenty-first century for us to continue to be governed by a document written so very long ago. It is time to begin contemplating, discussing, and ultimately drafting a new constitution.

11

If Nothing Changes, Can and Should the *United* States Survive?

The Ominous Shadow of Secession

What if nothing changes and the problems with American democracy become worse? What if the low public confidence in the government sinks further, the federal government becomes even less effective, and political polarization grows much greater? I predict that Americans will seriously talk about whether the United States should stay together as one country. Talk of secession is now a murmur, but it will become louder and more insistent. I do not know when that moment will be, but we all know that no democracy lasts forever, and there will be a point where ours is seriously questioned.

Indeed, if a conservative Republican is elected president with Republicans in control of both houses of Congress, I have no doubt that states like California will see serious talk of secession. Likewise, a liberal Democratic president and Democrats in control of both houses Congress will fuel talk of secession in places like Texas. Sharp ideological disagreements among the states have always existed. For the first seventy-five years of American history, they clashed over slavery, which ultimately led to the Civil War. In the twentieth century, Americans vehemently disagreed over the civil rights movement. But the current gulf between the blue states and the red states is enormous, toxic, and growing.

To be clear, I am not advocating secession. Quite the contrary, my strong sense is that it would be an enormously painful process that would make us worse off. And we need to exercise great care even in using the word. Our immediate image of secession is of a violent event, leading to civil war. But to think separation can be achieved only through violence is a mistake. Other countries have seen voluntary separations. And it is crucial to remember that secession need not mean splitting the United States into two or more countries. It could, for example, entail a significant devolution of power to the states, except as to military matters and foreign affairs, where a national government would remain. That kind of secession could be much more like creating the European Union than the Civil War.

But if the country continues on the current path, the question will and should be raised: is what unites us as a country still greater than what divides us? The most conservative red states and most liberal blue states fundamentally disagree over values. It will become important to think about whether it makes sense for the country to remain the *United* States in the way that it has for over two centuries.

Lest it seem misguided to even talk about this subject, a 2021 poll administered by the University of Virginia Center for Politics found that four out of ten (41 percent) of Biden voters and half (52 percent) of Trump voters "somewhat agree" it would be best to split the country by red and blue states.[1] Some form of secession is in people's minds, and it will not go away unless dramatic changes are made in American government. We must confront the issue.

We must consider, first, whether the Constitution allows for secession; what lessons we can learn from foreign countries; and what secession might mean. Only then should we consider whether it is worth talking about at all.

Does the Constitution Allow for Secession?

The Constitution says absolutely nothing about states choosing to opt out of the United States. It neither prohibits secession nor creates a mechanism for it. Perhaps this omission was an oversight, as those in Philadelphia were focused on devising a blueprint for government. The framers did not foresee the need to specify mechanisms for states that had ratified the Constitution to change their minds and opt out. Perhaps this was a deliberate choice, though not articulated. The new union was going to be fragile at best. Ratification was uncertain, and the states disagreed deeply over every major issue. In these circumstances, the framers might have thought it best to say nothing about how the union that they were creating could be dissolved.

Secession was occasionally mentioned in the state ratifying debates, but those discussions offer no clear conclusions. As my colleague Berkeley law professor Dan Farber notes, the scattered statements made there about the impermanence of the union "are hard to interpret. They might have referred to a legal right to revoke ratification. But they equally could have referred to an extraconstitutional right of revolution, or to the possibility that a new national convention would rewrite the Constitution, or simply to the factual possibility that the national government might break down."[2] Those drafting and ratifying the Constitution were in the process of replacing one government with another. They followed no blueprint but created their own. They could easily have imagined that the time might come to replace the Constitution that they were creating.

The Constitution does not prohibit states from seceding. If the framers meant to forbid it, they could have said so. They imposed other limits on state government power. For example, Article I, Section 10 forbids states to enter into treaties or coin money or interfere with the obligation of contracts. The framers could have expressly prohibited states from seceding. Or they might have added a prohibition of secession to Article VII, which specifies how the Constitution would be deemed ratified.

In the 1850s, when the constitutionality of secession was raised, the federal government initially said that there was no constitutional limit on it. Harvard law professor Noah Feldman explains that "James Buchanan's administration has produced a report stating bluntly that the federal government had no constitutional authority to act if the states seceded. Nothing in the Constitution authorized war to save the union."[3]

The eleven states that seceded in 1861 precipitated, by their action, the Civil War. President Lincoln labeled it a "rebellion" and used military force to stop it. He declared the secession unlawful and waged war against the states that had formed a new country. But that choice does not resolve the underlying constitutional issue. In fact, Feldman powerfully argues that President Lincoln lacked the authority to do this under the Constitution and that he "broke" the Constitution to save the union.

The Supreme Court had no occasion to consider the constitutionality of secession until after the Civil War. In 1869 in *Texas v. White*, the Court opined on the constitutionality of the secession that had occurred.[4] The case is always cited to support the proposition that secession is unconstitutional, but actually the decision is more equivocal than that and indeed actually recognizes the permissibility of secession under the Constitution.

In that case, the Reconstruction government of Texas sued the Confederate Texas state legislature, claiming that it had illegally sold U.S. bonds during the Civil War. The Supreme Court, in an opinion by Chief Justice Salmon Chase, ruled that Texas remained a state within the United States from the time it joined the country in 1845, despite its joining the Confederate States of America and despite it being under military rule at the time of the litigation before the Supreme Court. The Court said that legally no state actually had seceded from the union despite their declarations of doing so.

Salmon Chase was a major figure in mid-nineteenth century American politics. He was a leading advocate for the abolition of slavery, forming anti-slavery societies and representing fugitive slaves in the courts. He had been governor of Ohio, then a senator, and he ran for the Republican presidential nomination in 1860. After being defeated by Abraham Lincoln, Chase became secretary of the treasury in Lincoln's cabinet.[5] He was part of what Doris Kearns Goodwin called Lincoln's "team of rivals"—one of Lincoln's adversaries who was part of his cabinet.[6] Chase succeeded brilliantly in that role, raising billions of dollars that were crucial to the Union victory in the Civil War.

In 1864 Lincoln named Chase to be the chief justice of the United States. In that role, he famously presided in 1868 over the Senate trial of President Andrew Johnson following his impeachment by the House of Representatives. Although Chase served as chief justice until his death in 1873, he never gave up his hope of becoming president.

He unsuccessfully sought the Democratic presidential nomination in 1868 and the Liberal Republican nomination in 1872.

It was no surprise then, given his background and politics, that Chief Justice Chase, writing for the Court in *Texas v. White*, ruled that states had no right to secede from the country. He was a Northerner and part of the Lincoln administration that had waged the war to save the Union. His opinion echoed Lincoln's view that secession was unlawful and the Southern states had never actually left the Union. In his majority opinion, Chase declared that the "Constitution, in all its provisions, looks to an indestructible Union, composed of indestructible States."[7] What was the basis for his conclusion that secession is not allowed? The only authority Chase invoked was the Preamble, which states, he said, that "the Constitution was ordained 'to form a more perfect Union.' It is difficult to convey the idea of indissoluble unity more clearly than by these words. What can be indissoluble if a perpetual Union, made more perfect, is not?"[8]

But that is a slender basis for concluding that secession is unconstitutional. The Preamble's important and majestic language says and implies nothing about secession. It stretches beyond credulity to say that the Preamble's commitment to a more perfect union implicitly prohibits states from seceding. A couple's promise to marry and pledge to spend a life together doesn't foreclose that things later can go sour and they might divorce.

More important, in an often-overlooked passage in his *Texas v. White* opinion, Chase actually acknowledged that secession was permissible under the Constitution. The Court declared: "The union between Texas and the other States was as complete, as perpetual, and as indissoluble as the union between the original States. There was no place for reconsideration, or revocation, except through revolution, or *through consent of the States*" (emphasis added).[9] So the very decision that is said to make secession impermissible explicitly says that it is allowed with "consent of the states." In other words, the Supreme Court's only precedent considering the constitutionality of secession would allow, in some form, a voluntary dissolution.[10] Even Salmon Chase, a leading foe of secession, recognized its permissibility.

Nonetheless, whenever the topic of secession is mentioned, legal scholars respond that *Texas v. White* makes it unconstitutional. In the early 2000s, the Alaskan Independence Party sought to put an initiative on the ballot in Alaska proposing that the state secede from the United States.[11] It obtained the requisite number of signatures to go before the voters, but the elections authority rejected the initiative as seeking an unconstitutional action. The Alaska Supreme Court agreed and concluded that "secession from the Union is clearly unconstitutional."[12]

But based on the text of the Constitution or the discussions during its drafting, that conclusion is impossible to justify. And the precedent of *Texas v. White* is questionable at best. We may want to believe that secession is unconstitutional, but nothing in the Constitution or its history supports that conclusion.

What Can We Learn from Foreign Countries?

In all historical truth, the United States came into existence by *seceding* from England. The secession was obviously violent, during the Revolutionary War. If there is to be a secession in the twenty-first-century United States—and again, it will be important to think carefully about what that means—I am sure that all desire and deeply hope that it would be nonviolent. In other countries, secessions have occurred peacefully and by mutual agreement. Any discussion of secession should bear this in mind to counter the image that our only path would be an unthinkable civil war.

Perhaps the most notable successful nonviolent secession in recent history was the dissolution of Czechoslovakia into the Czech Republic and Slovakia. Since 1990 there have been at least three secessions of the same kind: Macedonia from the Socialist Federal Republic of Yugoslavia (SFRY) in 1991, and Estonia and Latvia from the USSR in 1991.[13]

The dissolution of Czechoslovakia into the Czech Republic and Slovakia is commonly referred to as the "Velvet Divorce" for its relatively smooth and peaceful sequence of events.[14] On November 17, 1989, eight days after the fall of the Berlin Wall, student protesters filled the streets of Prague. Police tried to beat them back, but the show of force only galvanized the resistance, as citizens of all ages joined the demonstrations.[15] Many remembered the events of 1968, when Soviet tanks quashed Czechoslovakia's hopes for independence. On November 20, 1989, a half-million Czechs and Slovaks filled the streets and took over Wenceslas Square.[16] The Communist government did not use force to retain power, and by the end of 1989, Czechoslovakia had an elected president for the first time since 1948.[17]

The post-1989 transition to a free market economy "led to significantly higher unemployment and a sharper decline in average living standards in Slovakia than in the Czech federal unit."[18] From 1990 to 1992, the division between the Slovak and Czech populations in Slovakia grew over the economy and nationalist concerns of visibility. Developments in the federalist structure of government aided this division.[19] Separate government ministers and cabinets were created for the two large populations, Czech and Slovak. In August 1992 Czech and Slovak negotiators set up the legal framework for the dissolution of the federation, which consisted of a series of separate agreements on the division of assets and on post-dissolution relations between the two republics and a law on the termination of the federation.[20]

The union was dissolved in 1992 by mutual consent of the ruling political elites but without the direct participation of the people in either the Czech Republic or Slovakia.[21] Public opinion polls conducted at the time indicated that the percentage of those wanting a split did not exceed 50 percent in either republic.[22] For instance, in Slovakia, a poll in late 1990 indicated that only 16 percent of the population favored secession.[23] No national referendum on the breakup took place.[24]

Crucial to the breakup was the neat dividing line between the two groups, their "clear, undisputed frontiers."[25] The existence of historical borders meant that there was "no fight for furniture."[26] Also, the Czech Republic and Slovakia are ethnically different and geographically compact: 81 percent of Czech Republic territory consists of Czech people and 86 percent of the Slovak territory consists of Slovaks.[27] Only 3 percent of the Czech population claimed to be of Slovak nationality, while Czech people made up only 1 percent of Slovakia.[28] This made a split-up of Czechoslovakia both easier and much more likely.

International recognition of the Czech Republic and Slovakia came after the central governments had agreed to the dissolution of their union.[29] Now both the Czech Republic and Slovakia are members of NATO and the European Union.

In an earlier example of peaceful secession, Norway broke away from Sweden in 1905. Unlike the movements for independence of the Czech Republic and Slovakia, and of Estonia, Latvia, and Macedonia, the division of Norway from Sweden was not precipitated by a fallen power. In 1814, the Danish crown had ceded Norway to Sweden. Sweden preserved the separate state and constitutional identity of Norway and gave it legislative autonomy.[30] But historically, relations between Norway and Sweden had always been tense. Through the latter half of the 1800s, Norway underwent a cultural renaissance that spurred a national revival of its unique history, language, folklore, art, and literature. As Norwegian national identity grew, so did public support for separation from Sweden.

By 1903 in Norway, there was no public opposition to a separation from Sweden.[31] By March 1905, the Norwegian government had the support of all the parties in the Swedish parliament and of all social strata in Norway for its proposed secession.[32] At first the Swedish government refused to recognize the unilateral act of secession, but ultimately it agreed to negotiate a secession, if a plebiscite were held in Norway and a majority supported secession.[33] The separation was finalized in the Karlsbad Agreement of 1905, and the major European powers subsequently recognized Norway as a separate country.[34]

Crucially, Norwegian public opinion and the political parties uniformly supported this act of unilateral secession.[35] The Swedish response, however, was not united. Some parliamentarians supported military action, and people demonstrated in support of the Swedish monarch in Stockholm, while the left-wing parties refused to condemn the secession.[36] But the secession was peaceful and is now over one hundred years old.

Other parts of the world have seen ongoing, long-standing secessionist movements: Quebec from Canada, Catalonia and Basque Country from Spain, and Scotland from the UK. There have been episodes of violence, particularly in the efforts at Basque secession. It is unclear whether the secessionists in these places will succeed. These movements have been characterized by ongoing "negotiations and concessions" along with demonstrations and referenda calling for independence.[37] But the calls for secession have been strongly resisted and are deeply divisive within these countries.

The history of other countries shows that peaceful secession is possible. In the United States, the memory of the Civil War causes us mistakenly to think that violence is the only path. An amicable, mutually agreed separation of states might someday be possible in the United States. But again, I don't want to be naïve. Secession efforts likely will be strongly opposed, and it is at best uncertain whether the divorce would be amicable or violent.

What Might Secession Mean?

Secession in the United States could take many different forms. It could mean one or more states separating from the United States. Some Texans and some Californians have talked of seceding, though from different ends of the political spectrum.

For more than a decade, the Texit movement has pushed for Texas to exit the Union and gain complete autonomy. Following the 2020 election, Texas Republican Party chairman Allen West proposed that Texas and other like-minded states leave the United States and form their own nation.[38] More recently, the Texas Republican platform has encouraged the legislature to allow Texans to vote on whether the state should secede from the United States. *The Platform and Resolutions Committee Report* section entitled "State Sovereignty" reads: "Pursuant to Article 1, Section 1, of the Texas Constitution, the federal government has impaired our right of local self-government. . . . Texas retains the right to secede from the United States, and the Texas Legislature should be called upon to pass a referendum consistent thereto."[39]

The CalExit movement, in turn, supports the idea of California leaving the United States. Setting aside for a moment the legal and political hurdles, California likely has the economic and natural resources to separate from the rest of the country. It has the world's sixth-largest economy and has a population that would put it thirty-sixth on the United Nations' list of countries.[40] Several organizations are advocating consideration of CalExit.

But secession need not mean a single state acting unilaterally. A peaceful divorce, by mutual agreement, might come about where two or more countries would emerge. The West Coast states—California, Hawaii, Washington, and Oregon—might form a nation that some have suggested could be called Pacifica. The blue states on the East Coast, and even Illinois in the Midwest, might join them. At first glance a country with noncontiguous states seems odd, but it is possible. Alaska and Hawaii are part of the United States even though they are not contiguous to the other forty-eight states. The red states in the South and Midwest might likewise come together as a separate country. By mutual consent, the separate countries could agree to allow free migration and to protect free trade between them.

Such a separation seems overwhelmingly difficult and likely would receive serious consideration only if the current political polarization and divide becomes far worse than it is now. But other paths to secession might be more plausible as well as more desirable. The possibility of the country coming apart raises the issues of the military and foreign policy. Dividing the military seems impossible, and the United States' role in the world, especially relative to superpowers like Russia and China, would likely be greatly weakened. It is easy to imagine those other powers stepping into the void in a way that almost all Americans would find very undesirable.

But these concerns could lead to consideration of a different form of secession: keep the United States and the federal government especially for the military and for foreign policy, but in other areas radically devolve power to the states. The states might form regional compacts or act independently for what they govern. Each region or state would have authority to decide for itself the meaning of the Constitution in its area. It might be a new constitution, created as described in the prior chapter, or it might be the existing Constitution. If California wanted to interpret the Constitution to protect abortion rights, to allow regulation of campaign finance, and to reject a right of individuals to have firearms, it could do so. But Texas could do just the opposite.

The practical challenges would be enormous. What powers would be left to Congress? When would the Supreme Court be able to act for the entire country? What would happen with federal programs like Medicare and Social Security? What about the reality that far more wealth exists in blue states than in red ones? What about the assets of the federal government that are located in the states, like military bases and national parks? What would be the impact on the economy of the world's richest country, and what would be the reverberations throughout the world? I do not minimize the daunting realities. But if we are going to talk about secession, it seems much better focused on this approach: keep the national government for the military and foreign policy and leave as much else as possible to the states. Dramatically reducing the size and scope of the federal government and returning much more governance to the states might, for different reasons, resonate with liberals and conservatives if ever there were serious calls for secession.

But were this type of secession to happen, liberals would have difficulty accepting what they regard as the repressive policies of the conservative states, and likewise those in red states would have difficulty accepting what they see as the misguided policies of progressive states. But that already is true, on issues of abortion, gay and lesbian and transgender rights, guns, and so many others.

The United States under this form of secession, with a limited national government and far more choices left to the states, would be quite different from the country since 1787. But it is not totally unfamiliar: it was the approach of the Articles of Confederation. The failure of that structure must be a cautionary tale. But the world was radically different then, especially in terms of communications and travel. Also, if ever the country were to go in that direction, important lessons can be learned from that failure. A major problem with the Articles, for example, was that states adopted protectionist laws and put up barriers to interstate commerce. The new countries or a new constitution could address that issue directly and agree on a solution. The European Union, which has not been without difficulties, can be a model for separate nations effectively functioning together. What if the United States remained in existence but operated under a structure much more like that of the European Union?

The European Union is an economic union of twenty-seven member states. It has a total population of 447 million people, significantly more than reside in the United States. It has the third-largest economy in the world, after the United States and China. It works by protecting the autonomy of nations, while as a confederation it protects free trade among them.

Is It Worth Talking About?

In the spring of 2023, I attended a scholarly conference at Columbia Law School where I suggested that it was possible to imagine serious talk of secession in our country. I was clear, as I have been in this chapter, that I was not advocating secession. I was just indicating that the country's current path might be leading there and that enough people are thinking about it that it should be part of discussions. The reaction was strong and disapproving. Even mentioning secession was denounced and declared "ridiculous." When I later described this reaction to my wife, her response was "Are any of them from California?"

I am not arguing in favor of secession or of developing a blueprint for how it might happen. But opinion polls, as we have seen, show that it is on many people's minds. Our deep ideological polarization is growing. Ignoring what is in people's minds does not make it go away. And I fear increasingly what unites us in this country will be outweighed by what divides us.

Nor should this question be off the table. States must have a better reason than inertia to remain in the United States. If someday the country carefully considers secession and then rejects it, that will be a powerful affirmation of the Union.

Discussing secession may have another, less obvious virtue. Even if people recoil, it could force us to pay serious attention to the types of changes that are needed to save the country. If the alternative of secession is considered intolerable, then adopting legislation, enacting constitutional amendments, and even drafting a new constitution may all seem more plausible and even realistic.

Coda

Change Can Happen

Our government is broken and our democracy is at grave risk, but I don't see any easy solutions. A book that describes problems ideally should offer realistic fixes, but none are apparent. I have tried to outline possible solutions, but the likelihood that any of them will be adopted right now seems dubious. I desperately want to be wrong, either about my premise (that American democracy faces a serious crisis), or my conclusion (that fixing the problems will be hugely difficult or even impossible). I want to feel and express optimism that our country's problems aren't so serious or that we can find a way to solve them. If nothing else, I hope that this book will challenge those who disagree with my premises to show that they are wrong. Even as we face the urgent and existential problem of climate change, the ability of our government to deal with it seems limited.

The past offers hope that change can happen. The United States has been through enormously difficult and divisive times before: a civil war, a great depression. A country that was founded to protect slavery, that lived through Jim Crow, and that is haunted by great racial inequalities still has deep disagreements over race, but we have made racial progress. The McCarthy era was a time of terrible political repression that thankfully has not been repeated. Rarely have Americans agreed on the nation's problems or their solutions, but still our country has prospered and overall succeeded.

Over the course of American history, our country has made great advances toward equality and freedom. I have seen that in my life-time. I was born in 1953, when state-mandated apartheid required separation of the races in much of the country. We have a long way to go to solve racial inequalities, but no one can deny the advances in civil rights in the last seventy years. Not that long ago, the idea that gay and lesbian individuals had a constitutional right to marry was unthinkable. Rights, like freedom of speech, are more secure and developed now than they have been at any point in American history, though other rights, like abortion and privacy more generally, are under assault.

The late Dr. Martin Luther King, Jr., was surely right when he declared, "The arc of the moral universe is long and it bends towards justice."

But we can achieve justice only if we acknowledge the difficult problems with our government and begin working toward solutions, as daunting as they inevitably will be to achieve. We must start by ending our veneration of the Constitution and acknowledging its deep flaws. We must recognize the serious threat to American democracy and understand that many of its problems can be traced to choices made in 1787 in drafting the Constitution. And we must begin to think about how to fix those defects, however difficult that task.

If I am wrong and the current crisis of democracy wanes—if consensus develops around major issues, if the toxic partisan divide lessens, if government becomes more effective, and if public confidence in it grows—then the country can put off facing the Constitution's flaws for years to come. But if my fears are justified, then it will be imperative to figure out how to fix the Constitution and save democracy.

The solutions will not come this year or next. But they will never come at all unless we start now, acknowledge the problems, and consider answers. That is why I wrote this book.

ACKNOWLEDGMENTS

This book was very difficult to write. I believe every word, but it is uncomfortable to write a book that I want to be wrong. I want to be wrong in my sense that American democracy is in crisis and that solutions are elusive. Many times along the way, I thought of abandoning the project because I don't have answers. But in the end, I think it is important to face where we are as a country, to discuss the problems, and to consider possible solutions.

I am enormously grateful to the many people who made this book possible. First and foremost, I want to thank my terrific editor, Bob Weil. He helped me formulate the thesis for the book, offered superb suggestions and criticisms, and was tremendously patient as I struggled to write and finish it. He is every author's dream editor, and I am fortunate to get to work with him.

My literary agent, Bonnie Nadell, was wonderful as always in working out all the details to make the book happen. We have worked together for over a decade now on many projects, and I hope there will be many more to come.

My work on this book, and everything else I accomplish, is made possible by my amazing executive assistant, Whitney Mello.

Several friends read parts of the manuscript including Joan Biskupic, Barry Friedman, Howard Gillman, Jon Gould, and Burt Neuborne. They all took time from their very busy schedules to offer terrific comments. Their suggestions were invaluable, and the book would have been better if I'd followed more of them. The errors, of course, are mine alone. I benefited greatly from a faculty workshop at Berkeley Law, and I presented some of Part I as the Cutler Lecture at William and Mary Law School, where I received great suggestions.

I was helped tremendously by a very talented group of research assistants: Margarita Akopyan, Nicole Antonuccio, Jordan Barton, Cameron Brown, Bailey Bryant, Danhong Cao, Josh Cayetano, Haleigh Cotton, Evan Jester, Allison Klei, Hunter Kolon, Benji Martinez, Lawrence Myung, and Russell Wirth.

Everything I do is enriched, more than words can express, by my wonderful family: Jeff, Kim, Andrew, Sarah, Amy, Adam, Katherine, Alex, and Mara.

I have dedicated this book to my wife, Catherine Fisk. She talked out with me every aspect of the book. She encouraged me to keep going when I had doubts. Most important, she fills every day with love and joy.

NOTES

Chapter 1: There Is a Crisis

1   Yascha Mounk and Roberto Stefan Foa, *This is How Democracy Dies*, Atlantic (January 29, 2020); Roberto Foa and Yascha Mounk, *Across the Globe, a Growing Disillusionment with Democracy*, New York Times (September 15, 2015); Robert D. Putnam et al., *Introduction: What's Troubling the Trilateral Democracies, in* Disaffected Democracies: What's Troubling the Trilateral Countries 6–7 (Susan J. Pharr and Robert D. Putnam eds., 2018) (drawing a "distinction between the effectiveness of specific democratic governments and the durability of democratic institutions per se," and finding that "earlier alarm about the stability of democracy itself . . . exaggerated"); *Public Trust in Government: 1958–2022*, Pew Research Center (June 6, 2022).

2   David Lauter, *Will Two Voter Groups Change American Politics*, Los Angeles Times (September 25, 2023), at 2.

3   Jason Lange, *Biden Approval Rises to 40 Percent, Highest in Two Months, Reuters/Ipsos Shows*, Reuters (August 9, 2022).

4   Lydia Saad, *Biden Job Approval Not Budging, U.S. Satisfaction Dips*, Gallup (June 22, 2022).

5   Jeffrey M. Jones, *Confidence in U.S. Supreme Court Sinks to Historic Low*, Gallup (June 23, 2022), https://news.gallup.com/poll/394103/confidence-supreme-court-sinks-historic-low.aspx.

6   Charles Franklin, *New Marquette Law School Poll National Survey Finds Approval of Supreme Court at New Lows, with Strong Partisan Differences over Abortion and Gun Rights*, Marquette University Law School Poll (July 20, 2022).

7   Amina Dunn, *Trump's Approval Ratings So Far Are Unusually Stable—And Deeply Partisan*, Pew Research Center (August 24, 2020).

8   Scott Powers, *Poll Finds Huge Democratic, Republican Divides on Pandemic, Corruption, Race, Debt*, Florida Politics (January 14, 2022).

9   Varieties of Democracy Institute (V-Dem), Autocratization Surges—Resistance Grows. Democracy Report 2020 (March 2020).

10 Economist Intelligence Unit, Democracy Index 2016 — Revenge of the "Deplorables" (2016).

11 Thomas Grey, The Constitution as Scripture 1, 3 (1984); *see also* Sanford Levinson, Constitutional Faith (1988); Max Lerner, *Constitution and Court as Symbols*, 46 Yale L. J. 1290, 1296 (1937).

12 4 Stat. 411 (law authorizing the president to exchange lands with the Indians residing in any of the states or territories and for their removal west of the Mississippi River).

13 *See* Cohen's Handbook on Indian Law § 1.03; *see generally* Francis Paul Prucha, The Great Father: The United States Government and the American Indians 179–269 (1984) (summarizing Indian removal).

14 Civil Rights Cases, 109 U.S. 3 (1883).

15 Hammer v. Dagenhart (the Child Labor Cases), 247 U.S. 251 (1918).

16 Printz v. United States, 521 U.S. 898 (1997).

17 U.S. Census Data, Resident Population for the 50 States, the District of Columbia, and Puerto Rico (2020).

18 Danielle Kurtzleben, *How to Win the Presidency with 23 Percent of the Popular Vote*, NPR (November 2, 2016).

19 Mara Liasson, *Democrats Increasingly Say American Democracy Is Sliding Toward Minority Rule*, NPR (June 9, 2021).

20 Rucho v. Common Cause 139 S.Ct. 2484 (2019).

21 James Madison, *Federalist Papers No. 39* (1776).

22 Vieth v. Jubelirer, 541 U.S. 267, 292 (2004).

23 Rucho v. Common Cause 139 S.Ct. 2484 (2019).

24 Shelby County, Ala. v. Holder, 570 U.S. 529 (2013).

25 558 U.S. 310 (2010).

26 John Creamer, *Inequalities Persist Despite Decline in Poverty for All Major Race and Hispanic Origin Groups*, U.S. Census Bureau (September 15, 2020).

27 Erwin Chemerinsky, We the People: A Progressive Reading of the Constitution for the Twenty-First Century 202 (2018).

28 Juliana Menasce Horowitz, Ruth Igielnik, and Rakesh Kochhar, *1. Trends in Income and Wealth Inequality*, Pew Research Institute (January 9, 2020).

29 Anshu Siripurapu, *The U.S. Inequality Debate*, Council on Foreign Relations (April 20, 2022).

30 Steven Levitsky and Daniel Ziblatt, How Democracies Die 227–230 (2017).

31 Andrew Marantz, *Does Hungary Offer a Glimpse of Our Authoritarian Future?* New Yorker (June 27, 2022).

32 Jennifer Rubin, *Opinion: The Truth About Many in the GOP Base: They Prefer Authoritarianism to Democracy*, Washington Post (June 29, 2021).

33 U. S. Global Change Research Program, Fourth National Climate Assessment, vol. 1, p. 10 (2017); Brief for Climate Scientists as *Amici Curiae* 8, in West Virginia v. Environmental Protection Agency, 142 S.Ct. 2587 (2022).

Chapter 2: The 1960s

1 Robert N. Clinton, *A Brief History of the Adoption of the United States Constitution,* 75 Iowa L. Rev. 891, 893 (1990).

2 *How Things Have Changed in Philadelphia Since the 1787 Convention,* National Constitution Center (May 25, 2016).

3 1 Max Farrand, The Records of the Federal Convention of 1787 30 (1911).

4 *Meet the Framers of the Constitution,* National Archives, https://www.archives .gov/founding-docs/founding-fathers/.

5 *Creating the United States: Road to the Constitution,* Library of Congress, https:// www.loc.gov/exhibits/creating-the-united-states/road-to-the-constitution .html/.

6 *Id. See also* The Major Debates at the Constitutional Convention, Teach Democracy (Fall 2009), (stating that the delegates quickly decided that their discussions should not be made public and that "nothing spoken in the House be printed, or otherwise published or communicated." Because of the secrecy rule, the public knew little of what was happening inside the Philadelphia statehouse); Margaret Wood, *May 1787: The Beginning of the Constitutional Convention,* Library of Congress Blogs (May 26, 2016) (stating "Although the proceedings of the convention were kept secret at the time, the Convention's Secretary, William Jackson, gathered up the journals and related papers and delivered them to George Washington, who in turn delivered the papers to the Department of State in 1796").

7 Farrand, *supra* note 3, at 76.

8 Kennedy v. Bremerton School Dist., 142 S.Ct. 2407, 2428 (2022) (quotation omitted).

9 I develop this point in Erwin Chemerinsky, Worse Than Nothing: The Dangerous Fallacy of Originalism (2022).

10 Chiafalo v. Washington, 140 S.Ct. 2316 (2020).

11 Matthew M. Hoffman, *The Illegitimate President: Minority Vote Dilution and the Electoral College,* 105 Yale L. J. 935, 943 (1996).

12 For a detailed description of what occurred at the Constitutional Convention, *see* Paul Finkelman, *The Proslavery Origins of the Electoral College,* 23 Cardozo L. Rev. 1145, 1151 (2002).

13 The Federalist No. 68, at 393 (Alexander Hamilton) (Isaac Kramnick ed., Penguin Books 1987).

14 Finkelman, *supra* note 12, at 1154.

15 2 Farrand, *supra* note 3, at 57; Finkelman, *supra* note 12, at 1155.

16 Finkelman, *supra* note 12, at 1155.

17 2 Farrand, *supra* note 3, at 32.

18 *See* Akhil Reed Amar, The Constitution Today: Timeless Lessons for the Issues of Our Era 333 (2016); Akhil Reed Amar, *Some Thoughts on the Electoral College: Past, Present, and Future,* 33 Ohio N.U.L. Rev. 467 (2007).

19 Gordon S. Wood, *Reading the Founders' Minds,* New York Review of Books (June 28, 2007).

20 *See, e.g.,* Reynolds v. Sims, 337 U.S. 533 (1964).

21 *Id.* at 568.

22 Robert A. Caro, Master of the Senate: The Years of Lyndon Johnson 33 (2002).

23 Jessie Kratz, *The 1824 Presidential Election and the "Corrupt Bargain,"* National Archives: Pieces of History (October 22, 2020).

24 Reynolds, 337 U.S. at 568.

25 *Id.*

26 Jesse Wegman, Let the People Pick the President, 149–50 (2020).

27 Robert M. Alexander, Representation and the Electoral College 111 (2019).

28 Jerry Schwartz, *Explainer: They Lost the Popular Vote but Won the Elections,* Associated Press (October 31, 2020).

29 *Id.*

30 *Id.*

31 Alexander, *supra* note 27, at 110.

32 Allen Guelzo, *In Defense of the Electoral College,* National Affairs (Winter 2018), 76.

33 *Id.* at 77.

34 *Id.*

35 *Id.* at 76–88.

36 *Id.*

37 1912 Electoral Vote Tally, February 12, 1913, National Archives, https://www .archives.gov/legislative/features/1912-election.

38 Drew Desilver, *Trump's Victory Another Example of How Electoral College Wins Are Bigger Than Popular Vote Ones,* Pew Research Center (December 20, 2016).

39 Denise Lu, *The Electoral College Misrepresents Every State but Not as Much as You May Think,* Washington Post (December 6, 2016).

40 Katy Collin, *The Electoral College Badly Distorts the Vote. And It's Going to Get Worse,* Washington Post (November 17, 2016) (citing Census Bureau urban population data, link in article).

41 *Id.*

42 *Id.*

43 Frederick Douglass, The Life and Times of Frederick Douglass 407 (2003).

44 Republican Party Platform of 1960, American Presidency Project.

45 Martin Pengelly, *LBJ OK? Historian Mark Lawrence on a President Resurgent,* Guardian (January 22, 2023).

46 Alexander, *supra* note 27, at 196.

47 Mark Muro and Sifan Liu, *Another Clinton-Trump Divide: High-output America vs Low-output America,* Brookings (November 29, 2016).

48 Wegman, *supra* note 26, at 186.

49 Tara Law, *These Presidents Won the Electoral College—But Not the Popular Vote,* Time, May 15, 2019.

50 Adam Jentleson, Kill Switch: The Rise of the Modern Senate 127 (2021).

Chapter 3: The 1970s

Parts of this chapter are drawn from Catherine Fisk and Erwin Chemerinsky, *The Filibuster*, 49 Stan. L. Rev. 181 (1997).

1 Ari Berman, *Voting Rights Bills Will Be Blocked by the Anti-Democratic System It Seeks to Reform*, Mother Jones (June 22, 2021).
2 Strategic use of extended debate apparently occurred both in the English Parliament and in the Roman Senate. *See* Robert Luce, Legislative Procedure: Parliamentary Practices and the Course of Business in the Framing of Statutes 277–78 (1922). The term *filibuster* did not become associated with the practice until the mid-nineteenth century. In fact, filibustering originally referred to mercenary warfare intended to destabilize a government, and thus the legislative term originally connoted disloyalty.
3 *See* Franklin L. Burdette, Filibustering in the Senate 14 (1940); 1 George H. Haynes, The Senate of the United States: Its History and Practice 399 (1960).
4 Burdette, *supra* note 3, at 14.
5 2 Robert C. Byrd, The Senate, 1789–1989: Addresses on the History of the United States Senate 94 (1991).
6 *See* Robert Luce, Legislative Procedure: Parliamentary Practices and the Course of Business in the Framing of Statutes 262 (1922).
7 Clay tried at least twice in 1841 to get the Senate to adopt restrictions on debate. He did this by proposing the adoption of the previous question and later by proposing a time limit, but both were rejected. On Clay's two 1841 efforts to limit debate, *see* Sen. Comm. on Rules and Admin., 99th Cong., Senate Cloture Rule, Limitation of Debate in the Congress of the United States and Legislative History of Rule XXII of the Standing Rules of the United States Senate (Cloture Rule) 12 (Comm. Print 1985); 1 Haynes, *supra* note 3, at 394.
8 On the tremendous sectional and party conflicts of the era, *see generally* Don E. Fehrenbacher, The Dred Scott Case: Its Significance in American Law and Politics 123–87 (1978); William W. Freehling, The Road to Disunion: Secessionists at Bay, 1776–1854, 308–565 (1990); David M. Potter, The Impending Crisis, 1848–1861 (1976).
9 Richard R. Beeman, *Unlimited Debate in the Senate: The First Phase*, 83 Pol. Sci. Q. 419, 421 (1968).
10 *Id.* at 422.
11 *Id.* at 424.
12 George H. Hoar, *The Conduct of Business in Congress*, N. Am. Rev. 126 (February 1879). Senator Hoar, a Republican with Whig roots, opposed Democratic filibusters. In 1890 he tried to get the Senate to adopt some form of cloture to end Democratic opposition to a bill proposing to use the army to supervise elections in the South. *See* Luce, *supra* note 6, at 291–92.
13 Hoar, *supra* note 12, at 126.
14 *Id.* at 126.
15 *Id.*

16 *Id.* at 128.
17 *See* 2 Byrd, *supra* note 5, at 96.
18 *See* Luce, *supra* note 6, at 283.
19 Walter J. Oleszek, Congressional Procedures and the Policy Process 269 (4th ed. 1996) (discussing the scheduling of legislation in the House and House floor procedure).
20 Walker even had himself inaugurated as president of Nicaragua in July 1856. *See* Robert E. May, *Young American Males and Filibustering in the Age of Manifest Destiny: The United States Army as a Cultural Mirror,* 78 J. Am. Hist. 857, 857 (1991).
21 Oleszek, *supra* note 19, at 269 n.56.
22 *See* Burdette, *supra* note 3, at 39.
23 *Id.* at 43.
24 *See id.* at 52–57.
25 *See id.* at 58–58.
26 *Id.* at 88.
27 *Id.*
28 *Id.* at 89.
29 *Id.*
30 *Id.* at 120.
31 For a detailed story of the filibuster, *see* Thomas W. Ryley, A Little Group of Willful Men (1975).
32 55 Cong. Rec. 45 (1917).
33 *See Complete List of Cloture Votes Since Adoption of Rule 22,* 32 Cong. Q. Wkly. Rep. 317 (February 9, 1974). The four successful cloture votes pertained to a Prohibition-related measure, the Glass-Steagall branch banking bill, the Versailles Treaty, and the World Court. *See* 68 Cong. Rec. 4986 (1927) (Prohibition bureau); 68 Cong. Rec. 3824 (1927) (branch banking); 67 Cong. Rec. 2678–79 (1926) (World Court); 58 Cong. Rec. 8555–56 (1919) (Versailles Treaty).
34 Cloture was obtained on the Civil Rights Act of 1964 and on a communications satellite bill in 1962. *Complete List of Cloture Votes Since Adoption of Rule 22, supra* note 34, at 317.
35 Charles Tiefer, Congressional Practice and Procedure 696 (1989).
36 Southerners successfully filibustered anti-lynching legislation in 1922, 1935, and 1938. *See* Burdette, *supra* note 3, at 133–37.
37 Anti-poll-tax legislation was filibustered in 1942, 1944, and 1946. *Complete List of Cloture Votes Since Adoption of Rule 22, supra* note 34, at 317.
38 Southerners filibustered assorted civil rights legislation in 1946, 1950, 1957, 1960, 1962, 1964, 1965, 1966, 1968, 1972, and 1975.
39 William E. Leuchtenburg, Franklin D. Roosevelt and the New Deal 186 (1963).
40 William Small, *Equality of Access for Broadcast Journalism, in* Congress and the News Media 66, 68–69 (Robert O. Blanchard ed., 1974).
41 Still, filibustering was not strictly a tool of conservatives. Liberals filibustered in 1947

against the anti-labor Taft-Hartley bill and in 1953 against a bill to allow oil explo-ration in coastal tidelands. *See* Bruce I. Oppenheimer, *Changing Time Constraints on Congress: Historical Perspectives on the Use of Cloture, in* Congress Reconsidered 393, 399 (Lawrence C. Dodd and Bruce I. Oppenheimer eds., 3d ed. 1985).

42 In 1971 some Southerners had a change of heart and voted for cloture, for the first time in their careers, to end the liberals' filibuster against an extension of the military draft. *See* Jacqueline Calmes, *"Trivialized" Filibuster Is Still a Potent Tool*, 45 Cong. Q. Wkly. Rep. 2120 (September 5, 1987).

43 *See* Gary Orfield, Congressional Power: Congress and Social Change 39–43 (1975).

44 *See* Oppenheimer, *supra* note 42, at 406. Mansfield devised this system when a cloture vote on employment discrimination legislation failed in 1972. *See id.*

45 Oppenheimer, *supra* note 42, at 399.

46 Memorandum from Richard S. Beth, Congressional Research Service, Filibus-ters in the Senate, 1789–1993, 5–7 (February 18, 1994).

47 Memorandum on the Huey Long filibuster of June 12–13, 1935 (March 3, 1940) (citing Wash. Daily News, June 13, 1935).

48 Of course, the presence of televisions may *cause* some filibusters that might not otherwise occur, as when a senator might wish constituents to see him stand-ing for some provision of particular interest to them. At the end of the 102nd Congress, for example, Senator Alphonse D'Amato held the floor for an entire night because a provision benefiting one of his corporate constituents was not included in a tax bill. He surely knew he would not succeed, but he was in a close race for reelection, and the filibuster signaled to voters his dedication to their interests. *See* 138 Cong Rec. S16,846-924 (October 5, 1992) (remarks of Senator D'Amato).

49 *See* Congressional Budget Act, Pub. L. No. 93-944, 88 Stat. 297 (1974) (codified as amended at 2 U.S.C. § 601–3, 651–58 (1996)).

50 *See* Heidi Glenn, *Budget Facelift Possible Next Year*, 1996 Tax Notes 1716, 1717. Forty percent of the Senate's business is now being conducted as reconciliation bills (which cannot be filibustered), budget resolutions (which, as concurrent resolutions, do not have the force of law), and appropriation bills (which can be filibustered). *See id.*

51 In addition to the Inflation Reduction Act (Biden's economic recovery bill), recent legislative priorities pushed through the reconciliation process include the Tax Cuts and Jobs Act of 2017 (Republican legislation cutting corporate tax rates), the Economic Growth and Tax Relief Reconciliation Act of 2001 (Bush administration tax reform legislation), and Republican attempts in 2017 to repeal the Affordable Care Act, which failed due to Senator John McCain's nay vote. Bill Heniff, Jr., Cong. Rsch. Serv., RL30862, The Budget Reconciliation Process: The Senate's "Byrd Rule" 8 (2022).

52 Claudia Grisales, *Senate Parliamentarian Rejects Immigration Reform in Dem-ocrats' Spending Bill*, NPR (December 16, 2021).

53 *See* Congressional Budget Act, *supra* note 50, at 297; *see also* 142 Cong. Rec. S8070–01 (July 18, 1996) (discussing the Byrd Rule); 141 Cong. Rec. S16,691-01 (November 3, 1995) (same). The germaneness requirement can be waived by a vote of 60 senators. *See* Congressional Budget Act, *supra* note 50, at 297.

54 Jonathan S. Gould, *Law Within Congress,* 129 Yale L. J. 1946 (2020).

Chapter 4: The 1980s and After

 1 Richard Labunski, James Madison and the Struggle for the Bill of Rights, 139–40 (2006).

 2 Elizabeth Kolbert, *Drawing the Line: How Redistricting Turned America from Blue to Red*, New Yorker (June 27, 2016). But this account has been challenged as untrue: *see* Thomas Rogers Hunter, The First Gerrymander?: Patrick Henry, James Madison, James Monroe, and Virginia's 1788 Congressional Districting, 9 Early Am. Studies 781 (2011).

 3 Jennifer Davis, *Elbridge Gerry and the Monstrous Gerrymander,* Library of Congress Blogs (February 10, 2017).

 4 Kolbert, *supra* note 2.

 5 *Historical Election Results Data*, North Carolina State Board of Elections (2022), https://www.ncsbe.gov/results-data/election-results/historical-election -results-data#by-precinct.

 6 Rucho v. Common Cause, 139 S.Ct. 2484, 2492 (2019).

 7 *Id.* at 2510 (Kagan, J., dissenting).

 8 *Id.* at 2513.

 9 *Id.*

10 *Id.*

11 *Id.* at 2512.

12 *Id.* at 2513.

13 Kolbert, *supra* note 2.

14 Sue Halpern, *America's Redistricting Process Is Breaking Democracy,* New Yorker (May 25, 2022).

15 *Id.*

16 *Id.*

17 *Id.*

18 Alexa Tausanovitch, *Voter-Determined Districts: Ending Gerrymandering and Ensuring Fair Representation,* Center for American Progress (May 2, 2019).

19 *Id.*

20 *Id.*

21 Arizona State Legislature v. Arizona Independent Redistricting Comm'n, 135 S.Ct. 2652, 2677 (2015).

22 Davis v. Bandemer, 478 U.S. 109, 165 (1986) (Powell, J., concurring).

23 Vieth v. Jubelirer, 541 U.S. 267, 314–15 (Kennedy, J., concurring).

24 Gill v. Whitford, 138 S.Ct. 1916, 1938 (Kagan, J., concurring).

25 Commission on Political Reform, Bipartisan Policy Center, Governing in a

Polarized America: A Bipartisan Blueprint to Strengthen our Democracy 30 (June 24, 2014).

26 Bandemer, *supra* note 22, at 131–32.
27 Rucho, *supra* note 6, at 2506–7.
28 *Id.* (Const., Art III, § 2, cl. 1.)
29 Rucho, *supra* note 6, at 2502.
30 *Id.* at 2506–7.
31 *Id.* at 2513 (Kagan, J., dissenting).
32 *Id.* at 2525.
33 Tim Henderson, *Bipartisan Commissions Cause Redistricting Pain for Democrats*, Pew Charitable Trusts (November 2, 2021).
34 Halpern, *supra* note 14.
35 *Id.*
36 These facts are described in Moore v. Harper, 143 S.Ct. 2065 (2023).

Chapter 5: The Twenty-First Century

1 Dobbs v. Jackson Women's Health Organization, 142 S.Ct. 2228, 2243 (2022).
2 Jennifer Agiesta, *CNN Poll: About Two-Thirds of Americans Disapprove of Overturning Roe v. Wade, See Negative Effect for the Nation Ahead*, CNN (July 28, 2022).
3 Max Farrand, The Framing of the Constitution of the United States, 79 (1913).
4 Farrand, *supra* note 3, at 104–5.
5 Farrand, *supra* note 3, at 79–80. For example, John Rutledge stated at the Convention, "The State Tribunals might and ought to be left in all cases to decide in the first instance the right of appeal to the supreme national tribunal being sufficient to secure the national rights [and] uniformity of judgments." Farrand, *supra* note 3, at 124.
6 *Id.*, at 27.
7 *Id.*
8 *Id.*, at 125.
9 *Id.*
10 There are revisionist views of Article III that argue that the Convention intended for lower federal courts to exist. *See* Julius Goebel, History of the Supreme Court: Antecedents and Beginnings to 1801, 247 (1971) (arguing that change in wording done by the Committee of Style is responsible for the language that appears to accord Congress discretion to decide whether to create lower federal courts); *see also* Robert N. Clinton, *A Mandatory View of Federal Court Jurisdiction: A Guided Quest for the Original Understanding of Article III*, 132 U. Pa. L. Rev. 741 (1984).
11 This question of whether federal courts are equal to state courts in their ability and willingness to protect federal rights is often referred to as the question of the "parity" between federal and state courts. *See* Burt Neuborne, *The Myth of Parity*, 90 Harv. L. Rev. 1105 (1977).

12 Jerome R. Corsi, Judicial Politics: An Introduction, 104 (1984).

13 *See* Williams-Yulee v. Florida State Bar, 575 U.S. 433, 437 (2015) ("in 39 States, voters elect trial or appellate judges at the polls").

14 *See, e.g.,* Martin H. Redish, *Constitutional Limitations on Congressional Power to Control Federal Jurisdiction: A Reaction to Professor Sager,* 77 Nw. U. L. Rev. 143 (1982); Neuborne, *supra* note 11, at 1124; *but see* Michael E. Solimine and James L. Walker, *Constitutional Litigation in Federal and State Courts: An Empirical Analysis of Judicial Parity,* 10 Hastings Const. L.Q. 213, 230–31 (1983) ("it does not follow, however, that elections of state judges . . . will influence subsequent decisions of elected judges").

15 Gwynn Guiford, *117 Years of Data Show Why Today's Supreme Court Nominees Have More Influence than Ever,* Quartz, July 10, 2018.

16 Linda Greenhouse, *How Long Is Too Long for the Court's Justices?,* New York Times (January 16, 2005).

17 David Fishbaum, *The Supreme Court Has a Longevity Problem, but Term Limits on Justices Won't Solve It,* Harv. Business Rev. (July 13, 2018).

18 I discuss this in detail in Erwin Chemerinsky, The Case Against the Supreme Court (2014).

19 *Race and Voting,* Constitutional Rights Foundation, 2023, http://www.crf-usa .org/brown-v-board-50th-anniversary/race-and-voting.html.

20 Michael J. Pitts, *The Voting Rights Act and the Era of Maintenance,* 59 Ala. L. Rev. 903, 909–10 (2008).

21 J. Morgan Kousser, The Shaping of Southern Politics: Suffrage Restriction and the Establishment of the One-Party South, 1880–1910, 67–68 (1974).

22 *Id.*

23 *Id.*

24 *Id.*

25 *Id.*

26 *Id.*

27 South Carolina v. Katzenbach, 383 U.S. 301 (1966).

28 Georgia v. United States, 411 U.S. 526 (1973); City of Rome v. United States, 446 U.S. 156 (1980); Lopez v. Monterey County, 525 U.S. 266 (1999).

29 *Fannie Lou Hamer, Rosa Parks, and Coretta Scott King Voting Rights Act Reauthorization and Amendments Act of 2006: Hearing on H.R. 9,* 152 Cong. Rec. (2006) (statement of Rep. F. James Sensenbrenner), https://www.congress.gov/ congressional-record/2006/7/13/house-section/article/h5143-2.

30 *Fannie Lou Hamer, Rosa Parks, and Coretta Scott King Voting Rights Act Reauthorization and Amendments Act of 2006: Congressional Purpose and Findings,* Pub. L. 109–246, § 2(b)(9), 109th Cong., July 27, 2006.

31 Shelby County, Alabama v. Holder, 133 S.Ct. 2612, 2639 (2013), *citing to* H.R. Rep. No. 109–478, at 21.

32 *Id.* at 2643.

33 *Election 2016: Restrictive Voting Laws by the Numbers,* Brennan Center for Justice at NYU Law, September 28, 2016.

34 *Id.*

35 Shelby County, *supra* note 31, at 2631.

36 Shelby County, Alabama v. Holder, 679 F.3d 848, 901 (D.C. Cir. 2012).

37 Shelby County, *supra* note 31, at 2625 (citations omitted).

38 *Id.* at 2624.

39 *Id.* at 2623–24

40 *Id.* at 2649 (Ginsburg, J., dissenting). Justice Ginsburg gave several examples of federal laws that treat some states differently from others.

41 Brnovich v. Democratic National Committee, 141 S.Ct. 2321, 2353 (Kagan, J., dissenting).

42 Mobile v. Bolden, 446 U.S. 55, 79–80 (1980).

43 Democratic Nat'l Comm. v. Hobbs, 948 F.3d 989, 999 (9th Cir. 2020).

44 Brnovich, *supra* note 41, at 2340 ("We also do not find the disparate-impact model employed in Title VII and Fair Housing Act cases useful here.")

45 *Id.* at 2338.

46 *Id.*

47 *Id.* at 2339.

48 *Id.*

49 *Id.* at 2351 (Kagan, J. dissenting).

50 *Id.* at 2356.

51 In June 2023, Allen v. Milligan, 143 S.Ct. 1487 (2023), did not change or weaken the law for when Section 2 can be used to challenge election districts as racially discriminatory. It was a 5–4 decision, and Justice Kavanaugh, one of the justices in the majority, suggested that Section 2 might be unconstitutional because it is no longer needed to deal with race discrimination.

52 Citizens United v. Fed. Election Comm'n, 130 S.Ct. 876 (2010).

53 *McConnell v. Fed. Election Comm'n*, 540 U.S. 93, 128–29 (2003).

54 Citizens United, *supra* note 52.

55 *Id.* at 907 (citations omitted).

56 *Id.* at 913.

57 *Id.* at 929 (Stevens, J., dissenting).

58 *Id.* at 948–49. Justice Scalia wrote a separate concurring opinion that responded to this and defended the protection of corporate political spending from an originalist perspective. *Id.* at 925 (Scalia, J., concurring).

59 *Id.* at 930.

60 *Id.* at 979 (Stevens, J., dissenting).

61 Georgia Lyon, *How Does the Citizens United Decision Still Affect Us in 2022?,* Campaign Legal Center, January 21, 2022.

62 Richard L. Hasen, *The Decade of* Citizens United, Slate (December 19, 2019).

63 McCutcheon v. Fed. Election Comm'n, 134 S.Ct. 1434, 1440–41 (2014).

64 Merrill v. Milligan, 142 S.Ct. 879 (2022).

65 *Id.* at 884 (Kagan, J., dissenting).

66 Singleton v. Merrill, No. 2:21-CV-1291-AMM, 2022 WL 265001, at *2 (N.D. Ala. Jan. 24, 2022), *cert. Granted sub nom. Merrill v. Milligan*, 142 S.Ct. 879 (2022).

67 Allen v. Milligan, 143 S.Ct. 1487 (2023).

68 Merrill, *supra* note 64, at 882 (Roberts, C. J., dissenting).

69 *Id.* at 879 (Kavanaugh, J., concurring).

70 Purcell v. Gonzalez, 549 U.S. 1, 3 (2006) (per curiam).

71 *Id.* at 5–6 (2006) (per curiam).

72 Republican Nat'l Comm. v. Democratic Nat'l Comm., 140 S.Ct. 1205, 1206–7 (2020) (per curiam).

73 *Id.* at 1209 (Ginsburg, J., dissenting).

74 *Id.* at 1207 (Kavanaugh, J., concurring).

75 *Id.*

76 Allen, *supra* note 67, at 1487.

Chapter 6: Yesterday and Today

1 Thurgood Marshall, *The Constitution's Bicentennial: Commemorating the Wrong Document?*, 40 Vand. L. Rev. 1337 (1987).

2 Brown v. Board of Education, 347 U.S. 483 (1954).

3 Marshall, *supra* note 1, at 1338.

4 *Id.*

5 *Id.* at 1340.

6 Michael Ovaska et al., *A Terrible Passage from Africa*, Reuters Graphics (August 2, 2019).

7 *African Americans in St. Augustine 1565–1821*, National Park Service (April 20, 2022).

8 *See* Nikole Hannah-Jones, The 1619 Project: A New Origin Story (2021); Beth Austin, *1619: Virginia's First Africans*, Hampton History Museum (December 2018).

9 1 U.S. Census Bureau, Bicentennial Edition: Historical Statistics of the United States, Colonial Times to 1970 14 (Helen E. Teir et al. eds., 3rd ed. 1975).

10 The Debates in the Federal Convention of 1787, Which Framed the Constitution of the United States of America 446 (Gaillard Hund and James Brown Scott eds., 1920) (James Madison, *Wednesday, August 22*).

11 *Id.*

12 Leonard L. Richards, The Slave Power: The Free North and Southern Domination, 1780–1860, 57 (2000).

13 Madison, *supra* note 10, at 446.

14 *Id.* at 442.

15 *Id.* at 360.

16 *Id.* at 444.

17 *Id.*

18 *Id.*
19 The other, discussed in Chapter 3, is the assurance that every state would have equal representation in the Senate.
20 *Id.*
21 Somerset v. Stewart, 98 ER 499 (1772).
22 Steven Lubet, Fugitive Justice: Runaways, Rescuers, and Slavery on Trial 18 (2010).
23 Madison, *supra* note 10, at 481.
24 Charles Cotesworth Pinckney, Speech in South Carolina House of Representatives, *in* 3 Records of the Federal Convention of 1787 252, 254 (Max Farrand ed., 1911).
25 For an excellent description of these cases and this history, *see* Robert M. Cover, Justice Accused: Antislavery and the Judicial Process (1975).
26 Prigg v. Pennsylvania, 41 U.S. (16 Pet.) 539 (1842).
27 *Id.* at 610.
28 Id. at 611.
29 Id.
30 Id. at 613.
31 Moore v. Illinois, 55 U.S. (14 How.) 13, 18 (1852).
32 See Donald L. Robinson, Slavery in the Structure of American Politics 1765–1820, 245–246 (1971).
33 Dred Scott v. Sanford, 60 U.S. (19 How.) 393 (1857).
34 Sanford's name is misspelled in the United States Reports as "Sandford."
35 Dred Scott, *supra* note 33, at 403.
36 Id. at 404–5.
37 Id. at 409.
38 Id. at 451–52.
39 For example, the famous Lincoln-Douglas debates involved extended arguments about the *Dred Scott* decision and its meaning. For an excellent discussion, *see* David Zarefsky, Lincoln, Douglas and Slavery: In the Crucible of Public Debate 51–53 (1990).
40 I develop this argument in Erwin Chemerinsky, We the People: A Progressive Reading of the Constitution for the Twenty-First Century (2018).
41 In Bolling v. Sharpe, 347 U.S. 497 (1954), the Supreme Court held that the Due Process Clause of the Fifth Amendment, which does apply to the federal government, implicitly includes a requirement for equal protection.
42 Plessy v. Ferguson, 163 U.S. 537 (1896).
43 Kriston McIntosh et al., *Examining the Black-White Wealth Gap*, Brookings Institution (February 27, 2020).
44 *Id.*
45 *Id.*
46 Liz Mineo, *Racial Wealth Gap May Be a Key to Other Inequalities*, Harvard Gazette (June 3, 2021).

47 Aditya Aladangady and Akila Forde, Wealth Inequality and the Racial Wealth Gap, Board of Governors of the Federal Reserve System (October 22, 2021).

48 *Id.*

49 Katherine Getchell, *Is Wealth Inequality Corroding American Democracy?*, Guardian (April 11, 2021).

50 Anshu Siripurapu, *The U.S. Inequality Debate*, Council on Foreign Relations (April 20, 2022).

51 Inequality in a Rapidly Changing World, United Nations Department of Economic and Social Affairs (2020).

Chapter 7: The 2010s and Beyond

1 Robert Mueller, Report on the Investigation into Russian Interference in the 2016 Presidential Election (2019).

2 U.S. Senate, Report No. 116-290, at 576 (2020).

3 *Id.*

4 *Id.* at 5.

5 *Senate Intel Committee Releases Bipartisan Report on Russia's Use of Social Media*, U.S. Senate Intelligence Committee (October 8, 2019).

6 Jon Greenberg, *Most Republicans Still Falsely Believe Trump's Stolen Election Claims*, Politifact: Poynter Institute (June 14, 2022).

7 Mark Scott and Rebecca Kern, *The Online World Still Can't Quit the "Big Lie,"* Politico (January 6, 2022); Mark Scott, *Post-election, Extremists Use Fringe Social Networks to Push Fraud Claims, Violence*, Politico (November 13, 2020).

8 Nicholas Riccardi, *Support of False Election Claims Runs Deep in 2022 GOP Field*, Associated Press (September 8, 2002).

9 Daniel Dale, *10 Trump Election Lies His Own Officials Called False*, CNN (June 16, 2022); Michael Balsamo, *Disputing Trump, Barr Says No Widespread Election Fraud*, Associated Press (June 28, 2022).

10 *Fact Check: Courts Have Dismissed Multiple Lawsuits of Alleged Electoral Fraud Presented by the Trump Campaign*, Reuters (February 15, 2021).

11 Red Lion Broad. Co. v. FCC, 395 U.S. 367, 375 (1969) (upholding the fairness doctrine based on broadcast spectrum scarcity).

12 Martha Minow, Saving the News: Why the Constitution Calls for Government Action to Preserve Freedom of Speech 14 (2021).

13 *Id.* at 12–17.

14 Eugene Volokh, Cheap Speech and What It Will Do, 104 Yale L. J. 1805, 1806–7 (1995).

15 Packingham v. North Carolina, 137 S.Ct. 1730 (2017).

16 David M. Howard, *Can Democracy Withstand the Cyber Age: 1984 in the 21st Century*, 69 Hastings L. J. 1355, 1373 (2018).

17 *Id.* at 1373; David M. Thompson, *Is the Internet a Viable Threat to Representative Democracy?*, 6 Duke L. & Tech. Rev. 1, 13 (2007–8).

18 Howard, *supra* note 16, at 1373.

19　*See* Lori Andrews, I Know Who You Are and I Saw What You Did: Social Networks and the Death of Privacy 121–35 (2011).

20　Danielle Keats Citron, Hate Crimes in Cyberspace 53 (2014).

21　*Id.* at 35–55.

22　Marlisse Silver Sweeney, *What the Law Can (and Can't) Do About Online Harassment*, Atlantic (November 12, 2014).

23　*When Egypt Turned Off the Internet*, Al Jazeera (January 28, 2011).

24　Ashcroft v. ACLU, 542 U.S. 656, 667 (2004).

25　*See* Mueller, *supra* note 1.

26　*See generally* American Psychological Association, *Misinformation and Disinformation*. (According to the APA, misinformation is "false or inaccurate information—getting the facts wrong," whereas disinformation is "false information which is deliberately intended to mislead—intentionally misstating the facts." *See* Bharat Dhiman, *Key Issues and New Challenges in New Media Technology in 2023: A Critical Review*, 5 J. Media & Mgmt. 1, 3 (2023).

27　William M. Brooks, *Democracy on the Edge: Use the First Amendment to Stop False Speech by Government Officials*, 53 Memphis L. Rev. 255, 270 (2023), *citing* Soroush Vosoughi, Deb Roy, and Sinan Aral, *The Spread of True and False News Online*, 359 Science 1146–51 (March 2018).

28　Dhiman, *supra* note 26, at 3; Andrea Butler, *Protecting the Democratic Role of the Press: A Legal Solution to Fake News*, 96 Wash. U. L. Rev. 419 (2018).

29　Dhiman, *supra* note 26, at 2.

30　*Id.*

31　*Id.*

32　*Id.*

33　New York Times Co. v. Sullivan, 376 U.S. 254 (1964).

34　*Id.* at 270.

35　*Id.* at 271.

36　*Id.* at 271–72.

37　United States v. Alvarez, 567 U.S. 709 (2012).

38　*Id.* at 715–16.

39　*Id.* at 715.

40　*Id.* at 725–26.

41　*Id.* at 718.

42　*Id.* at 719.

43　*See, e.g.,* Cent. Hudson Gas and Elec. Corp. v. Pub. Serv. Comm'n of N.Y., 447 U.S. 557, 566 (1980).

44　Hustler Magazine, Inc. v. Falwell, 485 U.S. 46, 52 (1988).

45　New York Times Co., *supra* note 33, at 271–72 (quoting NAACP v. Button, 371 U.S. 415, 433 (1963)).

46　Alvarez, *supra* note 37, at 723.

47　*Community Standards Enforcement Report Q4 2021*, Meta. Much of this moderation is either performed by algorithms or aided by algorithms. In the second and third quarters of 2022 alone, Facebook acted against 24.1 million posts containing hate speech. *Community Standards Enforcement Report Q3, Hate Speech*, Meta. It attributed its moderation actions in part to improved "proactive detection technology." *Id.* For discussion of algorithmic moderation, see, for example, Hannah Bloch-Wehba, *Automation in Moderation*, 53 Cornell Int'l L. J. 41 (2020); Evelyn Douek, *Governing Online Speech: From "Posts-as-Trumps" to Proportionality and Probability*, 121 Colum. L. Rev. 759, 791 (2021); Tim Wu, *Will Artificial Intelligence Eat the Law? The Rise of Hybrid Social-Ordering Systems*, 119 Colum. L. Rev. 2001 (2019); Aziz Z. Huq, *A Right to a Human Decision*, 106 Va. L. Rev. 611 (2020).

48   Douek, *supra* note 47, at 791.

49   *See, e.g.,* Mueller, *supra* note 1.

50   *Id.*

51   Indictment, United States v. Internet Research Agency, LLC, No, 1:18-cr-00032-DLC (D.D.C. February 16, 2018), 2018 WL 914777.

52   Sheera Frenkel and Katie Benner, *To Stir Discord in 2016, Russians Turned Most Often to Facebook*, New York Times (February 17, 2018).

53   Scott Shane, *Russia Isn't the Only One Meddling in Elections. We Do It Too*, New York Times (February 17, 2018).

54   *Id.*

55   Raphael Satter, *Inside Story: How Russians Hacked the Democrats' Emails*, Associated Press (November 4, 2017).

56   First Nat. Bank of Bos. v. Bellotti, 435 U.S. 765, 767–68 (1978).

57   *Id.* at 776–77 (emphasis added).

58   Citizens United v. Fed. Election Comm'n, 558 U.S. 310, 319 (2010).

59   *Id.* at 350, 394.

60   Pac. Gas and Elec. Co. v. Pub. Utils. Comm'n of Cal., 475 U.S. 1, 8 (1986) (plurality opinion).

61   Blauman v. FCC, 800 F. Supp. 2d 281, 284 (D.D.C. 2011), *aff'd*, 565 U.S. 1104 (2012).

62   *Id.* at 288.

63   McIntyre v. Ohio Elections Comm'n, 514 U.S. 334, 357 (1995).

64   *Id.* at 341–42.

65   *Id.* at 342.

66   Dhiman, *supra* note 26, at 3. *See also* Cass R. Sunstein, #republic: Divided Democracy in the Age of Social Media 70–71 (2017).

67   Dhiman, *supra* note 26, at 3. *See also* Seth Oranburg, *Social Media and Democracy After the Capital Riot, or, A Cautionary Tale of the Giant Goldfish*, 73 Mercer L. Rev. 591, 609 (2022); Helen Margetts, *Rethinking Democracy with Social Media*, 90 Pol, Q. 107, 113 (2019).

68   Dhiman, *supra* note 26, at 3. *See also* Oranburg, *supra* note 67, at 610; Gregory P. Magarian, *How Cheap Speech Underserves and Overheats Democracy*, 54 UC Davis L. Rev. 2455, 2474.

69 Dhiman, *supra* note 26, at 3. *See also* Sunstein, *supra* note 66, at 76–79.

70 Dhiman, *supra* note 26, at 3; *See also* Margetts, *supra* note 67, at 113; Oranburg, *supra* note 67, at 610.

71 Margetts, *supra* note 67, at 113.

Chapter 8: What Can Be Done Without Changing the Constitution?

1 Steven Levitsky and Daniel Ziblatt, How Democracies Die 9 (2018).

2 *Id.* at 1.

3 Yascha Mounk and Roberto Stefan Foa, *This Is How Democracy Dies*, Atlantic (January 29, 2020); Roberto Foa and Yascha Mounk, *Across the Globe, a Growing Disillusionment with Democracy*, New York Times (September 15, 2015); Robert D. Putnam et al., *Introduction: What's Troubling the Trilateral Democracies, in* Disaffected Democracies: What's Troubling the Trilateral Countries 6–7 (Susan J. Pharr and Robert D. Putnam eds., 2018) (drawing a "distinction between the effectiveness of specific democratic governments and the durability of democratic institutions per se," and finding that "earlier alarm about the stability of democracy itself . . . exaggerated"); *Public Trust in Government: 1958–2022*, Pew Research Center (June 6, 2022).

4 Caroline Kane et al., *Why the House of Representatives Must Be Expanded and How Today's Congress Can Make It Happen*, Fordham L. Arch. Scholarship & Hist. 7 (January 2020).

5 *Id.*

6 For a proposal of how to calculate the size of a larger House of Representatives, *see* id.

7 Kriston McIntosh et al., *Examining the Black-White Wealth Gap*, Brookings Institution (February 27, 2020).

8 For a compelling defense that a ban on such deepfakes would be constitutional, *see* Bobby Chesney and Danielle Citron, *Deep Fakes: A Looming Challenge for Privacy, Democracy, and National Security*, 107 Calif. L. Rev. 1753 (2019).

9 *See, e.g.*, Citizens United v. Fed. Election Comm'n, 558 U.S. 310 (2010) (upholding disclosure requirements in the Bipartisan Campaign Finance Reform Act).

10 Bolling v. Sharpe 347 U.S. 497 (1954).

11 Wesberry v. Sanders, 376 U.S. 1, 8 (1964).

12 Bush v. Gore, 531 U.S. 98, 104 (2000).

13 This was a core insight of John Hart Ely, Democracy and Distrust (1980).

14 Reynolds v. Sims, 377 U.S. 533 (1964).

15 *The Warren Court: An Editorial Preface*, 67 Mich. L. Rev. 219, 220 (1968).

16 Note, *Rethinking the Electoral College Debate: The Framers, Federalism and One Person One Vote*, 114 Harv. L. Rev. 2526 (2001).

17 Matthew M. Hoffman, *The Illegitimate President: Minority Vote Dilution and the Electoral College* 105 Yale L. J. 935, 937 (1996).

18 Congressional Budget Act, Pub. L. No. 93-944, 88 Stat. 297 (1974) (codified as amended at 2 U.S.C. § 601–3, 651–58 (1996)).

19 *See id.* at § 313; *see also* 142 Cong. Rec. S8070-01 (July 18, 1996) (discussing the Byrd Rule); 141 Cong. Rec. S16,691-01 (November 3, 1995) (same). The germaneness requirement can be waived by a vote of sixty senators. *See* Pub. L. No. 93-944, § 904, 88 Stat. 297 (1974).

20 Article I, Section 3 provides that the Senate may remove an officer after an impeachment if two-thirds of the senators concur. U.S. Constitution, Article I, Section 3, Clause 6. Article I, Section 5 allows either House to expel a member if two-thirds agree. U.S. Constitution, Article I, Section 5, Clause 2. Article I, Section 7 provides that to override a presidential veto requires a two-thirds vote of both the House and the Senate. U.S. Constitution, Article I, Section 7. Article II, Section 2, Clause 2 gives the president the power to make treaties provided that two-thirds of the senators approve it. Article V provides that for Congress to propose a constitutional amendment both Houses must approve it by a two-thirds vote. Section 3 of the Fourteenth Amendment provides that those who have engaged in insurrection or rebellion cannot be elected to Congress or hold any office, but says that Congress by a two-thirds vote of both Houses may remove such a disability. Finally, the Twenty-fifth Amendment, Section 4, creates a procedure whereby Congress, by a two-thirds vote of both Houses, can determine a President to be disabled. *See also* Benjamin Lieber and Patrick Brown, Note, On Supermajorities and the Constitution, 83 Geo. L. J. 2347, 2350 (1995).

21 *See* Bruce Ackerman et al., *An Open Letter to Congressman Gingrich*, 104 Yale L. J. 1539 (1995) (seventeen law professors argue that a recently adopted House rule requiring a supermajority vote for a tax increase is contrary to the framers' intent and is unconstitutional).

22 United States v. Ballin, 144 U.S. 1, 6 (1891).

23 Gabe Roth, *Supreme Court Term Limits Do Not Require a Constitutional Amendment,* USA Today (September 24, 2020).

24 Rebecca Kaplan, *Perry: Term-Limit Judges, Make Congress a Part-Time Job,* CBS News (November 15, 2011).

25 Kermit Roosevelt, *Court Reform and the Biden Commission,* Harv. J. Law & Public Pol. (February 24, 2022).

26 *Id.*

27 Supreme Court Tenure Establishment and Retirement Modernization Act of 2022, S. 4706, 117th Cong. (2022).

28 Dobbs v. Jackson Women's Health Org., 142 S.Ct. 2228 (2022).

29 Students for Fair Admissions v. President & Fellows of Harvard Coll., No. 20-1199, slip op. at 1 (S.Ct. Jun. 29, 2023). C

30 Citizens United, *supra* note 9, at 310.

31 Rucho v. Common Cause, 139 S.Ct. 2484 (2019).

32 Shelby County v. Holder, 570 U.S. 529 (2013).

33 *See, e.g.,* Washington v. Davis, 426 U.S. 229 (1976); City of Mobile v. Bolden, 446 U.S. 55 (1980); McCleskey v. Kemp 481 U.S. 279 (1987) (all discussed below).

34 See text accompanying notes 57–65 (discussing this in the areas of crack cocaine sentencing, the death penalty, and schools).

35 As explained in Chapter 2, if there is racial discrimination, the government must meet strict scrutiny and show that its action is necessary to achieve a compelling purpose. The government usually loses. But when the government action needs only to meet a rational basis test—being rationally related to a legitimate government purpose—the government almost always wins.

36 The Supreme Court has said that if a decision is provably "motivated in part by a racially discriminatory purpose," the burden shifts to the government to prove that "the same decision would have resulted even had the impermissible purpose not been considered." Village of Arlington Heights v. Metropolitan Housing Development Corp., 429 U.S. 252, 270–71 n.21 (1977).

37 Washington, *supra* note 33, at 229.

38 *Id.* at 239 (emphasis in original).

39 *Id.* at 242 (citation omitted).

40 McCleskey, *supra* note 23, at 279.

41 *Id.*

42 *Id.* at 292 (emphasis in original).

43 *Id.* at 298.

44 The Court also has held that proving a violation of 42 U.S.C. § 1982 and the Thirteenth Amendment requires proof of a discriminatory purpose. In *Memphis v. Greene*, 451 U.S. 100 (1981), the Court found no constitutional violation when a city closed down a street that was used mainly by blacks. The Court said that "the record discloses no racially discriminatory motive on the part of the City Council [and] a review of the justification for the official action challenged in this case demonstrates that its disparate impact on black citizens could not [be] fairly characterized as a badge or incident of slavery." *Id.* at 126.

45 Washington, *supra* note 33, at 239.

46 Laurence H. Tribe, American Constitutional Law 1516–19 (2d ed., 1988).

47 *See* Daniel R. Ortiz, *The Myth of Intent in Equal Protection*, 41 Stan. L. Rev. 1105 (1989).

48 Charles Lawrence, *The Id, the Ego, and Equal Protection: Reckoning with Unconscious Racism*, 39 Stan. L. Rev. 317, 355 (1987).

49 *See, e.g.,* Anthony G. Greenwald and Linda Hamilton Krieger, *Implicit Bias: Scientific Foundations*, 94 Calif. L. Rev. 945, 946 (2006); *see also* Laurie A. Rudman et al., *"Unlearning" Automatic Biases: The Malleability of Implicit Prejudice and Stereotypes*, 81 J. Personality & Soc. Psychol. 856, 856 (2001); Annika Jones, *Implicit Bias as Social-Framework Evidence in Employment Discrimination*, 165 U. Pa. L. Rev. 1221 (2017).

50 Greenwald and Krieger, *supra* note 49, at 946.

51 Linda Hamilton Krieger, *The Content of Our Categories: A Cognitive Bias Approach to Discrimination and Equal Employment Opportunity*, 47 Stan. L.

Rev. 1161 (1995) (discussing the notion that people categorize information as they receive it as part of the central premise of social cognition theory).

52 Lawrence, *supra* note 48, at 322–23.

53 Christine Jolls and Cass R. Sunstein, *The Law of Implicit Bias*, 94 Calif. L. Rev. 969, 976 (2006).

54 *See* David Strauss, *Discriminatory Intent and the Taming of Brown*, 56 U. Chi. L. Rev. 935 (1989).

55 *Crack Cocaine Sentencing Policy: Unjustified and Unreasonable*, Sentencing Project (1997).

56 *See, e.g.,* United States v. Clary, 34 F.3d 709 (8th Cir. 1994), cert. denied, 115 S.Ct. 1172 (1995) (reversing the district court's conclusion that the disparity between crack and powder cocaine violated equal protection.) *See* David Sklansky, *Cocaine, Race, and Equal Protection*, 47 Stan. L. Rev. 1283, 1284 (1995) (explaining why the disparity between crack and powder cocaine sentencing could not be challenged under equal protection; "Federal appellate courts have uniformly rejected these challenges, based on a largely mechanical application of the equal protection rules developed by the Supreme Court.")

57 Sklansky, *supra* note 56, at 184.

58 McClesky, *supra* note 23, at 279.

59 *See* U.S. General Accounting Office, Death Penalty Sentencing: Research Indicates Pattern of Racial Disparities (1990) (analyzing twenty-eight studies involving cases from 1972 to 1988), in 136 Cong. Rec. S6873, 6889 (1990); David C. Baldus et al., *Racial Discrimination and the Death Penalty in the Post-Furman Era: An Empirical and Legal Overview, with Recent Findings from Philadelphia*, 83 Cornell L. Rev. 1638, 1738 (1998); Samuel R. Gross and Robert Mauro, *Patterns of Death: An Analysis of Racial Disparities in Capital Sentencing and Homicide Victimization*, 37 Stan. L. Rev. 27, 108 (1984) (finding "a remarkably stable and consistent" pattern of racial discrimination in the imposition of the death penalty in Arkansas, Florida, Georgia, Illinois, Mississippi, North Carolina, Oklahoma, and Virginia); Gennaro F. Vito and Thomas J. Keil, *Capital Sentencing in Kentucky: An Analysis of the Factors Influencing Decision-Making in the Post-Gregg Period*, 79 Crim. L. & Criminology 483 (1988) (finding that Kentucky prosecutors were more likely to seek death in white-victim cases); Leigh J. Bienen et al., *The Reimposition of Capital Punishment in New Jersey: The Role of Prosecutorial Discretion*, 41 Rutgers L. Rev. 27, 63 n.129 (1988) (finding pronounced race-of-victim and race-of-defendant disparities unexplained by non-racial variables).

60 Matt Ford, *Racism and the Execution Chamber*, Atlantic (March 24, 2014).

61 *See* Griggs v. Duke Power Co., 401 U.S. 424 (1971) (Title VII, which prohibits employment discrimination based on race, sex, or religion, allows liability based on proof of disparate impact).

62 *See* Texas Dept. of Housing & Community Affairs v. Inclusive Communi-

ties Project, 135 S.Ct. 2507 (2015) (Fair Housing Act allows liability based on disparate impact).

63   These were enacted to overrule the Supreme Court's decision in Mobile v. Bolden, 446 U.S. 55 (1980). *See* Thornburg v. Gingles, 478 U.S. 30, 43–44 (1986) (purpose of 1982 Amendments to the Voting Rights Act was to overrule Mobile v. Bolden).

64   *See* Bobby Chesney and Danielle Citron, *Deep Fakes: A Looming Challenge for Privacy, Democracy, and National Security*, 107 Calif. L. Rev. 1753 (2019).

65   *See, e.g.*, Common Cause v. Biden, 909 F. Supp. 2d 9 (D.C.C. 2012); Judicial Watch v. U.S. Senate, 432 F.3d 359 (D.C. Cir. 2005); Page v. Shelby, 995 F. Supp. 23 (D.D.C. 1998).

Chapter 9: Can the Constitution Be Fixed?

1   This point is discussed in detail in Chapter 3.

2   Eric Posner, *The U.S. Constitution Is Impossible to Amend*, Slate (May 5, 2014). For a more optimistic assessment, that "we are due for a new wave of constitutional change in coming years," *see* John F. Kowal and Wilfred U. Codrington III, The People's Constitution 8 (2021).

3   National Prohibition Case, 253 U.S. 350, 386 (1920) ("The two-thirds vote in each house which is required in proposing an amendment is a vote of two-thirds of the members present – assuming the presence of a quorum – and not a vote of two-thirds of the entire membership, present and absent.")

4   *Id.* at 385.

5   *Id.*

6   *Id.*

7   *Measures Proposed to Amend the Constitution*, U.S. Senate, n.d.

8   Constitution of the United States: Amendments, U.S. Senate, n.d.; Richard Albert, *The World's Most Difficult Constitution to Amend?* 110 Calif. L. Rev. 2005, 2010 (2022). This number represents only the amendments introduced in Congress, not those introduced in the various state legislatures.

9   *Id.*

10   *Id.*

11   Laurence Tribe, American Constitutional Law 10 (3d ed. 2000).

12   The analogy to Ulysses is developed in Jon Elster, Ulysses and the Sirens: Studies in Rationality and Irrationality (1979). The story of Ulysses is from Homer, Odyssey (Harper Colophon ed. 1985) (bk. 12).

13   Stephen Carter, *Constitutional Interpretation and the Indeterminate Text: A Preliminary Defense of an Imperfect Muddle*, 94 Yale L. J. 821, 842 (1985).

14   *See* The Records of the Federal Convention of 1787 at 557–59 (Max Farrand ed. 1911) [hereinafter Farrand's Records] (Madison's notes, September 10, 1787).

15   Richard Albert, *The World's Most Difficult Constitution to Amend?*, 110 Calif. L. Rev. 2005, 2010 (2022).

16	Farrand's Records, *supra* note 14, at 558.
17	Albert, *supra* note 15, at 2020.
18	Articles of Confederation, National Archives; Albert, *supra* note 15, at 2009.
19	Farrand's Records, *supra* note 14, at 629–31.
20	Gavin W. Anderson, Constitutional Rights After Globalization 156 (2005).
21	Jason Mazzone, *Unamendments*, 90 Iowa L. Rev. 1747, 1767 (2005).
22	Anderson, *supra* note 20, at 160.
23	Farrand's Records, *supra* note 14, at 121–22, 202–3.
24	Anderson, *supra* note 20, at 156.
25	*Id.*
26	Farrand's Records, *supra* note 14, at 629.
27	Federalist No. 85 (Alexander Hamilton); Letter from Alexander Hamilton to James Duane (September 3, 1780).
28	Federalist No. 85 (Hamilton).
29	*Id.*
30	Farrand's Records, *supra* note 14, at 558.
31	*Id.*
32	*Id.*
33	*Id.*
34	*Id.*
35	*Id.*
36	*Id.* at 630–31.
37	*Id.*
38	*Id.* at 629.
39	*Id.* at 629–30.
40	*Id.* at 630.
41	*Id.*
42	*Id.*
43	*Id.*
44	Federalist No. 43 (James Madison).
45	Federalist No. 22 (Alexander Hamilton).
46	Francis Newton Thorpe, The Constitutional History of the United States 2:222 (1901).
47	Federalist No. 85 (Hamilton).
48	*Id.*
49	Mazzone, *supra* note 21.
50	*Id.* at 1771 (quoting Federalist No. 85, at 590 [Hamilton] [Jacob E. Cooke ed., 1961]).
51	*Id.*
52	*Id.*
53	Albert, *supra* note 15, at 2016.
54	Vicki C. Jackson, *The (Myth of Un)amendability of the US Constitution and the Democratic Component of Constitutionalism*, 13 Int'l J. Const. L. 575, 576 (2015).

55 Citizens United v. Fed. Election Comm'n, 558 U.S. 310 (2010).
56 For a description of several of these proposals, see Citizens Take Action, "Constitutional Amendment Proposals to Overturn Citizens United," citizenstakeaction.org.

Chapter 10: Is It Time for a New Constitution?

1   New York State Rifle & Pistol Ass'n, Inc. v. Bruen, 142 S.Ct. 333 (2021).
2   United States v. Rahimi, 61 F.4th 443 (5th Cir. 2023).
3   United States v. Price, No. 2:22-CR-00097, 2022 WL 6968457 (S.D.W. Va. October 12, 2022).
4   *See* Miller v. Bonta, 542 F. Supp. 3d 1009 (S.D. Cal. 2021).
5   U.S. Constitution, Article VII.
6   Akhil Reed Amar, *The Consent of the Governed: Constitutional Amendment Outside Article V*, 94 Colum. L. Rev. 457 (1994); *but see* Sanford Levinson, *The Political Implications of Amending Clauses*, 13 Const. Comment. 107, 114 (1996) (criticizing Amar's approach).
7   Richard H. Fallon, Jr., *Legitimacy and the Constitution*, 118 Harv. L. Rev. 1787, 1804 n.56 (2005).
8   Ratification at a Glance, Center for the Study of the American Constitution at the University of Wisconsin-Madison.
9   *Id.*
10 *Id.*

Chapter 11: If Nothing Changes, Can and Should the *United* States Survive?

1   *New Initiative Explores Deep, Persistent Divides Between Biden and Trump Voters,* Center for Politics, University of Virginia (September 30, 2021).
2   Daniel A. Farber, Lincoln's Constitution 83 (2004).
3   Noah Feldman, The Broken Constitution 5 (2021).
4   Tex. v. White, 4 U.S. (7 Wall.) 700 (1869).
5   *See* Walter Stahr, Salmon Chase: Lincoln's Vital Rival (2022).
6   Doris Kearns Goodwin, Team of Rivals: The Political Genius of Abraham Lincoln (2006).
7   Tex., *supra* note 4, at 700, 725.
8   Id. at 725.
9   Id. at 726 (emphasis added).
10 In other cases such as Williams v. Bruffy, 96 U.S.176 (1878), the Court repeated that secession was not allowed.
11 Kohlhaas v. State, 223 P.3d 105 (Alaska 2010).
12 *Id.* at 112.
13 *Id.* at 65.
14 *Id.* at 75.
15 Andy Kopsa, *Czechoslovakia's Velvet Revolution Started 30 Years Ago—But It Was Decades in the Making,* Time (November 16, 2018).
16 *Id.*

17 *Id.*
18 Aleksandar Pavkovic and Peter Radan, The Ashgate Research Companion to Secession 185 (2011).
19 *Id.* at 75.
20 *Id.* at 77.
21 *Id.* at 355 n. 17.
22 *Id.*
23 *See* Milica Z. Bookman, *War and Peace: The Divergent Breakups of Yugoslavia and Czechoslovakia,* 31 J. Peace Rsch. 176 (1994).
24 *Id.*
25 Ahsan I. Butt, Secession and Security 194 (2017).
26 *Id.* at 194–95.
27 *See* Bookman, *supra* note 23, at 184.
28 *Id.*
29 Pavkovic and Radan, *supra* note 18 at 261.
30 *Id.*
31 *Id.* at 71.
32 *Id.* at 72.
33 *Id.* at 72–73.
34 *Id.* at 73.
35 *Id.* at 72.
36 *Id.*
37 *See* Butt, *supra* note 25, at 184; David Gardner, *Why Basques and Catalans See Independence Differently,* Financial Times (July 12, 2019).
38 Tommy Beer, *Texas GOP Chairman Slammed After Suggesting Secession from United States,* Forbes (December 12, 2020).
39 Texas GOP, Report of the Permanent 2022 Platform and Resolutions Committee 6 (2022).
40 United Nations Department of Economic and Social Affairs, *World Population Prospects, 2023 Revision* (July 11, 2023).

INDEX

Page numbers in *italics* refer to illustrations.
Page numbers after 186 refer to notes.